BLACK AMERICA SERIES

JACKSON COUNTY
FLORIDA

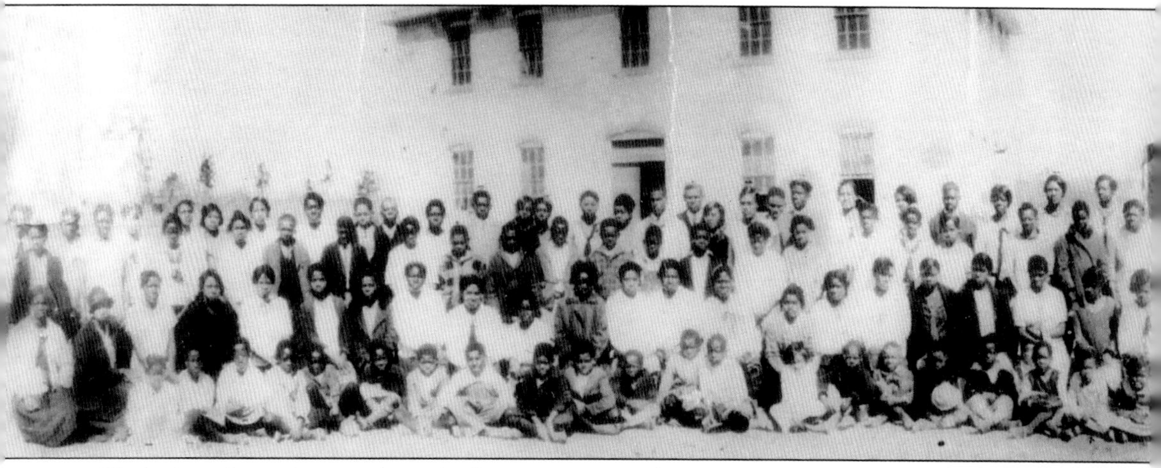

Blacks in Jackson County always had an interest in education. Pictured above is the faculty and staff of West Florida Baptist Academy that was constructed in 1925. Between 300 and 400 students were enrolled in the Academy. Rev. K.D. Britt was its founder and president. Faculty members were Rev. K.D. Britt, D.D.; Rev. L.C. Herring, secretary; Rev. M.N.M. Bennett, teacher of theology in music; Professor M.L. Clay, principal, academic department; Hattie E. Smith, primary grades teacher; Ester Livington, primary grades teacher; and Stella Martin, instructor in handicraft work. With few advantages, the teachers and students rose triumphantly above all obstacles and with untiring zeal and character went on to take their places in society. The founder, Reverend Britt, had an unusual drive and insatiable desire to help others make things better through education. In 1939 or 1940, the Baptist Academy became the Jackson County Training Elementary School.

Black America Series

Jackson County Florida

History and Publication Committee of the
Gilmore Academy-Jackson County Training School Alumni Association, Inc.

Arcadia Publishing

ISBN 978-0-7385-0098-0

Published by Arcadia Publishing
Charleston, South Carolina

Printed in the United States of America

Library of Congress Catalog Card Number: Applied for.

For all general information contact Arcadia Publishing at:
Telephone 843-853-2070
Fax 843-853-0044
E-mail sales@arcadiapublishing.com
For customer service and orders:
Toll-Free 1-888-313-2665

Visit us on the Internet at www.arcadiapublishing.com

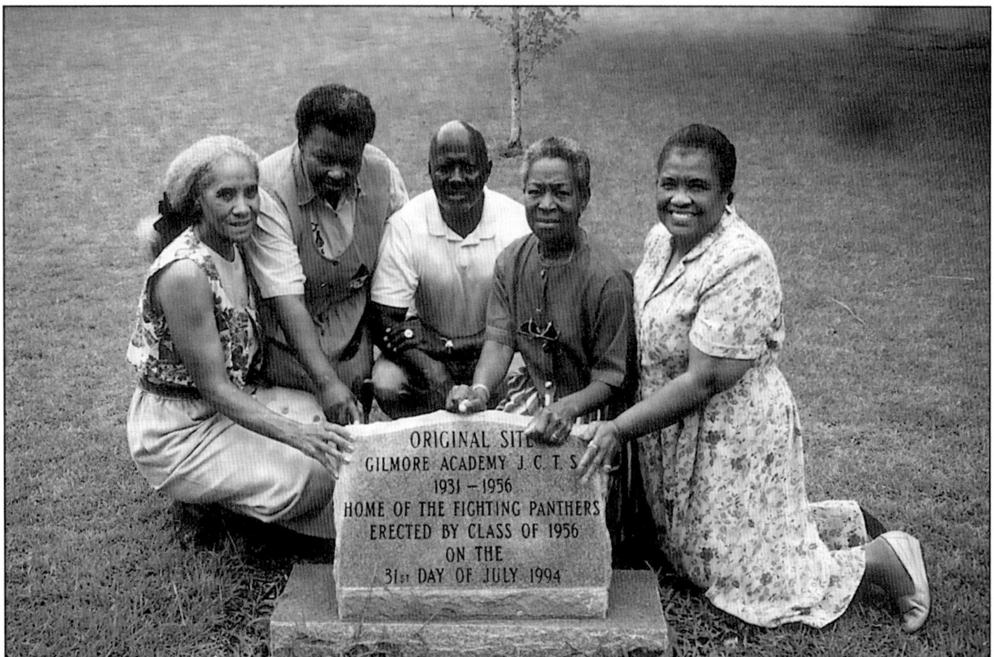

The members of the Gilmore Academy-Jackson County Training School History and Publication Committee are pictured at the marker erected on the original site of Gilmore Academy by the Class of 1956. Pictured, from left to right, are Lucy S. Hawthorne, Barbara H. Dixon, Roy L. Roulhac, Sarah S. Pender, and Queen B. Brown.

Contents

Acknowledgments		6
Introduction		7
1.	Slavery, Reconstruction, and "Jim Crow"	11
2.	Marianna Scenes	23
3.	Family Life	31
4.	Religious Life	43
5.	Places of Work	57
6.	Black Businesses	67
7.	Pre-School Education	79
8.	Jackson County Training School: Sports and Classes	85
9.	Union Grove and County Schools	107
10.	Clubs and Organizations	119

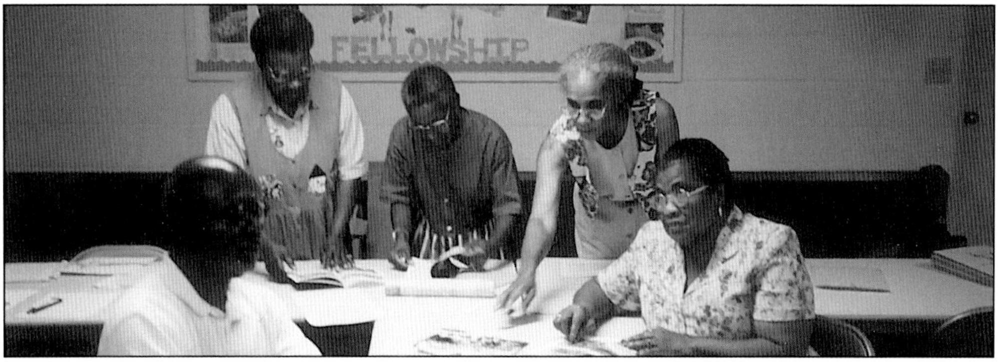

The members of the Publication and History Committee are pictured at work on the layout of *Jackson County, Florida* in the *Black America* series.

Acknowledgments

This visual history is our attempt to capture some of the memories of a community that provided opportunities for social, economic, and educational advancement. We are eternally grateful to the supporters and well wishers from across the county for their cooperation and support. We are especially indebted to the following: Judge Roy L. Roulhac, president of the Gilmore Academy-Jackson County Training School Alumni Association, Inc., for his vision, coordination, and dedication to this project; Sarah Speights Pender for her devotion, unlimited hours spent, and unselfish service rendered in completing this publication; the Gilmore Academy-Jackson County Training School Alumni Association for embracing the idea and providing financial support for this publication; St. Luke Missionary Baptist Church and the Jackson County Public Library for allowing the committee to use their facilities for meetings and planning; John Brewer, of John Brewer's Studio, Marianna, for sharing his early Jackson County photographs and for packaging material for mailing; and the Florida State Archives, Library of Congress, and the National Archives in College Park, Maryland, for making their photographic collections Internet accessible.

Special thanks go to the following persons for willingly donating pictures, information, or other assistance: Christine Anderson, Maggie P. Atwater, Attorney Harriet P. Birk, Annie H. Bradwell, Mary Roulhac Brown, Reola M. Bryan, Mary V. Burns, Elmer R. Clay, Willie Cooper, Lavonia Dupont, Karen Koonce Edwards, Ethel Ellis, Lillian Eumar, Grady Faulk, Katrina W. Florence, Alphonso Forrest, Aaron Granberry, Gertrude Green, Gussie Harrington, Annie J. Harvey, Lambert Hawthorne, Leila B. Hawthorne, Robert B. and Barbara Johnson, Linda D. Jones, William "Stack" Jones, LaFlorence Long, Carol "Cookie" Marks, Sheryl McGriff, Willie Hazel Morris, the late Robert Moultrie, Eva H. Patton, Robert J. Pender, Eva Pittman, Ora Mae Peterson, Roberta E. Pressley, Earlene Robinson, Johnny Robinson, Lillie G. Robinson, Donnie and Shirley Roulhac, Johnny Sansome, Vestivure Smith, Inez Speights, Johnny and Leola Speights, Sarah L. Speights, Amy Summerwell, Charles and Lula Vann, Leo Washington, Evelyn Wilson, Nellie Wilson, Callie Wooden, and Betty Worlds.

This publication cannot include every detail of each picture. It is our aim to stimulate memories and conversation. We wish to express sincere gratitude to the dedicated committee whose individual contributions helped to make the production of this book possible:

Sarah Speights Pender, Chairperson
Queen Bowers Brown, Vice Chairperson
Lucy Speights Hawthorne, Secretary
Barbara Harley Dixon, Member
Elmore Bryant, Member

Eulice Bryant, Member
Gwendolyn P. Godwin, Member
Roy L. Roulhac, Editor

Introduction

When I was invited to the Gilmore Academy-Jackson County Training School's first all-school reunion in Marianna, Florida on July 4-7, 1996, I was an eager participant. Over 500 former students, faculty, and staff came. With few opportunities for economic advancement, most had left Jackson County as soon after high school as possible to explore career opportunities in the North or in South Florida. In 1962, I went to Washington, D.C., where I waited tables at the National Press Club while studying part-time at Howard University. Others enrolled in college full-time or joined the military. Some remained in Jackson County. With the decline in Northern rust-belt economies in the 1970s, a few had returned home. Several had returned to Jackson County, as retirees, after long careers in different cities. We all welcomed the chance to renew friendships and reminisce about old times. The stories we shared were rich and plentiful, and thanks to the oral tradition, the memories, though blurred, were not lost. However, many of us were disturbed because we had made no effort to document and preserve our history. We decided it was time to act, and the following year the alumni association was incorporated and 216 people joined as charter members. This publication represents our first attempt to tell our story. We dedicate it to the present and future generations.

The presence of Africans in the Florida territory pre-dates the 1822 creation of Jackson County. The first fugitive slaves reached St. Augustine, the Florida capital under Spanish rule, in 1687. For a few years, the Spanish granted freedom to blacks who embraced the Roman Catholic religion. By 1763, when the Spanish ceded Florida to Great Britain, there were 429 blacks and mulattoes in the territory—79 free and 350 crown or private slaves. During the 20 years of British rule, from 1763 to 1783, and particularly during the Revolutionary War, African fugitives developed important alliances with the pro-British, anti-American Seminoles. Although Native Americans also enslaved the fugitives, they treated them more humanely. They were admitted into the Seminoles' family life and served as counselors and advisors. Additionally, they had mutual interests. The Seminoles hoped to avoid forced removal from Florida, and the blacks feared re-enslavement.

Generally, African Americans in Florida were either free because of protection offered by Spanish law; slaves on plantations; or "Indian Negroes" who were purchased by Seminoles or escaped from plantations. The presence of free blacks and refugee slaves among the Spanish and the Seminoles was discomforting to Georgia, South Carolina, and Florida slave owners. They were viewed as a source of unrest among the slaves and as potential leaders during insurrections. This fear was made apparent during the first Seminole War, when the might of the army and navy was visited upon about 300 African Americans and a few Seminoles and Choctaws who had made their home in an abandoned British fort at Prospect Bluff, 15 miles north of the Apalachicola River. In 1816, the fort and land extending 50 miles up and down the

Apalachicola River became a haven for slave fugitives. The fort's existence was short-lived.

After the Spanish governor rebuffed protests by Andrew Jackson to destroy the fort, the army and navy and the Lower Creeks made its destruction a top priority. Determined to avoid capture and re-enslavement, the runaways, led by black chief Garcon, repelled a July 17, 1816, attack by ambushing a navy vessel and killing three sailors, including an officer. Ten days later, the fort was destroyed, and 270 persons were killed when a red-hot cannonball landed in the fort's magazine. Garcon and the Choctaw chief were captured and murdered, and the blacks who survived were re-enslaved.

By 1825, three years after Spain ceded Florida to the United States, over 860 slaves were already in Jackson County. The county, established from Escambia County and named for Andrew Jackson, borders Alabama and Georgia to the north and is surrounded by Gadsden, Bay Washington, Holmes, Calhoun, and Liberty Counties. These counties, along with Walton, were created from Jackson County. Florida's territorial government wasted no time in enacting legislation to dehumanize and control those enslaved. In 1828, a law was enacted which proclaimed that, "slaves shall be deemed, held and taken as personal property, for every purpose whatever." In the same year, the legislature declared that any African American involved in a riot, quarrel, fight, or in the possession of firearms would be subject to a fine of up to $20 and up to 39 lashes. They could only testify in court as witnesses in cases for or against other blacks or mulattoes, and if it were discovered that they did not tell the truth, they were whipped or their ears were nailed to a post. As personal property slaves were taxed at 25¢ each until 1839, when it was raised to 50¢.

By 1838, the number of enslaved persons in Jackson County had increased to 1,130. The state census also included 35 free "colored" citizens whose status was little different from their slave cousins. In 1829, a law was enacted limiting their number to those already in the territory. They were taxed at $1 per year until 1845, when the amount was increased to $3. In 1848, shortly after Florida was admitted to the Union, legislation was enacted that required the appointment of guardians for free blacks. Rather than comply, some free blacks in Pensacola (the capital of the West Florida territory) voluntarily left their homes and resettled in Tampico, Mexico. In 1858, free blacks were allowed to select their own masters and become slaves.

The onset of the Civil War marked the beginning of the end of the "peculiar institution." Volumes have been written about the gallant efforts of the Confederates during the September 27, 1864 Battle of Marianna. These accounts barely mention the bravery displayed by African-American Union soldiers or their participation in the Battle. On September 15, 1864, a mounted cavalry, including 43 enlisted men of the 82nd U.S. Colored Infantry and 30 from the 86th U.S. Colored Infantry, left Fort Barrancas, near Pensacola, along with three battalions of the 2nd Maine Cavalry and a battalion of the First Florida Cavalry, for a raid into Northwest Florida. The official record of the Union and Confederate Armies describes the 30-minute Battle of Marianna as follows:

"Arrived at Marianna at 10a. The town was held by some 400 of the enemy, 150 of whom were cavalry. The rest home guards under command of Col. Alexander B. Montgomery . . . They were strongly posted behind building . . . Our troops were ordered to charge into the town. The advance Battalion from the 2nd Maine faltered and halted. The 2nd Battalion went bravely forward and through the town in chase of the enemies' cavalry, who were hastily decamped on our approach. The colored detachment were promptly brought up in front of the [St. Luke] Episcopal Church, behind which one company of home guards were posted. They [the "colored" troops] dismounted under a galling fire of buck ball delivered at a range of thirty yards and, fixing their bayonets, charged over the church yard fence compelling the enemy's company to surrender, killing and wounded some eighteen."

Over 600 enslaved persons left plantations in Jackson County and followed the troops. During the ensuing months, many Jackson County men enlisted in the 82nd and the 86th.

The May 20, 1865 surrender of the Confederate forces at Tallahassee did not dramatically change conditions for the freedmen. The ghost of U.S. Supreme Court Chief Justice Roger

Taney still haunted the Jackson County environs. Taney, in his 1857 Dred Scott decision, wrote that "at the time of the Declaration of Independence, and when the Constitution of the United States was framed and adopted . . . [blacks] had no rights which the white man was bound to respect." Most whites were still unwilling to accept blacks as equals and, during the Reconstruction period, made every effort, including violence, to keep them in their "place." Jackson County developed a reputation as the place "where Satan has his seat."

Although African Americans in Jackson County had encountered intense hostility since the end of the Civil War, it escalated against them and their Republican allies during a two-year period of lawlessness between 1869 and 1871. The already strained racial tensions in Jackson County had been heightened by the election of Emanuel Fortune and Homer Bryan, both former slaves, as delegates to the 1868 constitutional convention and Fortune's and Jesse Robinson's elections to two of three Jackson County seats in the state house. Homer Bryan was appointed Jackson County tax assessor, and Calvin Rogers was elected Marianna constable. At least 170 persons, primarily African Americans and unionists, were killed, compared to 20 in Madison, 16 in Columbia and Alachua, and between 4 and 10 in Lafayette, Taylor, Hamilton, and Suwannee Counties. It began on February 17, 1869. Dr. John L. Finlayson, the Republican clerk of the court, was killed, and William Purham, the former Bureau agent for Jackson County who had been elected to the state house, was severely wounded as they walked on Main Street from a concert staged by members of the 9th U.S. Colored Infantry. Then in early March, a white farmer was shot to death, a few days later an African-American man was found floating in the Chipola River, and in late April another white man was killed.

Six months later, on the morning of September 28, 1869, Calvin Rogers, who as constable was the only elected local official in Jackson County, and about 23 African-American women and children were ambushed at the Robinson sugar-house as they headed to a picnic at Robinson Springs. Wyatt Young (also known as Wyatt Scurlock), Washington Rivers, and a two-year old boy, Steward Livingston, were killed. Rogers, who was believed to have been the next target of the Ku Klux Klan, was grazed in the arm. By October 11, nine people had been killed, two whites and seven African Americans, including Oscar Granberry, Matt Nichols, his wife, Maria, and their son, Matt Jr., who were shot dead in a lime-sink. Samuel Fleischman, a Jewish merchant, who had been generous in extending credit to blacks farming their own land, was escorted out of Jackson County. Refusing to be run off, he was murdered as he re-entered the county. Before the end of the year, Calvin Rogers was killed. In April 1871, Jonathan Dickinson, who had been appointed to replace Finlayson as clerk of court, was killed in almost the same spot as Finlayson two years earlier. Richard Prosser (who had been appointed to replace Rogers), Deputy Sheriff Joseph Nelson, Emanuel Fortune, Homer Bryan, and Henry Reed were forced to leave Jackson County to protect themselves and their families. Fortune completed his term of office as state representative in Jacksonville.

Between 1871 and 1876, several other African Americans represented Jackson County in the state house of representatives: Robert H. Dennis in 1875, Benjamin F. Livingston from 1871 to 1875, and William K. Robinson in 1872. Washington Pope served in the state senate from 1873 to 1875, and Fuller M. White served for a brief period in 1876. Thereafter, full participation in the political process was restrained. No other African American would be elected or appointed to office in Jackson County for almost 110 years. Elmore Bryant was elected to Marianna's city commission in 1984 and was subsequently appointed its first black mayor. He was followed by Howard Milton in 1986, and E. Roger Clay 1988. Willie Spires was elected to the Jackson County commission in 1992. The predominately African-American community of Jacob, near Campbellton, was incorporated in 1994, and African Americans filled all of its public offices. David Pittman was the first mayor. He was followed by the late Isaac Pittman. Rev. Riley J. Henderson is the present mayor.

The end of Reconstruction in 1877 marked the beginning of the Jim Crow era with government sanctioned policies designed to put blacks "back in their place." The U.S.

Supreme Court's 1896 *Plessy v. Ferguson* decision, announcing the "separate but equal" doctrine, was the most notable. However, through it all, our ancestors survived. By 1900, African Americans in this country owned 40,000 businesses, including 55 banks, and controlled 70% of the business that served the black community. This trend was also reflected in Jackson County. African Americans owned and operated a number of businesses in downtown Marianna and without significant support from the county or state, had already established a system for educating their children.

Interest in education by African Americans had always been intense. In August 1867, two years after the Civil War, a Colored School Society was created. A committee, which included Jessie Waller, Emanuel Fortune, and John Livingston, petitioned the state board of education to establish a school in Marianna. The construction plans for a "Northern-type" school were approved, but the school was never built. Church-supported elementary schools were established in most communities. For over 50 years, they remained the primary source of education for black students.

In 1922, Robert T. Gilmore donated 3 acres of land to construct a union school, grades one through twelve. The Gilmore Academy, located at Orange and Clay Streets, was a two-story limestone building. The first floor contained four classrooms. The second floor housed three classrooms, the principal's office, and a large auditorium for daily assembly. Gilmore Academy graduated its first class in 1931, with three students—the late Ethel Massey and Susie Leeks Baker, and Maggie Pender Keith Atwater, who still lives in Marianna. The Academy successfully operated until 1932, when it became Jackson County Training School, the first publicly-supported school for African Americans in the county.

In 1939 or 1940, the school was separated and grades one through six were relocated to the Baptist Academy on Pennsylvania Avenue. In 1952, a new elementary school building was completed on South Street. The school was the first to be built by the County for black students. It was followed by the construction of a new high school on the same site in 1956. The class of 1970 was the final graduating class bearing the name, Jackson County Training School. Today, it serves as Marianna Middle School.

We are the alumni of Gilmore Academy-Jackson County Training School. We take seriously our obligation to use our time, knowledge, and talents to give back to our community. We stand on the shoulders of ancestors who struggled through the Middle Passage, slavery, Reconstruction, and the Jim Crow era so that we could have a better life. They were a strong and proud people who recognized that where there was life, there was hope. Their unyielding faith was perceptively captured by James Weldon Johnson in *Lift Every Voice and Sing*, which became known as the Negro national anthem. In the last stanza, he prays:

> *God of our weary years, God of our silent years,*
> *Thou who has brought us thus far on the way;*
> *Thou who has by thy might, led us into the light,*
> *Keep us forever in thy path, we pray.*
> *Lest our feet stray from the places, our God,*
> *where we met Thee.*
> *Lest our hearts, drunk with the wine of the world*
> *we forget Thee.*
> *Shadowed beneath Thy hand, may we forever stand,*
> *true to our God, true to our native land.*

We aspire to learn more about our history, not for the pleasure of knowing but for the lessons it teaches. By understanding our ancestors' reality, we can better understand our place on the map of human geography and our mission in the 21st century.

—Roy. L. Roulhac

One

Slavery, Reconstruction, and "Jim Crow"

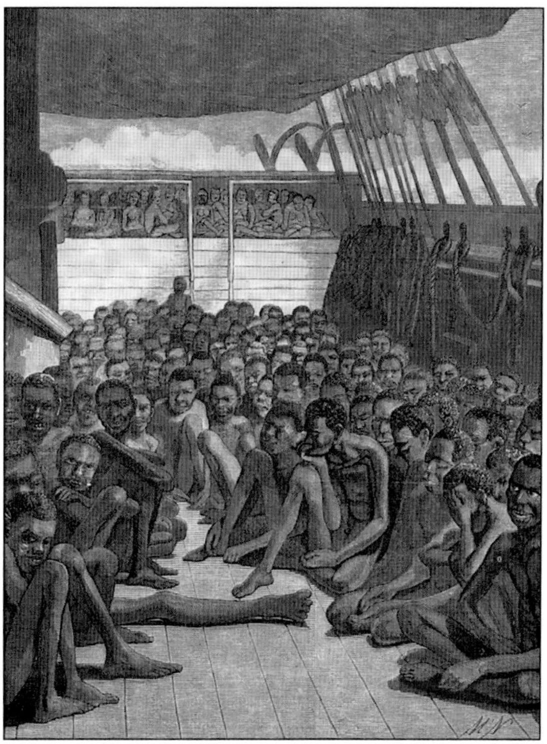

The treatment of Africans during the Middle Passage ranks among the most brutal the world has ever seen. Men, women, boys, and girls were snatched from the homelands and loaded upon ships bound for the West Indies and the Americas. The average ship had the capacity to hold over 500 people. Because they had been purchased by different traders, many were branded like cattle with red hot irons with marks of different forms. The journey across the Atlantic took from 17 to 30 days. The enslaved were enclosed under grated hatchways between decks. The space was so low that they sat between each other's legs with no possibility of lying down or changing their position. Although the foreign slave trade was abolished in 1808, the domestic trade continued until the Civil War. Pictured are slaves aboard the bark, *Wildfire*, as it was brought into Key West, Florida on April 30, 1860. (Florida State Archives Photographic Collection.)

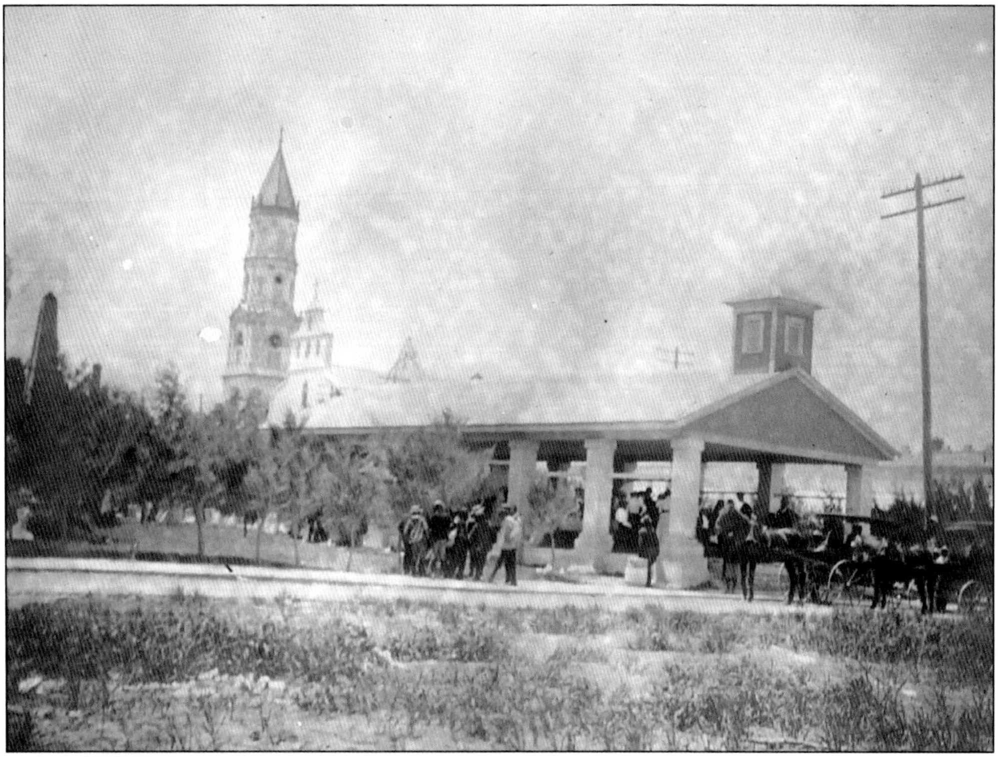

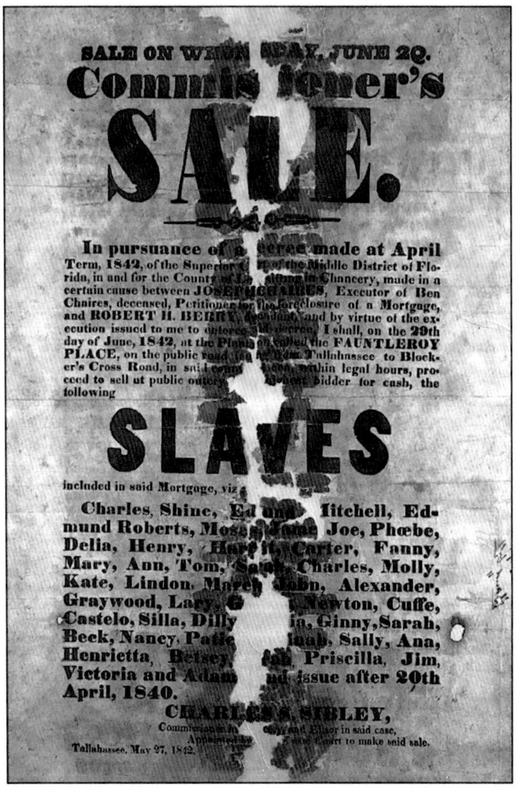

SALE ON WE[illegible]AY, JUNE 29.

Commis[illegible]ioner's

SALE.

In pursuance of a [illegible]cree made at April Term, 1842, of the Super[illegible] of the Middle District of Florida, in and for the County [illegible] in Chancery, made in a certain cause between JOSEPH CHAIRES, Executor of Ben Chaires, deceased, Petitioner for the foreclosure of a Mortgage, and ROBERT H. BERRY, [illegible] and by virtue of the execution issued to me to [illegible] decree, I shall, on the 29th day of June, 1842, at the Plan[illegible] called the FAUNTLEROY PLACE, on the public road [illegible] Tallahassee to Blocker's Cross Road, in said [illegible] within legal hours, proceed to sell at public out[illegible] bidder for cash, the following

SLAVES

included in said Mortgage, viz

Charles, Shine, Ed[illegible] Mitchell, Edmund Roberts, Mose[illegible] Joe, Phœbe, Delia, Henry, [illegible] Carter, Fanny, Mary, Ann, Tom, [illegible] Charles, Molly, Kate, Lindon, Ma[illegible] John, Alexander, Graywood, La[illegible] Newton, Cuffe, Castelo, Silla, Dilly [illegible]ia, Ginny, Sarah, Beck, Nancy, Pati[illegible] Sally, Ana, Henrietta, Betsey, [illegible] Priscilla, Jim, Victoria and Adam [illegible] issue after 20th April, 1840.

CHARLES S. SIBLEY,

Commissioner in [illegible] and Elisor in said case,
Appointed by [illegible] Court to make said sale.

Tallahassee, May 27, 1842.

People at the slave market in Cathedral Plaza, St. Augustine, Florida, are pictured May 13, 1895. In exchange for blacks' efforts against an English invasion of St. Augustine in 1728, the governor of Spanish Florida, Antonio de Benavides, did away with the slave market. (Florida State Archives Photographic Collection.)

Rev. Daniel J. Payne, in one of the first militant speeches by a black American against slavery, observed in June 1839, "Does a man take the calf from the cow and sell it to the butcher? So slavery tears the child from the arms of the reluctant mother, and barters it to the soul trader for a young colt, or some other commodity!" Reverend Payne was elected a bishop in the A.M.E. Church in 1852. (Florida State Archives Photographic Collection.)

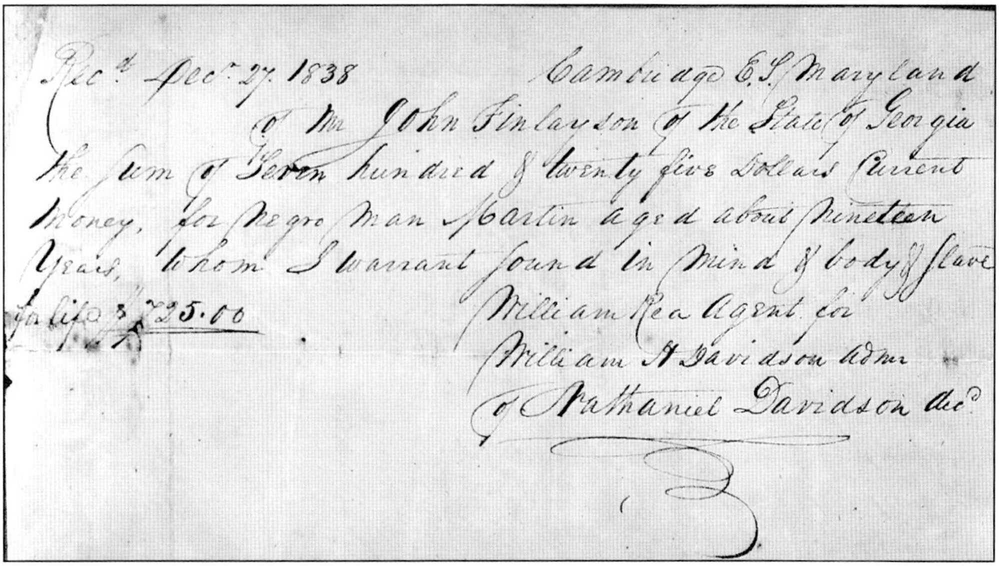

Recd Decr 27 1838 Cambriage E.S. Maryland
Of Mr John Finlayson of the State of Georgia
the Sum of Seven hundred & twenty five Dollars Current
Money, for Negro Man Martin aged about Nineteen
Years, whom I warrant sound in mind & body & slave
for life $725.00
William Rea Agent for
William H Davidson Adm
of Nathaniel Davidson decd

The law prohibited slaves from reading, writing, or possessing anything written or printed. They could not legally marry, testify against a white person, or assemble for worship, except in the presence of whites. (Florida State Archives Photographic Collection.)

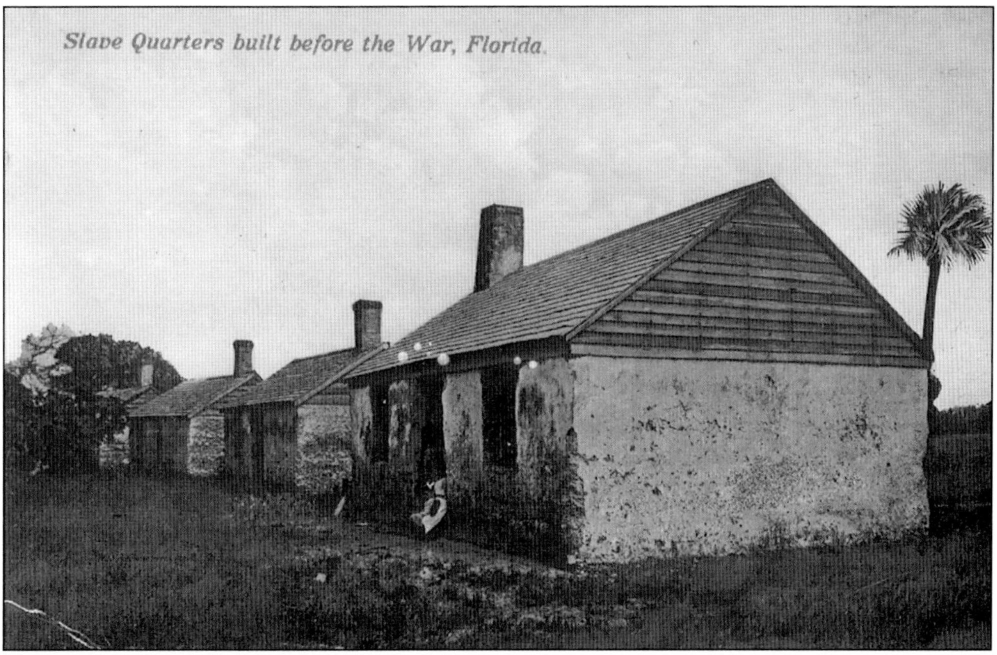

Inadequate housing and clothing were the rule. Most huts were without windows or floors, and slaves slept on straw or old rugs. Among the largest slave owners in Jackson County in 1838 were S.J. Baker (70), S.C. Bellamy (60), Joseph Russ Sr. (52), Benjamin Wynn (48), Daniel Smith (39), Julia Ferrier (36), J.J. Pittman (35), William and J.T. Russ (34), and T.B. Baker (32). (Florida State Archives Photographic Collection.)

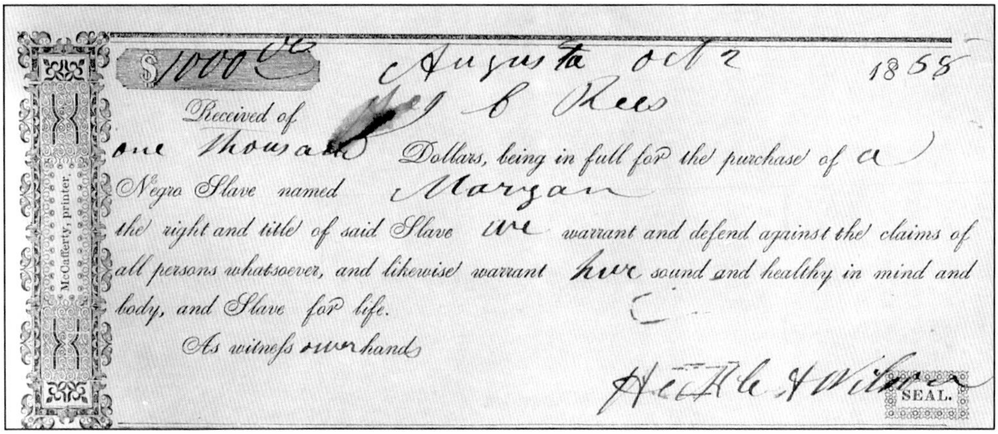
$1000 00 Augusta Oct 2 1858

Received of J. B. Rees

one thousand Dollars, being in full for the purchase of a Negro Slave named Margan

the right and title of said Slave we warrant and defend against the claims of all persons whatsoever, and likewise warrant her sound and healthy in mind and body, and Slave for life.

As witness our hand

[illegible] SEAL.

McCafferty, printer.

Although legally classified as chattel, slaves maintained their humanity and dignity. (Florida State Archives Photographic Collection.)

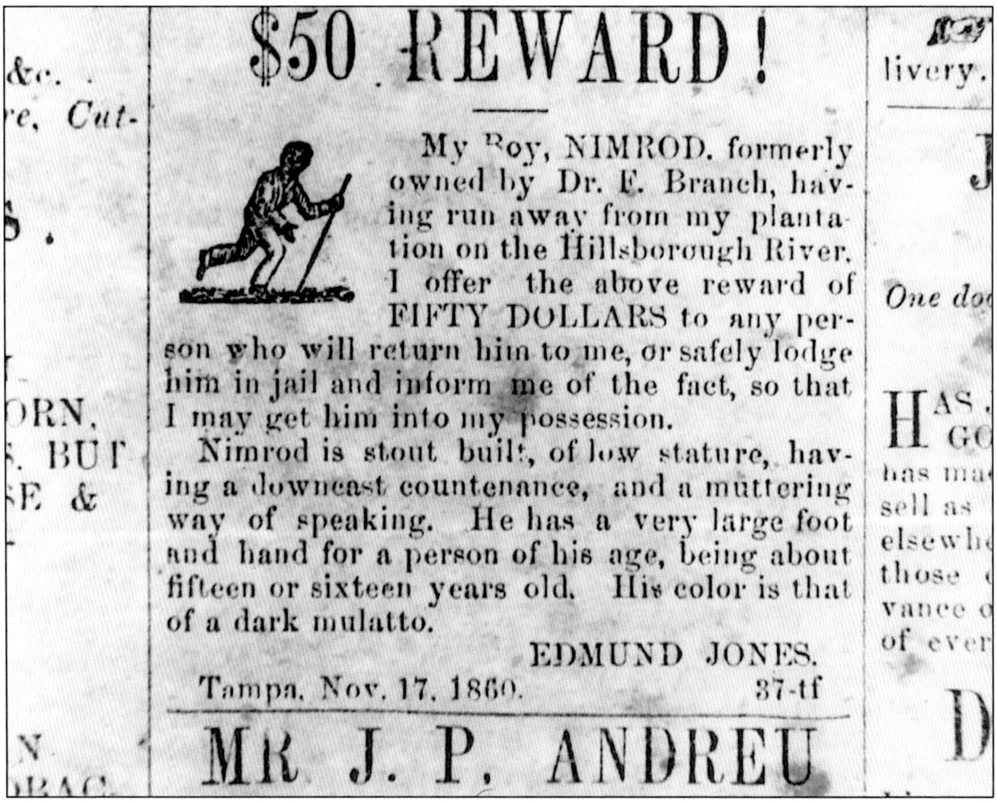
$50 REWARD!

My Boy, NIMROD, formerly owned by Dr. F. Branch, having run away from my plantation on the Hillsborough River, I offer the above reward of FIFTY DOLLARS to any person who will return him to me, or safely lodge him in jail and inform me of the fact, so that I may get him into my possession.

Nimrod is stout built, of low stature, having a downcast countenance, and a muttering way of speaking. He has a very large foot and hand for a person of his age, being about fifteen or sixteen years old. His color is that of a dark mulatto.

EDMUND JONES.

Tampa, Nov. 17, 1860. 37-tf

MR. J. P. ANDREU

Runaways from Georgia and South Carolina often fled into Spanish Florida and formed alliances with the Seminoles. In 1821, after the First Seminole War, Congress allocated $250,000 to pay Georgia slaveholders for slaves who had fled to the Seminole tribes. Bloodhounds were imported from Cuba to track them down. (Florida State Archives Photographic Collection.)

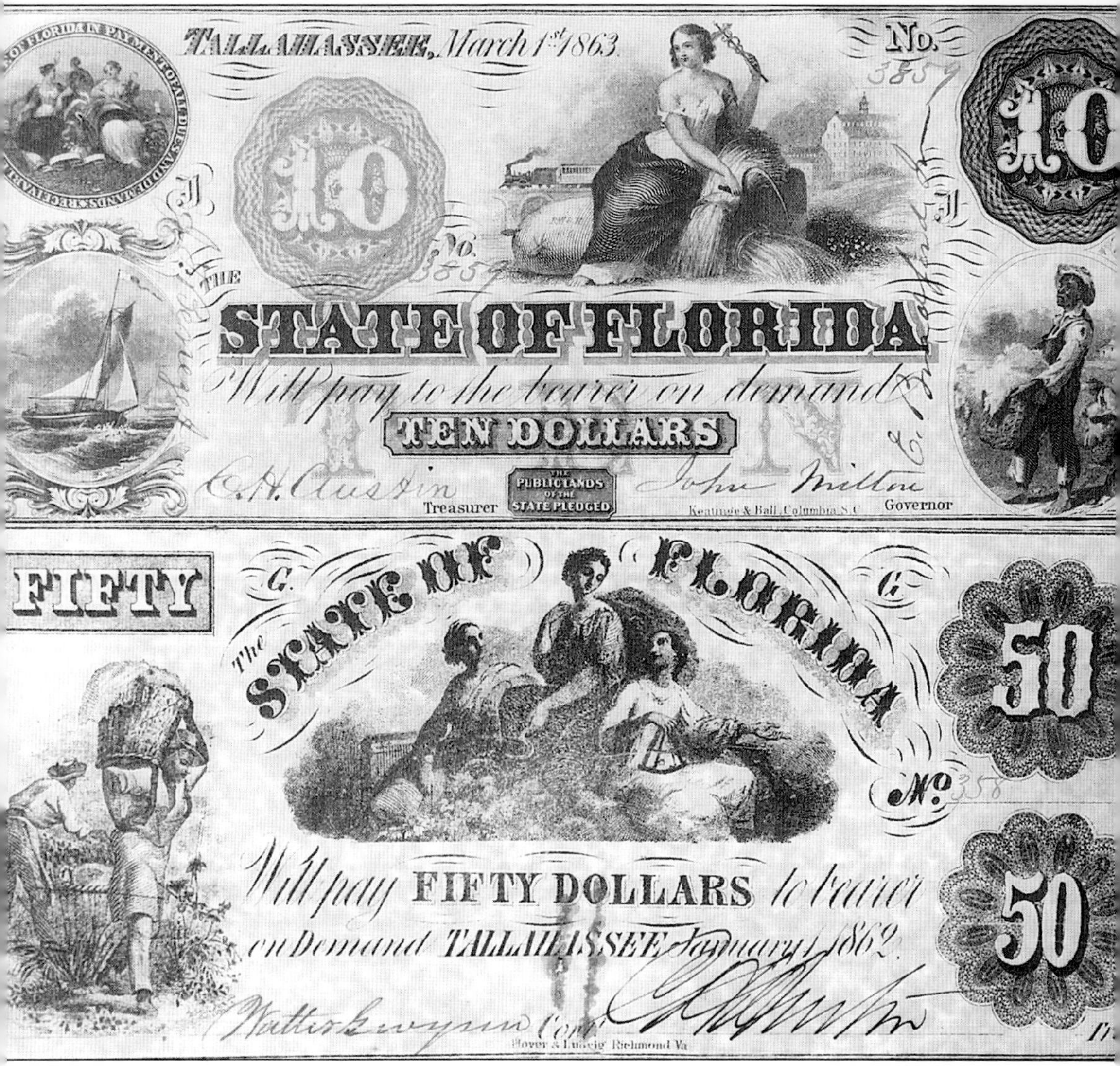

In February 1861, after 15 years of statehood, Florida joined the Confederate States of America. It began issuing its own money in 1862. Slave labor and cotton remained its most valuable resource. "Coon cards" were also used to ridicule blacks. (Florida State Archives Photographic Collection.)

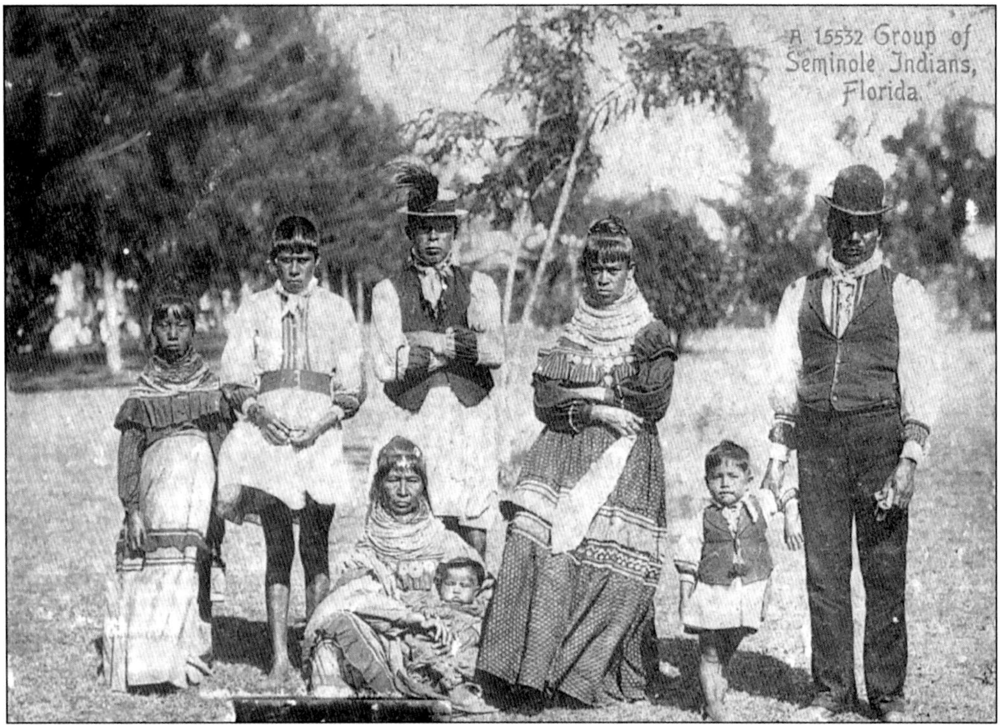

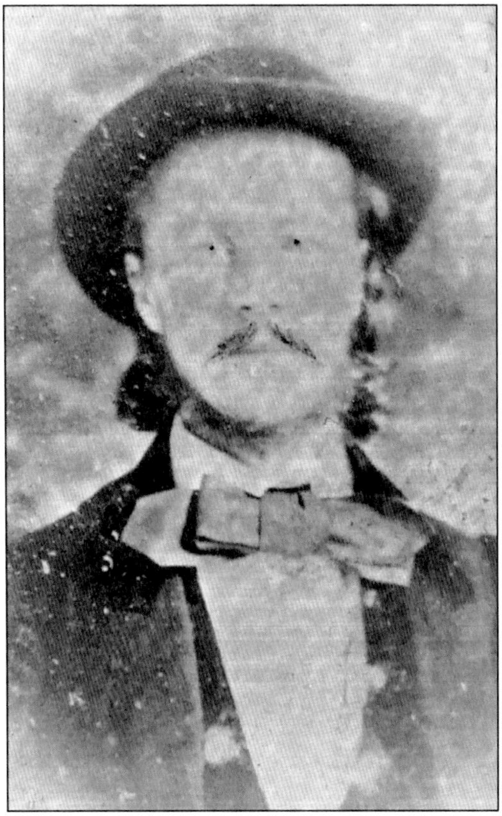

Runaway slaves from Georgia and South Carolina found much greater freedom among the Florida Seminoles. They intermarried and fought against attempts by American forces to expel the Seminoles from Florida and return them to slavery. Several black chiefs played leading roles during the Second Seminole War, 1835-1842. Black chief Abraham was one of the most noted. He helped bring an end to the war by negotiating an agreement with the U.S. military, which called for the Seminoles to surrender and leave Florida and for black Indians to join the Seminoles on the Trail of Tears and avoid re-enslavement. (Florida State Archives Photographic Collection.)

Dr. John L. Finlayson, a staunch defender of the rights of blacks during the period of Reconstruction, attended to the medical needs of blacks and operated the first night school in the county. He was murdered on February 17, 1869.

Born in 1832 on the Waddell Plantation, north of Marianna, Emanuel Fortune was a shoemaker before being elected to the 1868 Constitutional Convention and to the legislature. He fled Jackson County in May 1869 because of the state of lawlessness and outrage, and he completed his term of office in Jacksonville. Emanuel Fortune was one of several witnesses who testified before a special committee of the 42nd Congress, which convened in Jacksonville on November 11, 1871, to investigate the violence in Jackson and other Florida counties. In the tradition of Henry George and Karl Marx, he decried racism and portrayed the African-American position in the South as worse than during slavery. (Florida State Archives Photographic Collection.)

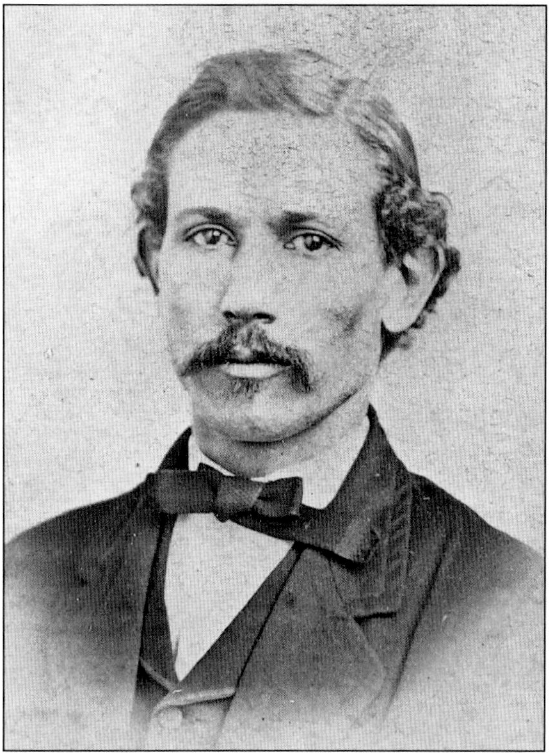

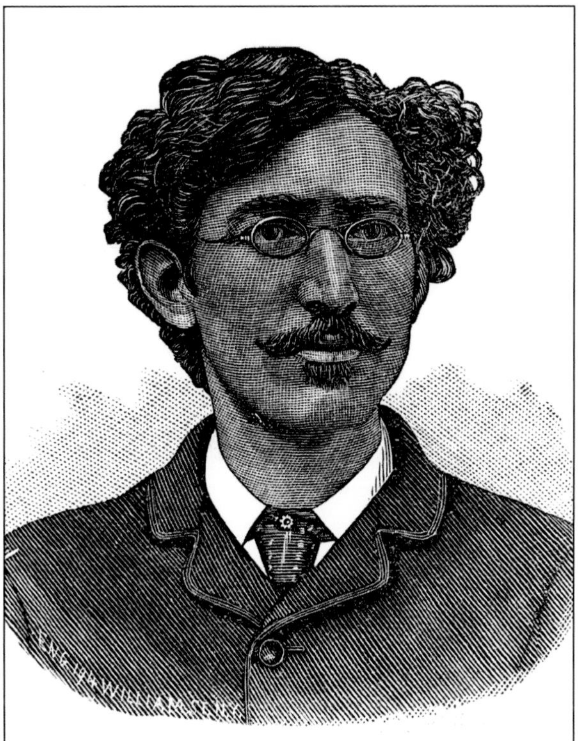

T. THOMAS FORTUNE.

Emanuel and Sarah Fortune's son, T. Thomas Fortune, formed the first black protest organization after Reconstruction, the Afro-American League. In 1881, he started the *New York Globe* which later merged with the *New York Age*, the leading African-American paper in the country during the 1880s and 1890s. In 1884, during the most radical phase of his career, Fortune wrote *Black and White: Land, Labor, and Politics in the South.* The untiring efforts of JCTS alumnus Clinton Black during the 1990s led to the placement of historic markers on Highway 90, at the county lines, acknowledging that T. Thomas Fortune was born in Jackson County. (Florida State Archives Photographic Collection.)

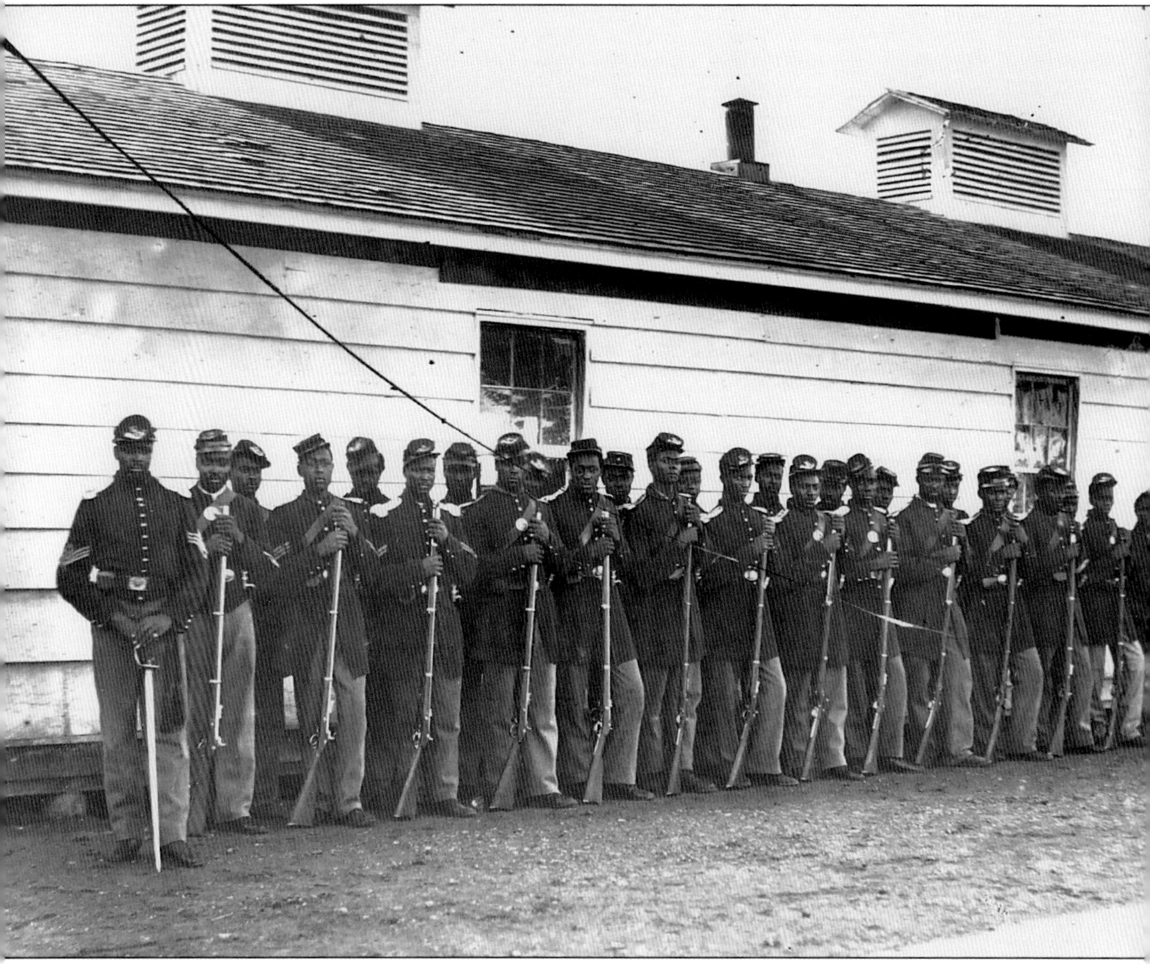

Following the Battle of Marianna on September 27, 1864, many Jackson County slaves joined the 82nd and 86th U.S. Colored Infantries, which had fought valiantly to liberate them. During the battle, Francis Nicholas of the 82nd was killed, and Isaac Anderson, Solomon Johnson, and James C. Breckenridge of the 86th were wounded. In the ensuing months, many Florida recruits enlisted in the 82nd and the 86th. The following ex-slaves joined the 82nd and listed Marianna or Jackson County as their birthplace: Andrew Barnes, Albert Bush, Winn Bryant, Frank Callahan, Ross Edward, Johnson Gibson, Pomprey Horne, James Mathias, Hampstone Robinson, Frank Russ, Augustus Wade, Robert Waddell, Robinson Washington, Henry Watson, Joseph Watson, James White, Fraser Williams, Edward Winn, Joseph Winn, Robert Winn, Jacob Wynn, and Wesley Wynn. Pictured above are members of Company E, 4th U.S. Colored Infantry, at Ft. Lincoln in Washington, D.C. (Florida State Archives Photographic Collection.)

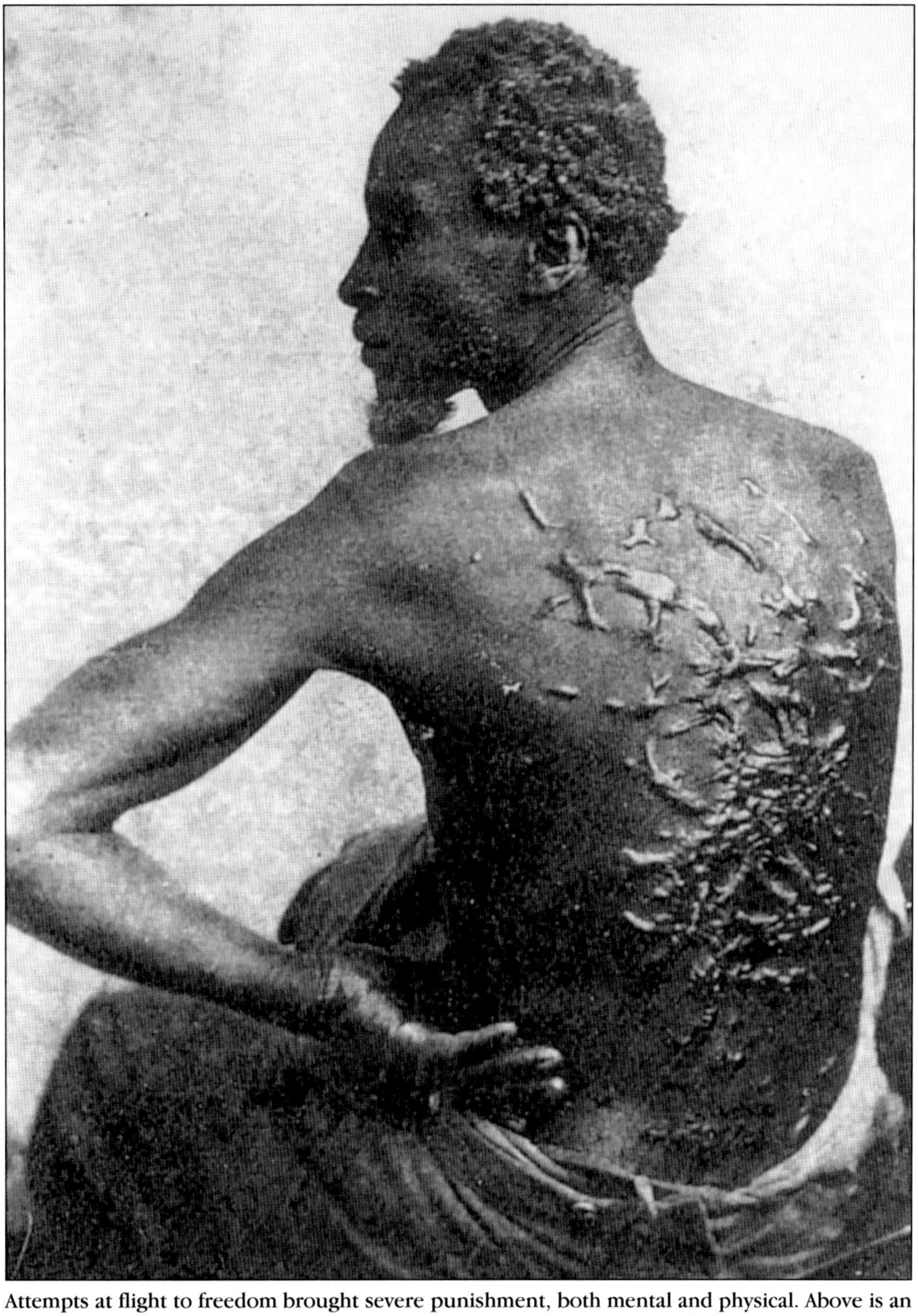

Attempts at flight to freedom brought severe punishment, both mental and physical. Above is an April 2, 1863 photograph of Peter, a slave on Captain John Lyon's Atchafaylya cotton plantation, near Washington, Louisiana. As he sat for this picture, he related to the photographer that he did not remember the beating, but was told he tried to shoot everyone, including his wife, burned all of his clothes, and was in bed sore for two months.

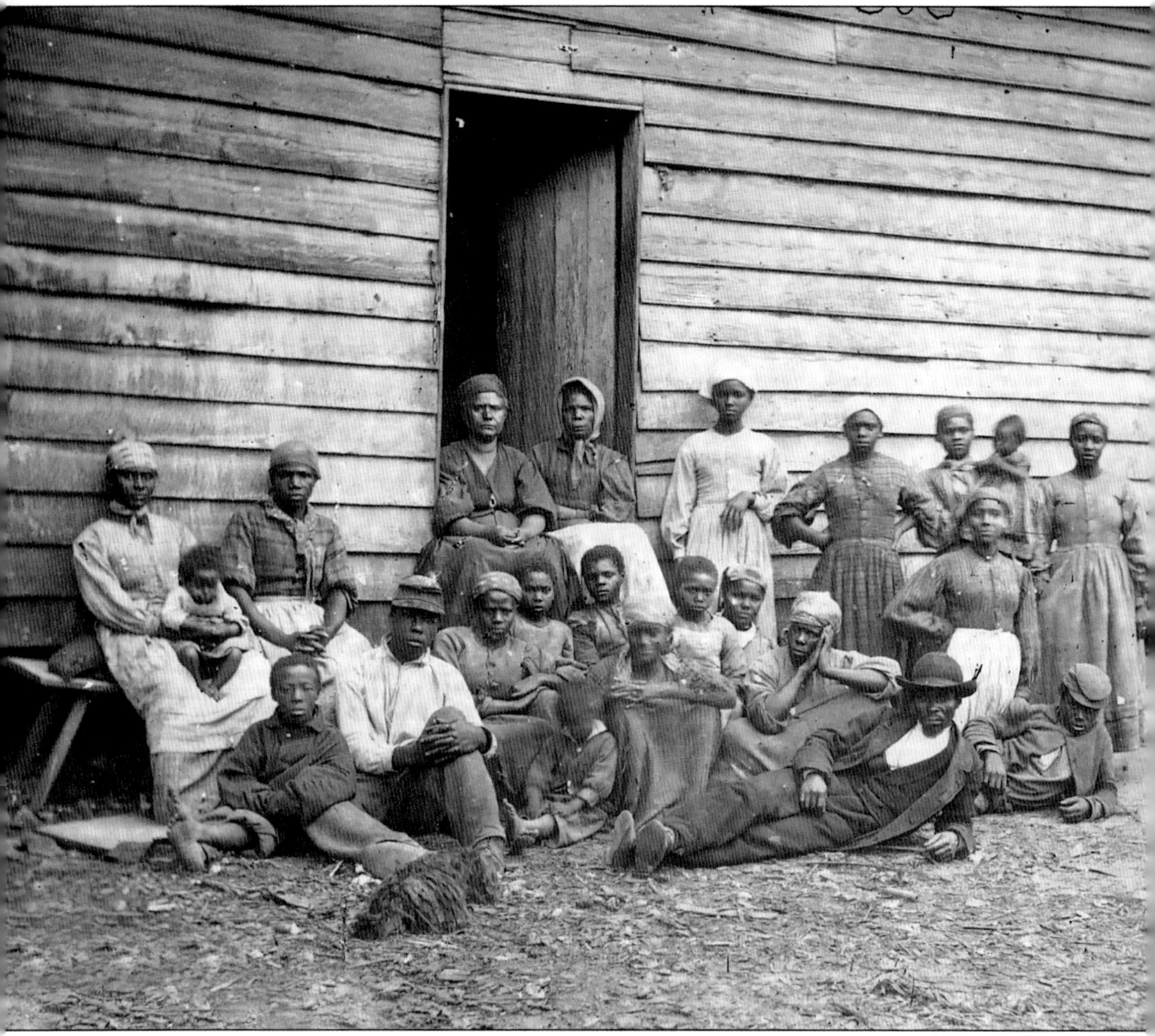

Slaves who left plantations and followed Union soldiers were referred to as "contraband of war." The term was coined in 1861 by Major General Benjamin F. Butler, who used fugitives at Fortress Monroe, Virginia, as laborers and spies rather than return them to plantations. (Library of Congress Photographic Collection.)

On October 19, 1934, 23-year-old Claude Neal, right, of Greenwood was arrested and taken into custody for the alleged rape and murder of Lola Cannaday, a white girl. Angry mobs at Chipley, in neighboring Washington County, where Neal was jailed, caused his removal to Panama City in Bay County. From there, Neal was transported by boat to Pensacola and across the state line to Brewton, Alabama, 210 miles from Marianna. In the early hours of October 26th, an armed mob of 100 men stormed the jail, seized Neal, and took him to a spot north of Greenwood. During Neal's 10 to 12 hours of torture before a group of 3,000 to 7,000 people from 11 Southern states, a rope was tied around his neck and he was pulled over a limb until he almost choked to death. The next morning. Neal's mutilated body was taken by the mob to Marianna, where he was rehung from an oak tree on the northeast corner of the courthouse square. Neal's lynching was investigated by the NAACP as part of its anti-lynching campaign. (Florida State Archives Photographic Collection.)

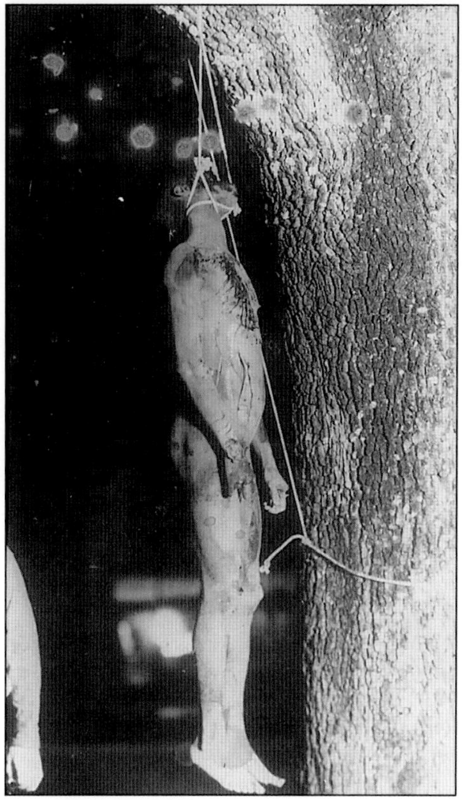

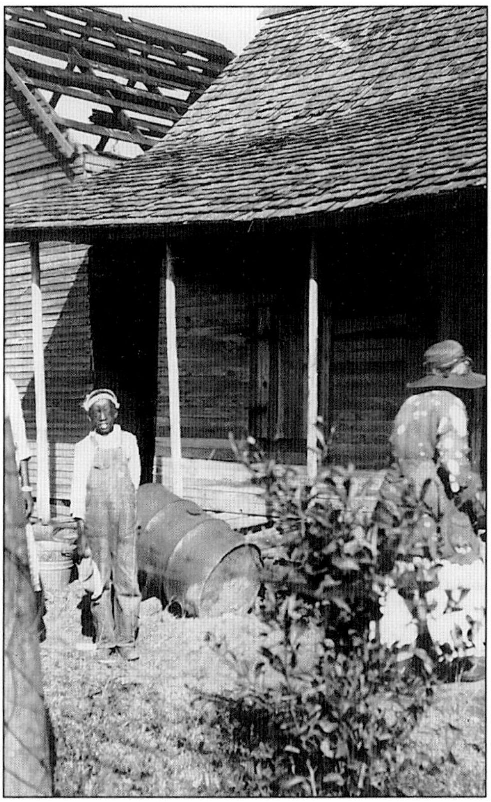

Claude Neal had lived with his mother, Annie Smith, and aunt, Sallie Smith, on a small farm across from the home of the alleged victim's family. The Smiths' home was burned and Neal's mother and aunt were arrested and taken out of the county. Between 1890 and 1943, at least eight other African Americans were lynched in Jackson County: Simmons Simpson, Marianna, 1890; unknown man, Sneads, 1900; Jon Sanders, Sneads, 1900; Doc Peters, Cottondale, 1905; Hattie Bowman and Edward Christian, victims of a double lynching, Graceville, 1910; Galvin Baker, Marianna, 1911; and Cellos Harrison, Marianna, 1943. (Library of Congress Photographic Collection.)

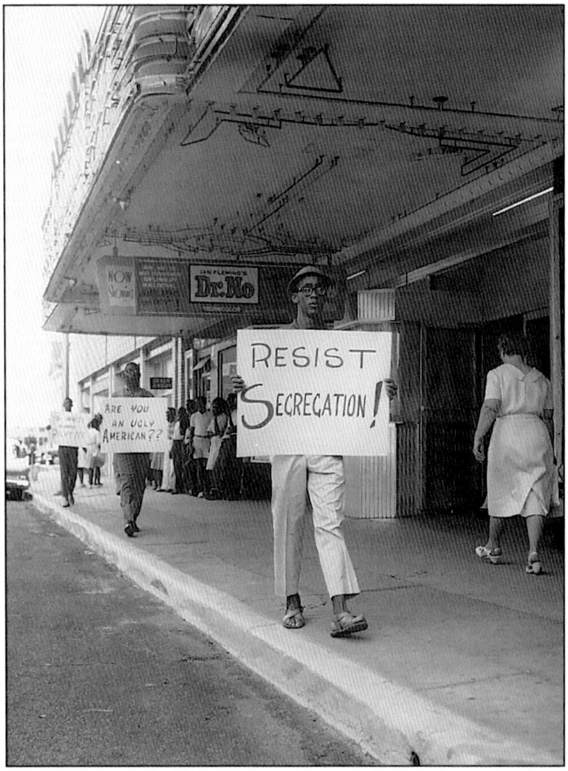

In 1954, the U.S. Supreme Court struck down the "separate but equal doctrine," the law of the land since the 1896 *Plessy v. Ferguson* decision. An adult branch and a youth council were established in Marianna in the early 1960s. The adult branch was led by Rev. C.S. Pope, Aaron Scott Marks, and Deacon Arthur Bryant. Earnest Williams and Anthony Swilley served as president and vice president, respectively, of the youth council. Other student activists included Shirley Bellamy, Juanita and Jessie Williams, Fred Bellamy, Adge Barnes, Aldric Borders, Walter Williams, and Carol, Daniel, and Richmond Marks. Other adult leaders included Lynn Collins, (Florida State Archives Photographic Collection.)

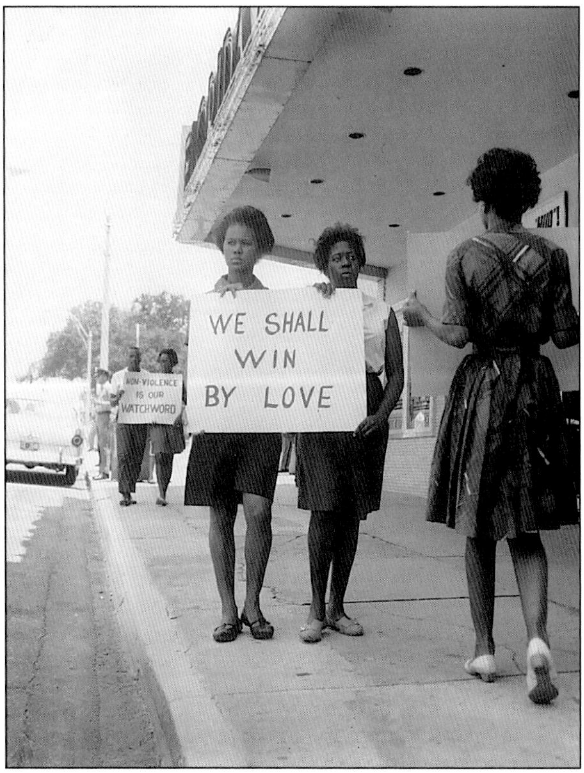

The youth council of the NAACP staged sit-ins at the soda fountains in Watson's Rexall and Hightower Drugstores and restaurants that refused to serve blacks. They picketed other Marianna businesses that did not employ blacks. A 1965 "swim-in" at the Blue Springs park ended tragically when Robert Clemons, on leave from military service, drowned while trying to save a youth protester. The Ritz and Gem movie houses in Marianna, like those in Tallahassee (pictured on this page), were segregated. Blacks were confined to the balconies and prohibited from entering the main floor lobby to purchase refreshments. (Florida State Archives Photographic Collection.)

Two

Marianna Scenes

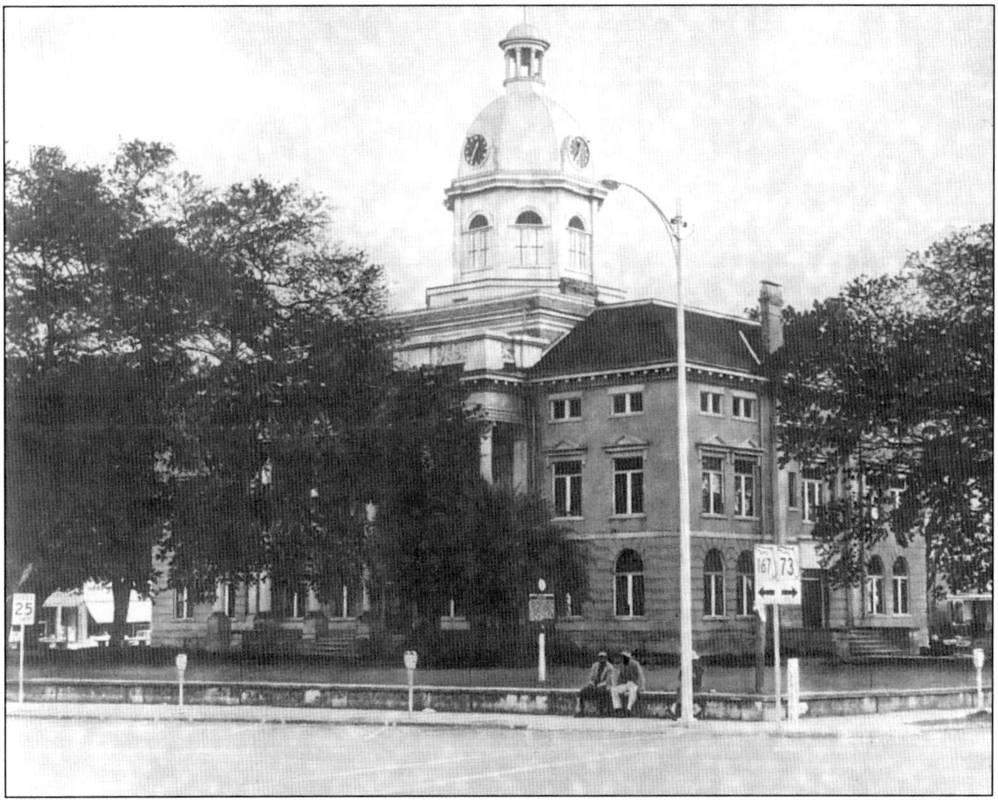

The Jackson County Courthouse is shown here as it appeared before it was remodeled in 1962. For years, "the Courthouse Square" served as a gathering place for many blacks who came to town on Saturdays to meet friends, shop, and peddle their produce. (Brewer's Studio.)

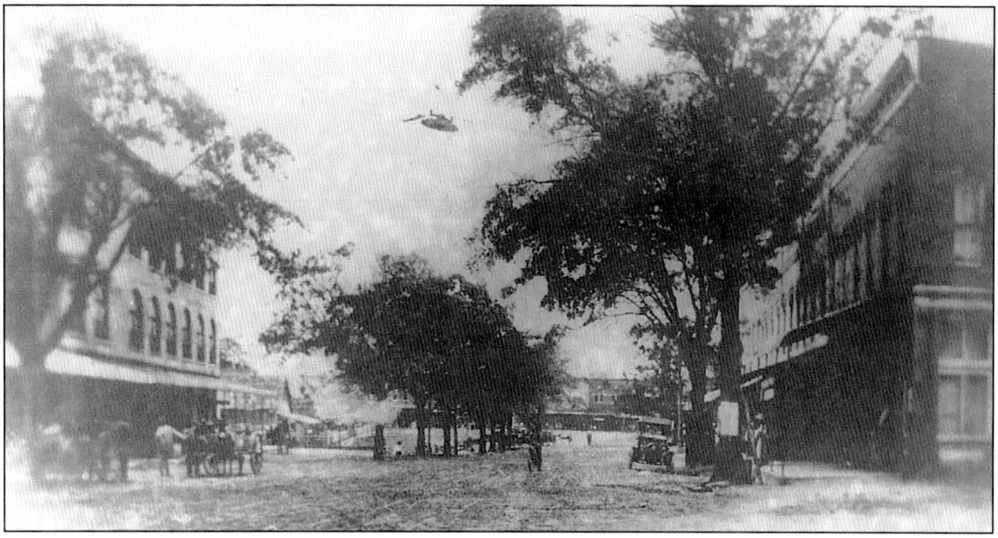

This is a 1915 view of Lafayette Street, Marianna, the county seat of Jackson County. Jackson County, in Florida's panhandle, is 70 miles west of Tallahassee. It is bordered on the north by Georgia and Alabama. The chief mode of transportation for blacks during this era was mule and wagon. (Brewer's Studio.)

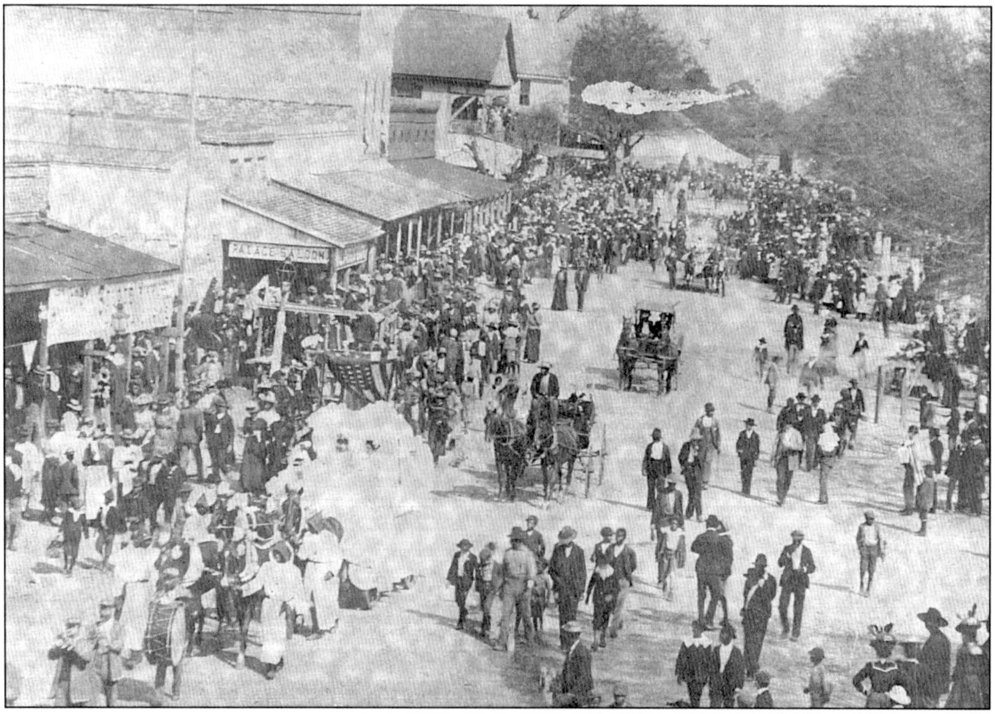

Downtown Marianna is pictured looking east at the May 20, 1901 Spring Parade. The May 20th celebrations were held throughout the county for many years, to mark the approximate time when blacks in Florida learned of their freedom. Blacks in Jackson County held their first parade on July 4, 1866, to celebrate their recently gained freedom. The display of the American flag and pictures of Abraham Lincoln by the black paraders caused quite a stir in the white community. (Brewer's Studio.)

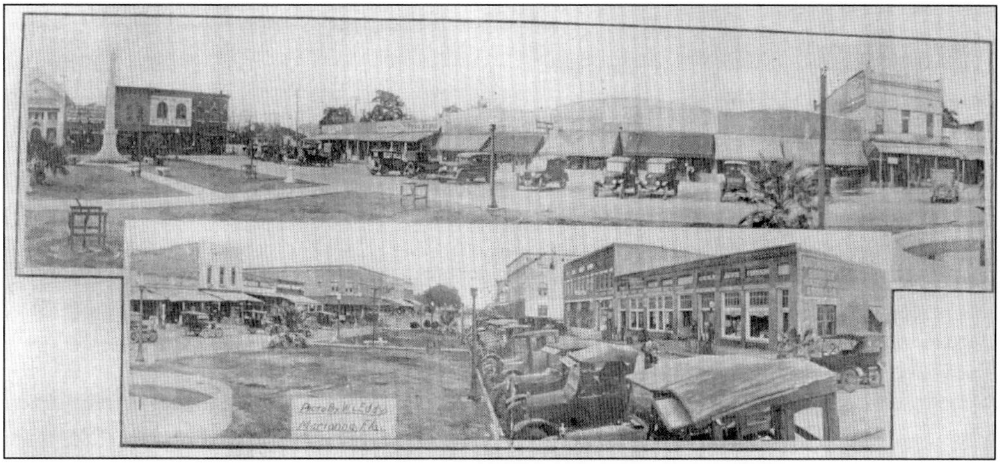

Pictured above is downtown Marianna and Confederate Park, along Highway 90. Many of the buildings remain but have been renovated and renamed. The building at top (on the extreme left) is the original First Bank Building. Adjacent to it is Harrison Chevrolet Company, which employed a few blacks, including Arthur "Sport" Crawford and Henry Jones. (Brewer's Studio.)

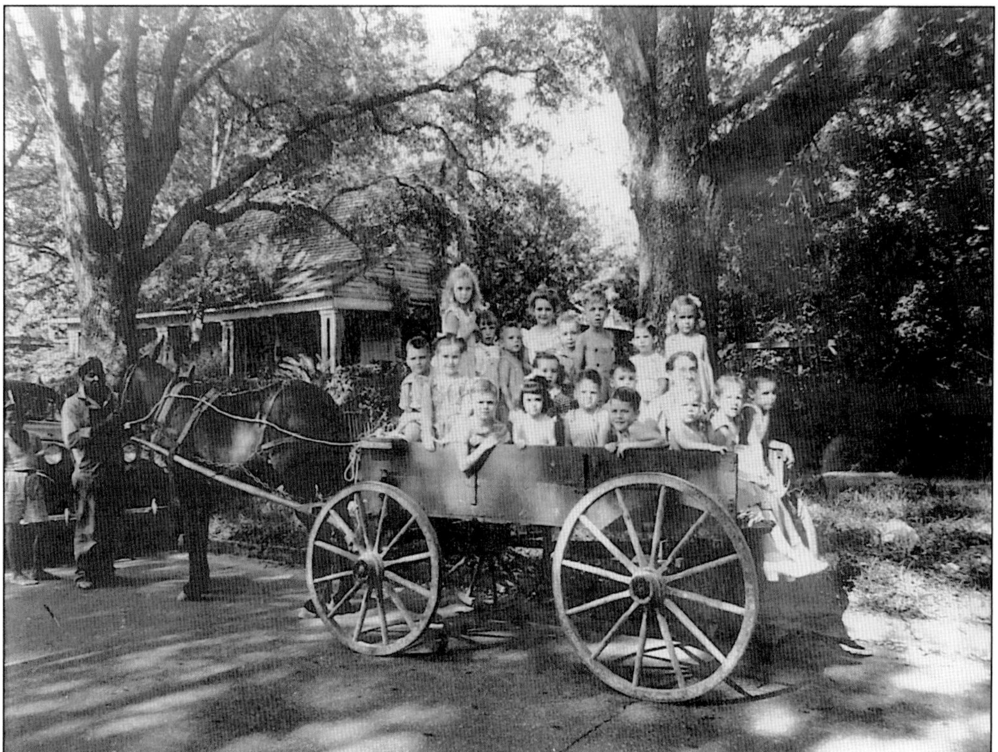

Many black men with little or no education were relegated to work as laborers, porters, and domestics. Others were forced to leave their families and find work in Panama City and Pensacola or South Florida, where opportunities were more plentiful. (Brewer's Studio.)

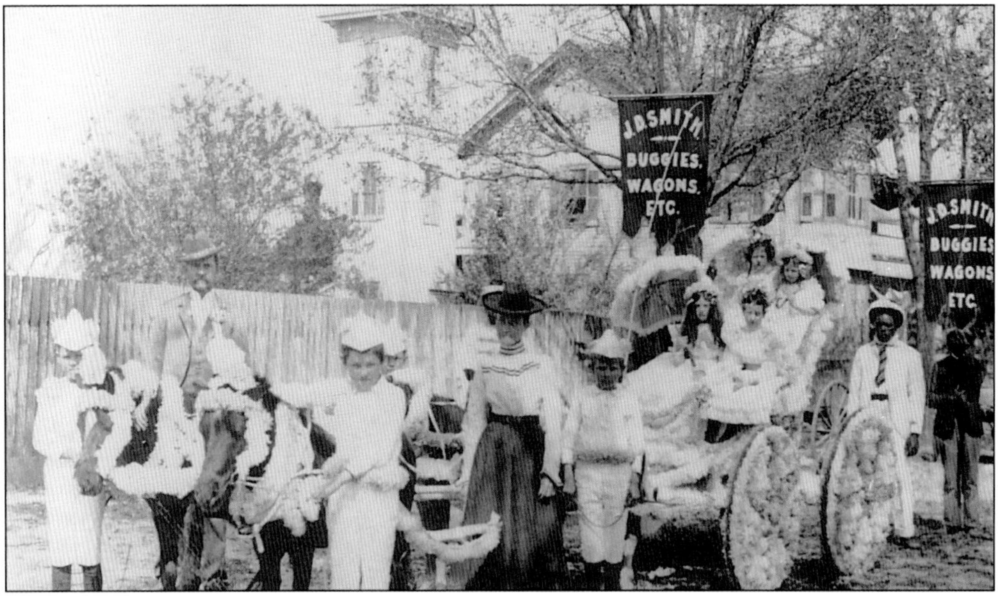

As late as the 1950s, many blacks were still sharecropping on the same lands as their ancestors labored during the times of slavery. As farms became mechanized and the need for labor diminished, many blacks in the rural areas joined the great migration north, while some became unskilled laborers in Marianna. The average hourly wage for domestics and laborers was 50¢.(Brewer's Studio.)

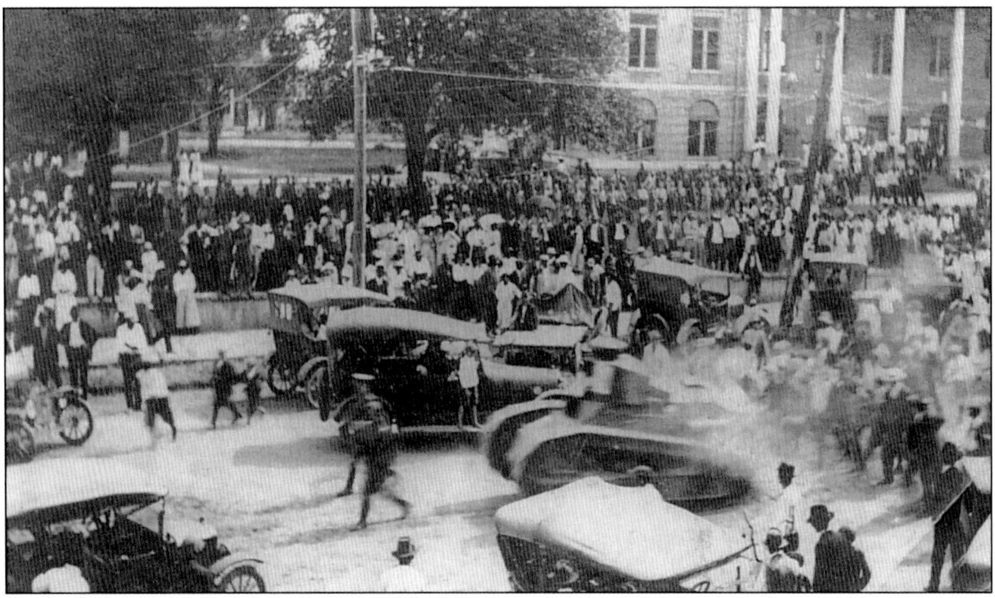

When America entered World War I on April 6, 1917, African Americans joined the military in record numbers. Of the 370,000 African Americans who enlisted, 458 were from Jackson County. Sixteen gave their lives. In 1919, Armstrong Purdee, the first black lawyer in Jackson County and editor of the *Florida Bugle*, appeared before the county commission and was granted approval to erect a monument on the courthouse square in memory of the black soldiers killed in France. The Confederate Memorial remains the only one on the square. (Brewer's Studio.)

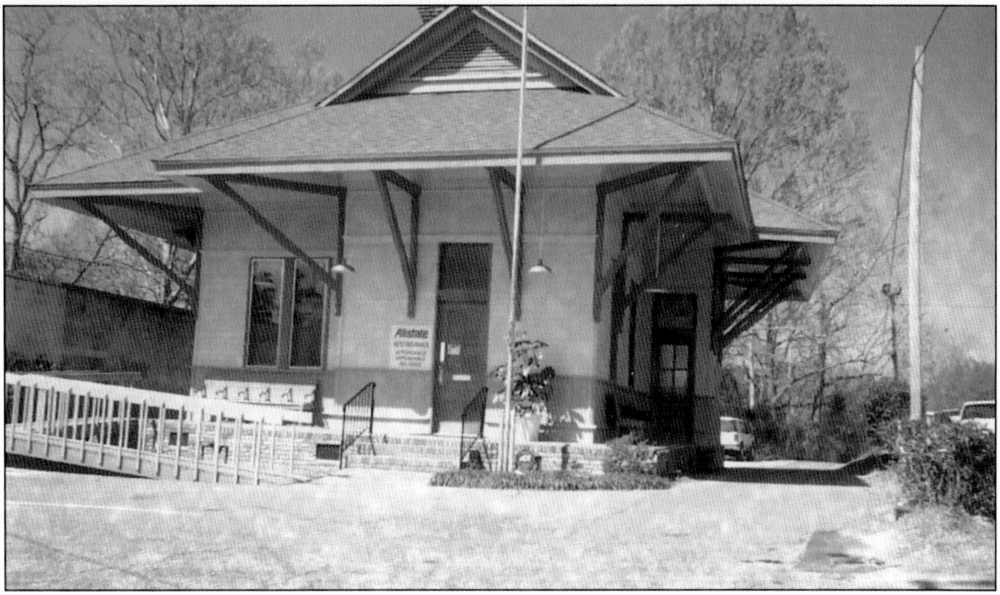

Pictured is a section of the old Louisville & Nashville train station that has been renovated and relocated. The door on the right led to the "Colored" waiting room. "White Only" and "Colored Only" signs were prominently displayed at drinking fountains, rest rooms, and many other places in Jackson County until the 1960s.

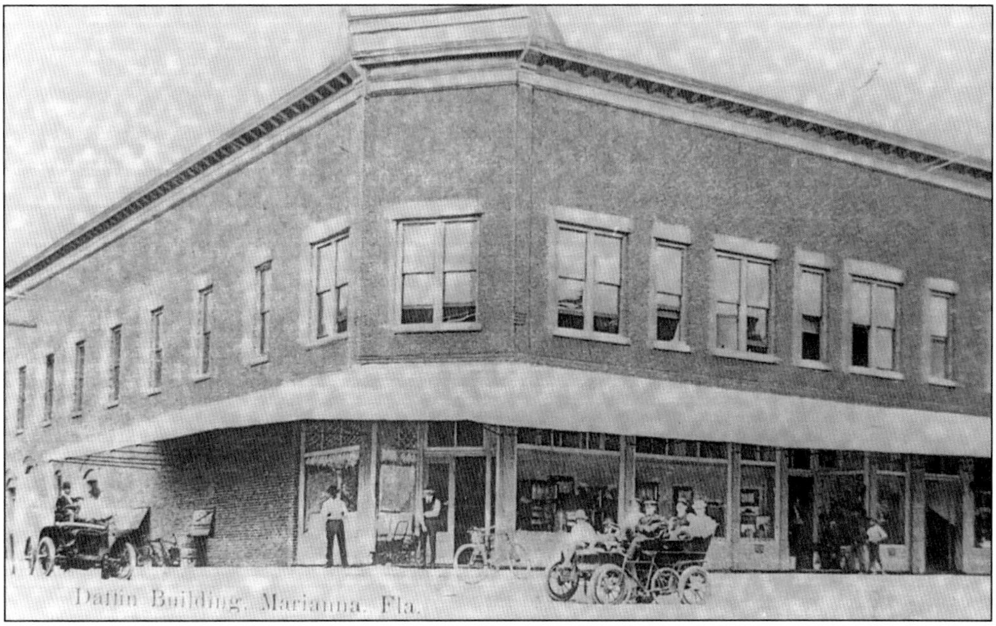

The F.C. Daffin building, located at the corner of Lafayette and Green Streets, is the oldest business in Jackson County. In its early history it served as a general merchandise store and employed a few African Americans, including Rev. Robert Roulhac, Joseph McLane, James Black, and Sam Bryant. McLane became successful in real estate and as a maitre d' in hotels in Jacksonville and several northern resorts. In 1934, he donated the land for McLane Park on the West End of Marianna. The park and community center provided the only recreational outlet for black children until the late 1970s. (Brewer's Studio.)

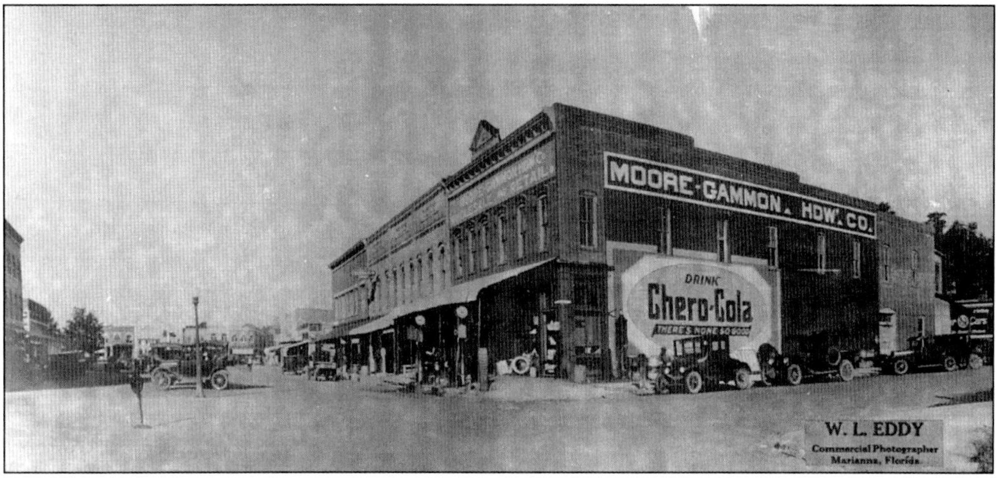

Moore-Gammon Hardware was located at the corner of Lafayette and Madison Streets in downtown Marianna. In the early 1900s, a number of blacks owned businesses on and around Madison Street. There were more black businesses in Marianna at the turn of the century than there are today. Black businesses suffered after the passage of the Civil Rights Act of 1964 and the integration of public facilities. (Brewer's Studio.)

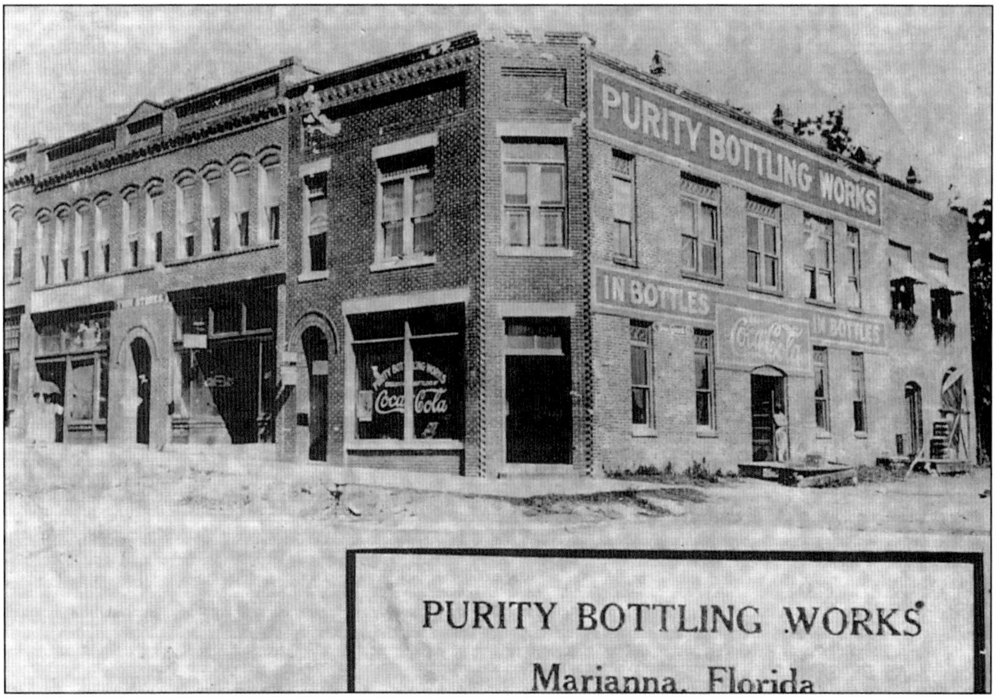

Purity Bottling Works was founded about 1912 and operated in downtown Marianna for years before becoming the Marianna Bottling Company. About the time Purity was established, the city embarked upon an extensive project to pave the downtown streets. Later, streets were paved and sidewalks were created in the white community. However, with the exception of the major streets—Orange, St. Andrews, and Old Cottondale Road—streets in the black community were not paved until the recent past. There are still no sidewalks anywhere in the black community. (Brewer's Studio.)

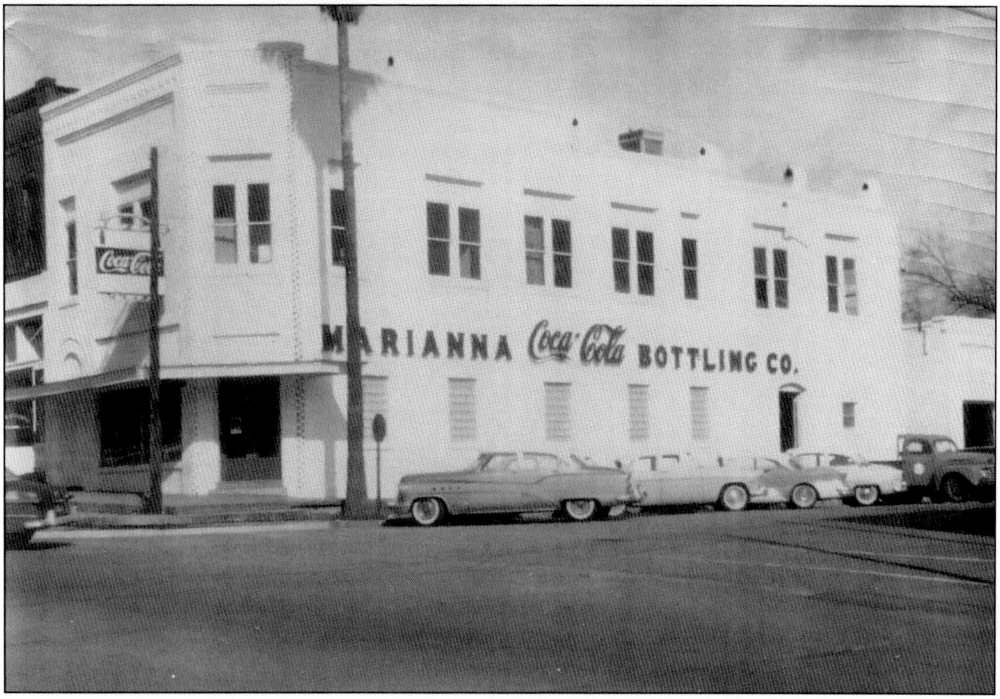

The Marianna Bottling Company provided employment for a number of African Americans, including Theodore Baker, Albert Robinson, and Rev. A.H. Parker. Today, part of the building is used as a beauty supply company that caters primarily to blacks. (Brewer's Studio.)

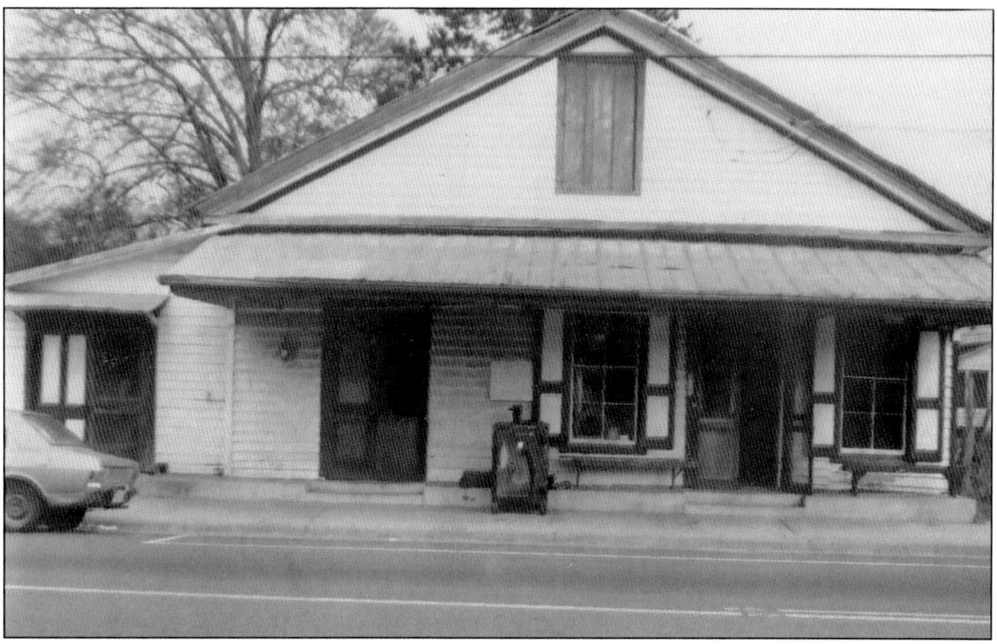

Pender's General Store, located in Greenwood, Florida, has been a trading place for blacks living in and around Greenwood since 1867. The store was built by Napoleon B. Long and Riley Cicero Long. (Florida State Archives Photographic Collection.)

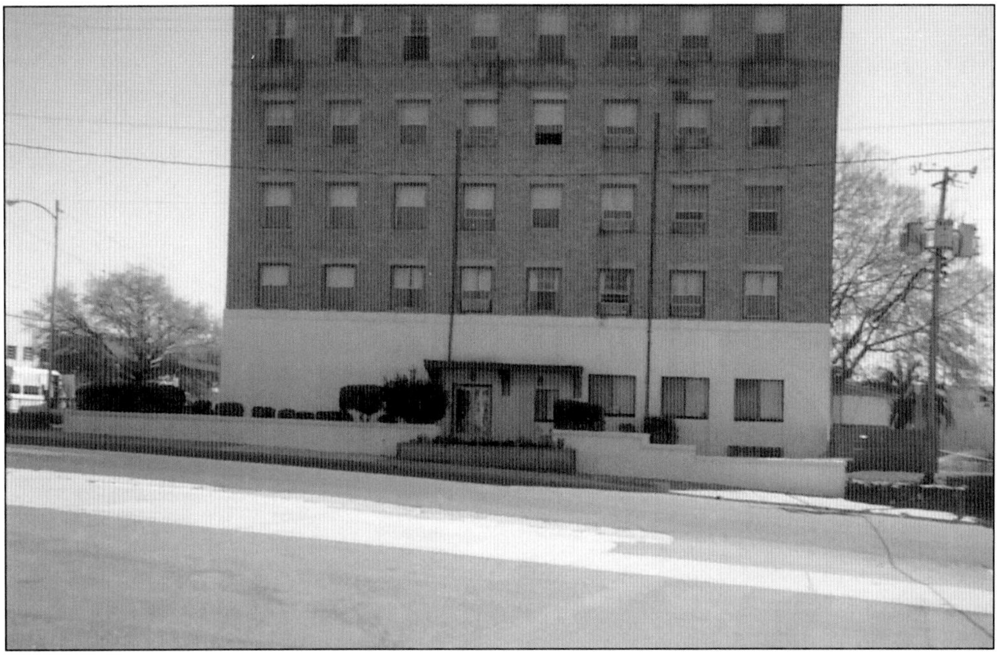

Chipola Hotel, located on the corner of Caledonia and Constitution Lane, was constructed in the 1880s. It has been remodeled several times. Blacks found employment there as cooks, maids, and porters. Benjamin "Buck" Pinkard and Matthew Huff were long time employees. The hotel has been converted to the Chipola Apartments.

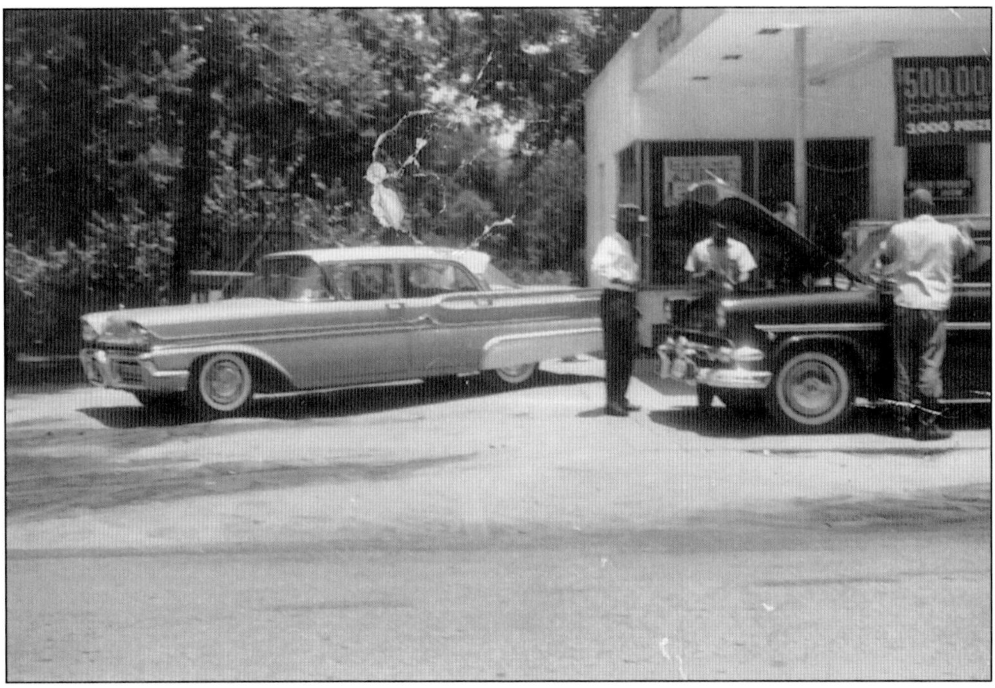

This scene took place at Johnny's Gulf Station, located on Orange Street on the "West End." African-American owner Johnny W. Sansome operated this full-service station with one full-time employee, Toney "Bish" Gilbert, and one part-time employee, Johnny Speights.

Three

FAMILY LIFE

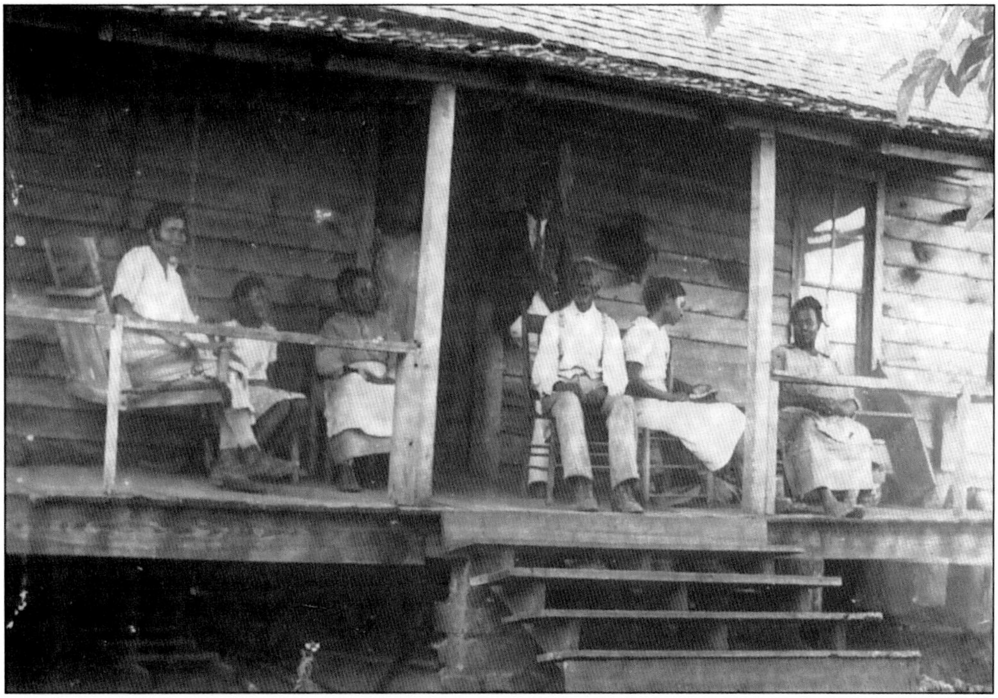

Anderson Baker, a former slave, was one of the first freedmen to be granted land under the 1862 Homestead Act. On November 30, 1878, he was granted 80 acres just north of Marianna in the Florida Caverns/Blue Hole area. He often shared with his granddaughter, Sarah Baker Speights of Marianna, many of his experiences. He told her that the cave was used by blacks to steal away for worship service, singing and praising God. He said, "the Blue Hole was not only used for fishing, but for the preservation of meat." He related that the low temperature of the underground "blue hole" provided an excellent environment to store food. Baker died in 1940 at the age of 104. His son, James Baker, lived to be 106 years old. The above picture of the Baker family and adult education teacher LeRoy Bell (standing) was taken on June 24, 1935. (Florida State Archives Photographic Collection.)

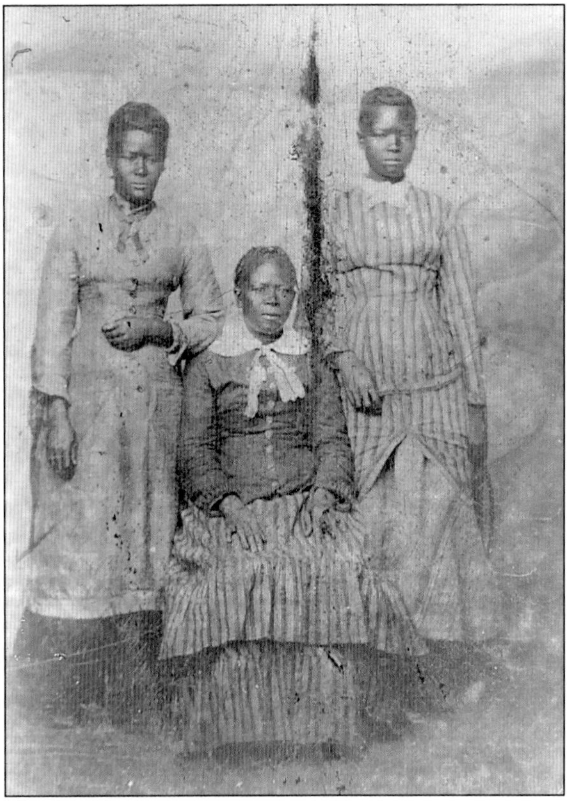

Former slaves Rebecca Gilbert, (seated) and daughters Bessie (left) and Lafuse (right), are seen in turn-of-the-century dresses sewn on a pedal sewing machine. They were raised in a community known as the Mt. Ararat or Rabb Valley, where pulp wood was an important industry. Log cabins homes were built by drawing the pulp from the logs.

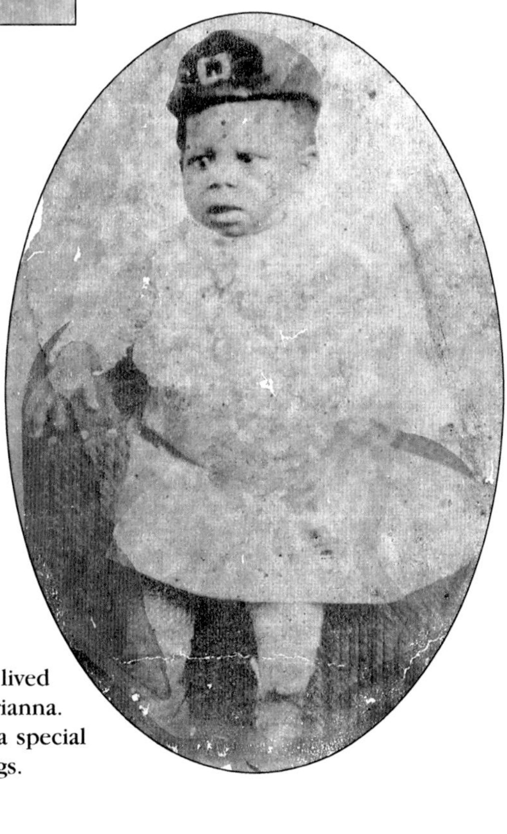

Shown at right is toddler Laura Colquitt, who lived on St. Andrews Street on the West End of Marianna. In this photo, she is appropriately attired for a special occasion with hat, a beautiful dress, and leggings.

Joe Dickens, a resident of the Whitesville Community, west of Marianna off Highway 90, was a sharecropper with Rudolph Hinson for many years before acquiring his own farm.

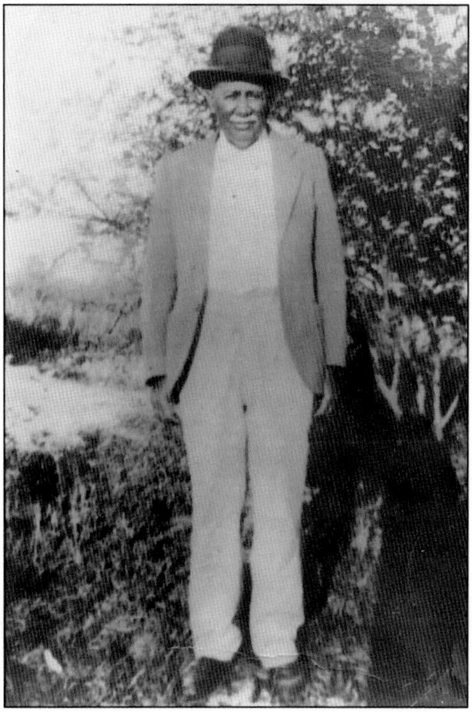

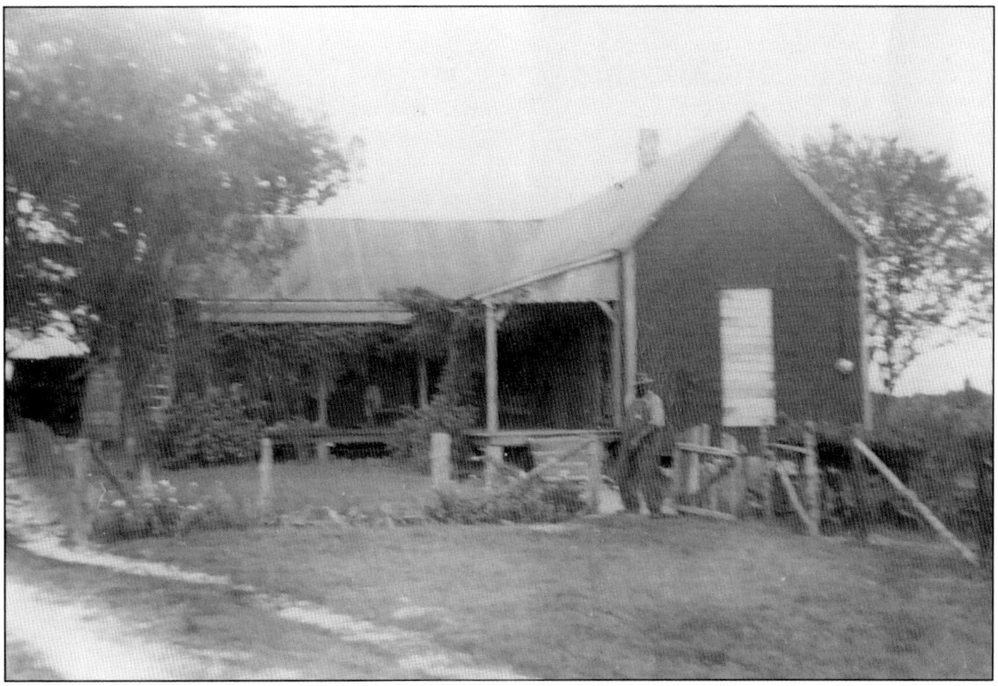

Charlie Speights and Tivis Speights' home place off Highway 73, northwest of Marianna city limits, was situated on a 40-acre tract of land. The family farm was the primary source of income for their eight children. They grew corn, cotton, peanuts, and raised hogs until the 1960s. Speights, in the foreground, was also a skilled carpenter. A son, Elmer Speights, still resides on his portion of the home place.

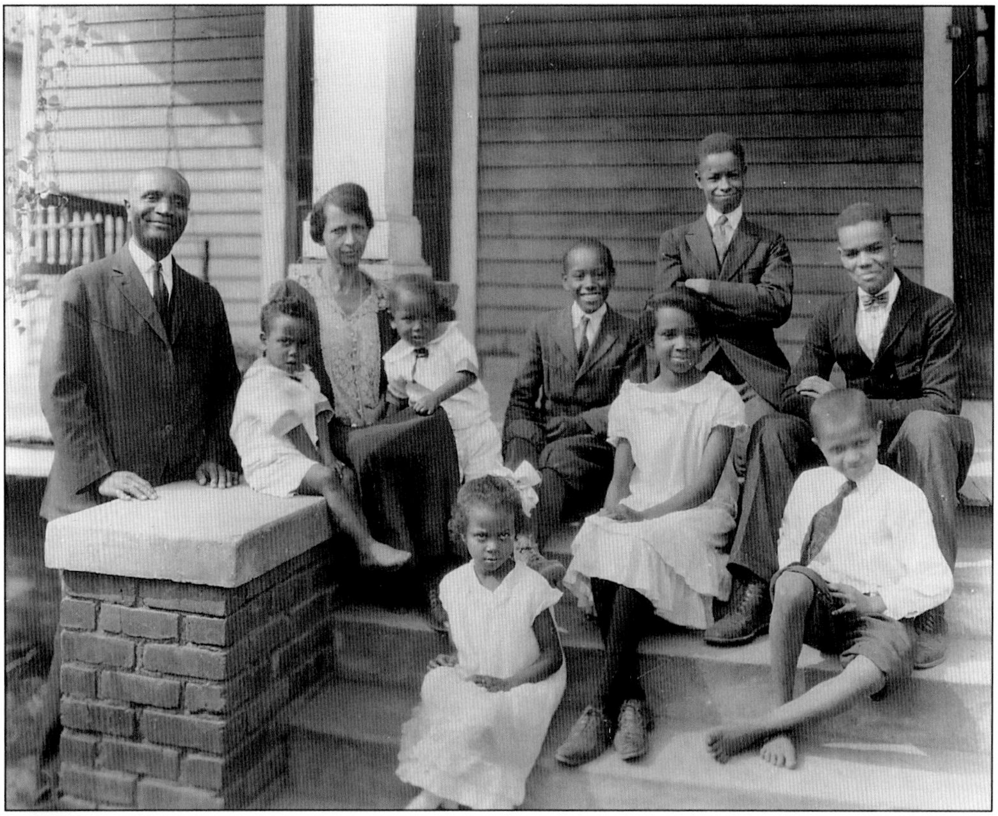

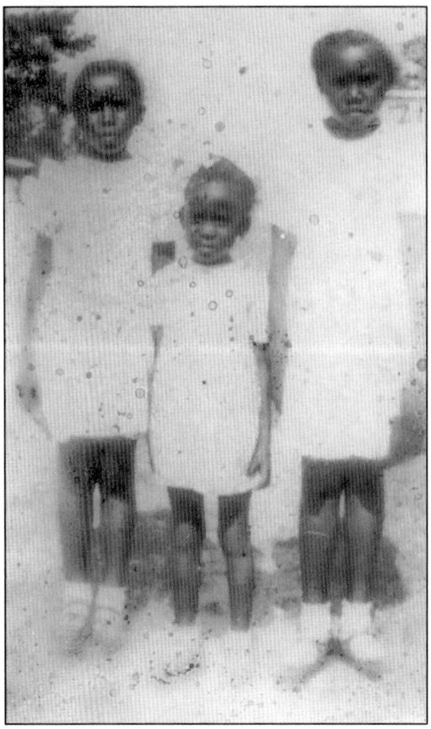

Rev. Robert Roulhac and his wife, Minerva Rhodes Roulhac, lived in Marianna until he graduated from Stillman College in 1905. They taught their children to stick together—if one has a penny, everyone has a penny; if one has a problem, everyone has a problem. He served as a Presbyterian minister in Selma, Alabama, before relocating to Detroit in the 1940s. Pictured, left to right, are twins Edgar and Edwin, Ruth, Simeon, Mary, Robert, John, and Joseph (without shoes).

Sisters Ora Mae Spires Peterson (left) and Otha Mae Spires Dickens (right) with first cousin Eldean Spires Nichols (center) were photographed by cousin Harvey Spears, the unofficial community photographer, at Antioch A.M.E. Church. Their Sunday best "Mary Jane" dresses were made by Willie Mae Spires, the community seamstress, on a pedal sewing machine. The young ladies picked blackberries for 25¢ a gallon to raise the money for the white voile material, and 50¢ for each dress to be made.

Lewis Benjamin was born a slave. He owned several hundred acres of land in the area of the present fair grounds and earned his living cutting logs and making cross ties for railroad beds and farming. He donated an acre of land to build a two-room school house which served as an adult night school and an elementary school for the Antioch, Rabb Valley, and Arberdeen communities. The school mysteriously burned in the late 1930s, after which the area A.M.E. churches provided school facilities. Benjamin brought produce to town on a mule and wagon and peddled it throughout the community. He died in 1959, at age 99.

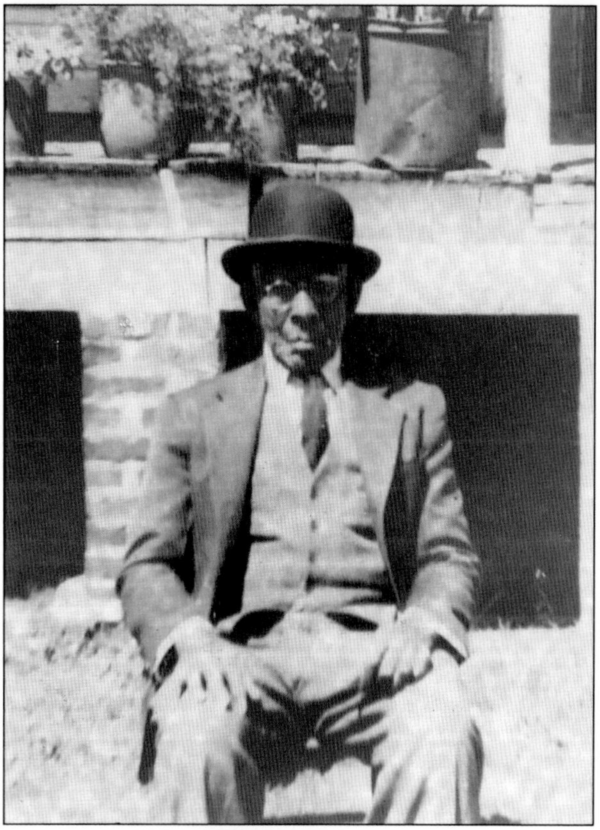

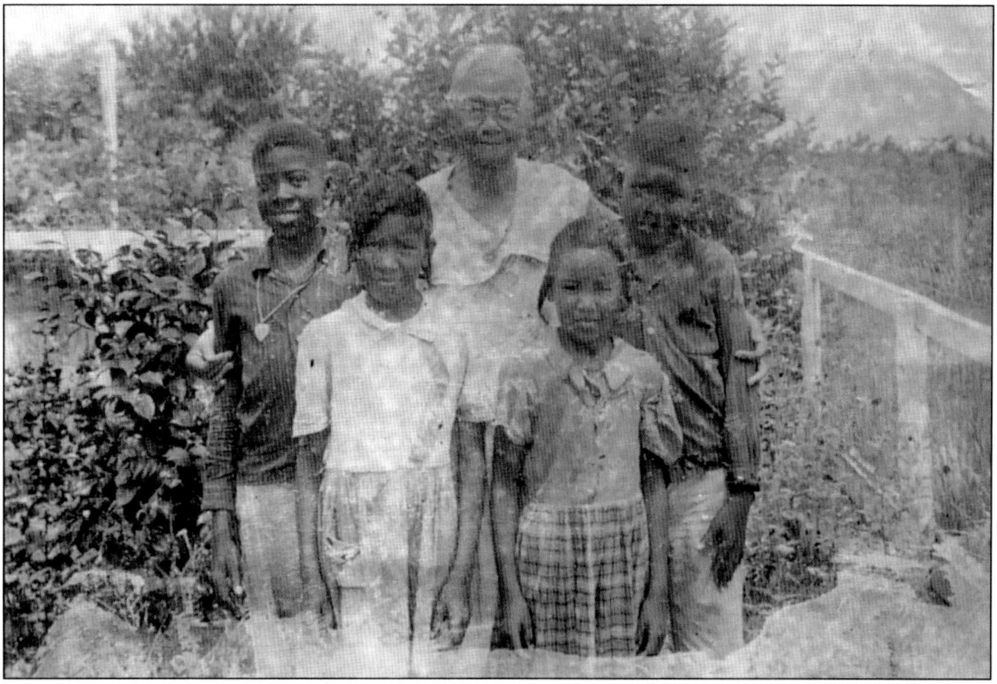

Nizy Gainer and grandchildren are pictured on the Gainer farm in the Browntown community.

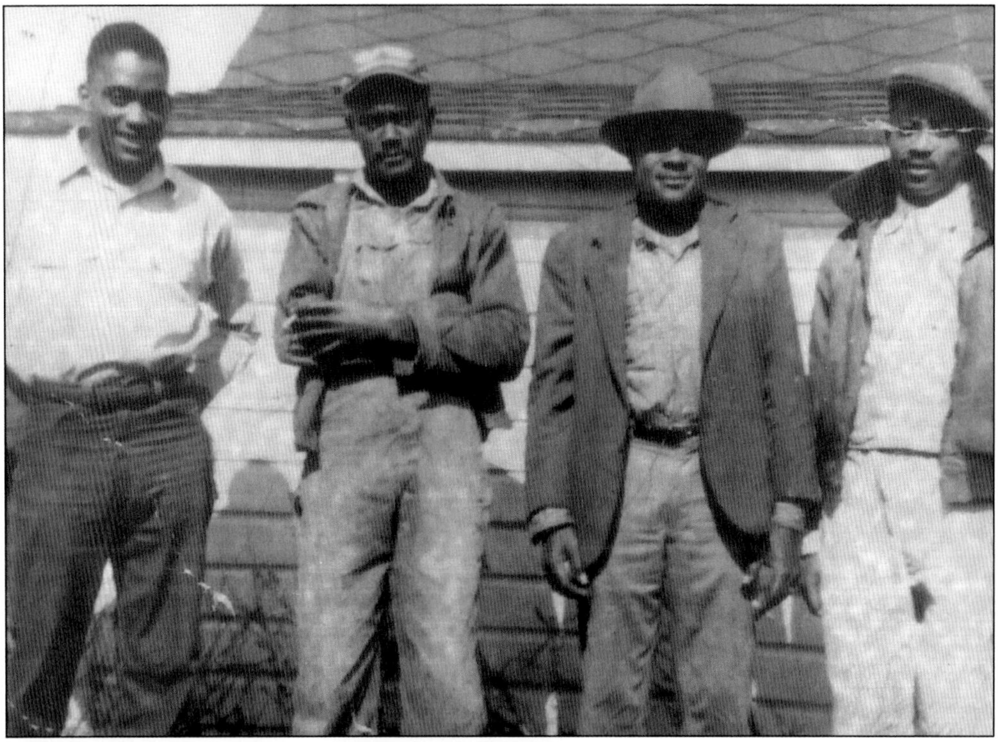

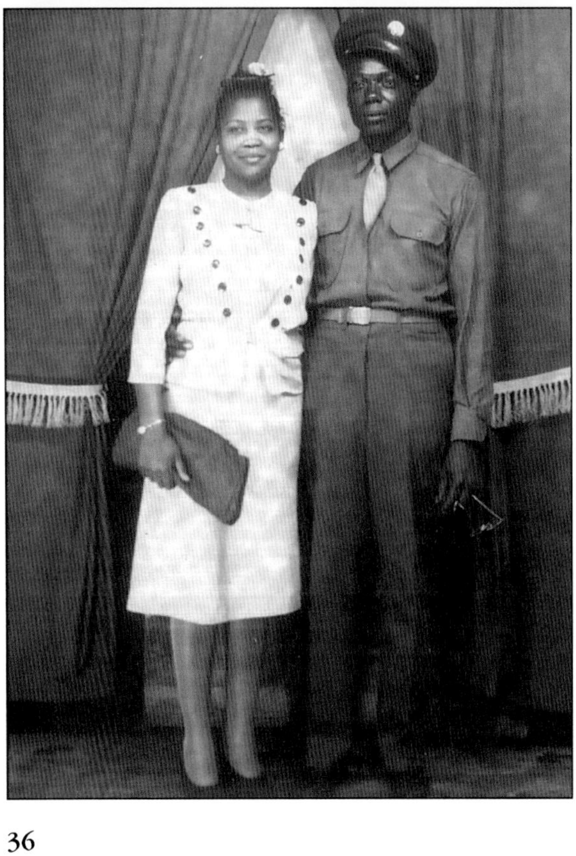

The Gainer brothers, sons of Will and Nizy Gainer, are an example of unity in the daily operation of a family farm. From left to right are Charlie, Willie, Rudy, and Thready Gainer.

Pictured are Sergeant and Dezzy Faulk and his wife, Grady. Sergeant Faulk was home on leave prior to going to Jefferson Barracks, Missouri, in the 1940s. Blacks have always been willing to take up arms in defense of the country and to win their own freedom.

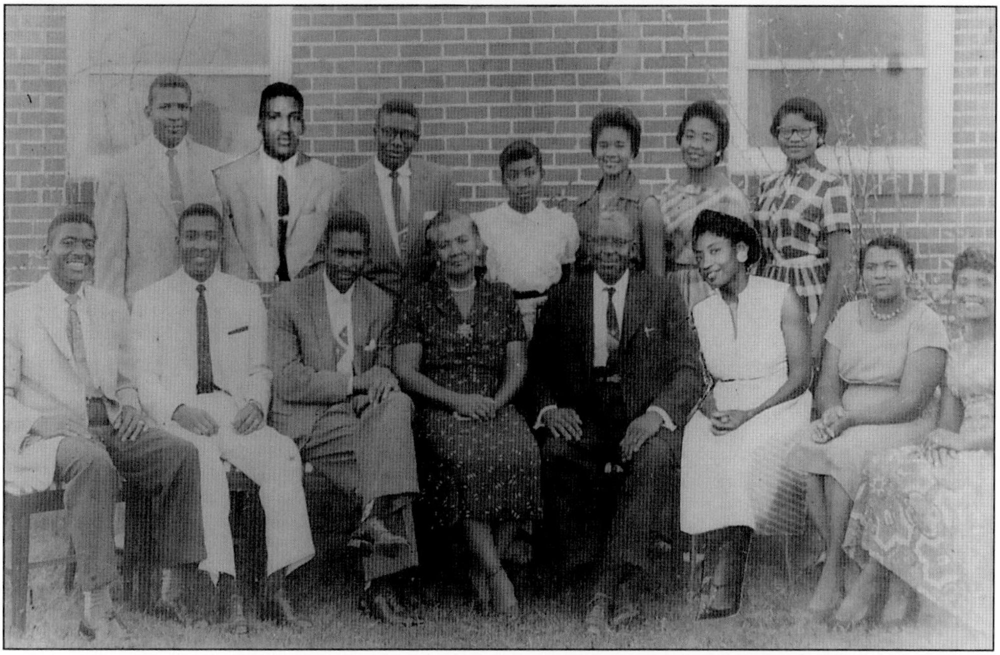

This photo, taken in 1952, includes Rev. Andrew H. Bowers Sr. his wife, Gertrude, and their 13 children. They owned and operated a farm in Bascom. Their children attended Jackson County schools and were members of Liberty Hill Missionary Baptist Church. Eleven children are graduates of Florida A&M University (FAMU). The other two sons pursued careers in business.

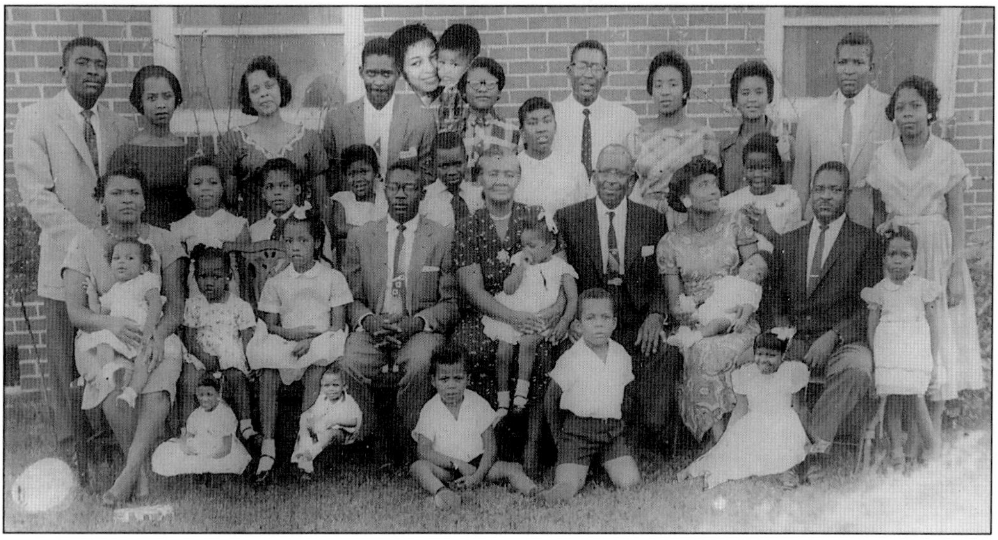

This 1952 photo includes Rev. and Mrs. Andrew H. Bowers (center), their children, children's spouses, and grandchildren. From their humble beginnings on the farm, their strong belief in God, and knowledge of the importance of hard work, the Bowers children were motivated to continue their undergraduate studies at FAMU. They have built careers in education, administration, law, medicine, real estate, farming, and financial management. The tradition continues with the grandchildren who have chosen careers as attorneys, engineers, doctors, accountants, journalists, artist, entertainers, information systems specialists, farmers, real estate brokers, entrepreneurs, and educators.

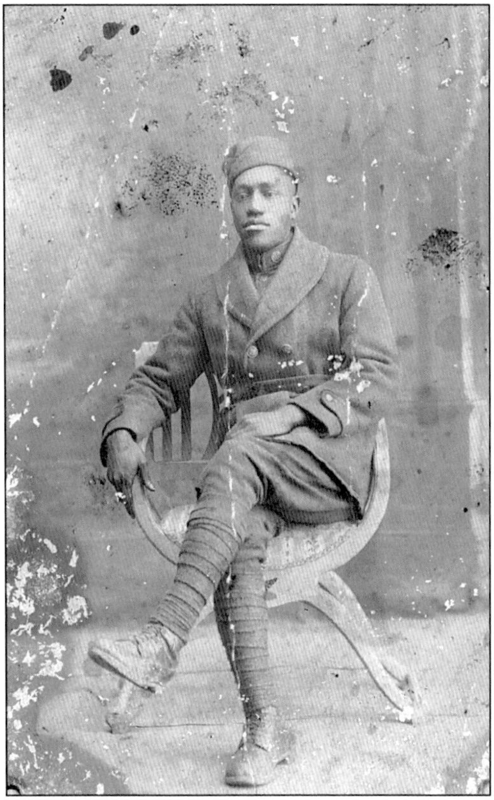

William Baker, son of Anderson Baker, was killed in the line of duty during World War I. In 1917 and 1918, males born between 1873 and 1900 were required to register for the draft. The registration cards contain valuable family history information, including the registrant's full name, place of birth, race, citizenship, occupation, description, and signature.

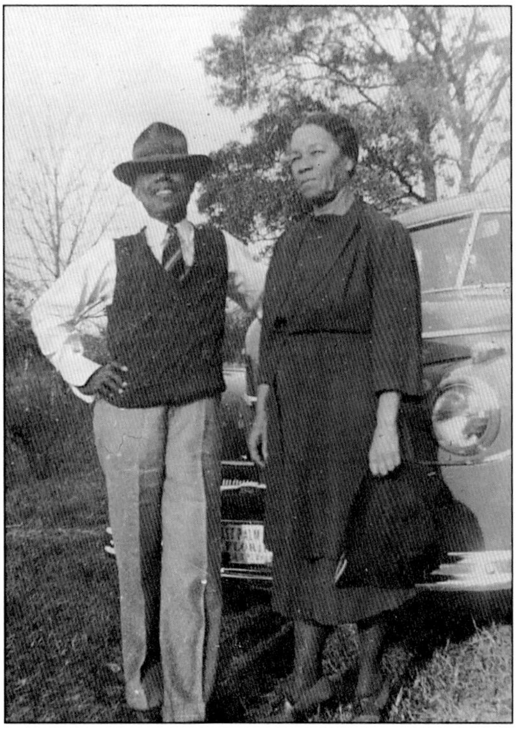

Johnny W. Sansome, a small business entrepreneur, is shown here with his mother, Ella Sansome, a former teacher in Jackson County.

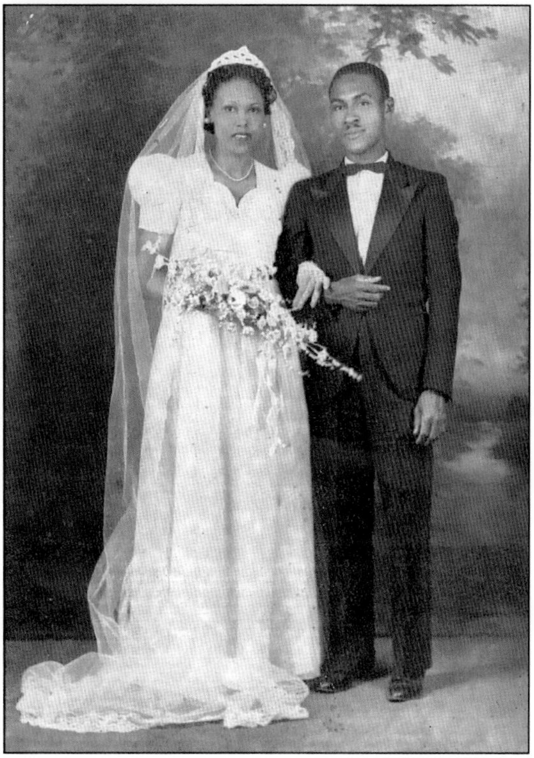

Pictured here is Lillian Knight, the daughter of Harmon and Mary Knight. She was the bride of Clinton Preston in a very simple and impressive traditional home wedding. Such weddings usually took place in the living room or on the front porch of the bride's home.

Presiding Elder Rev. E. Harley and his wife, Annie B. Harley, celebrate their 50th anniversary in the dining room of their family residence.

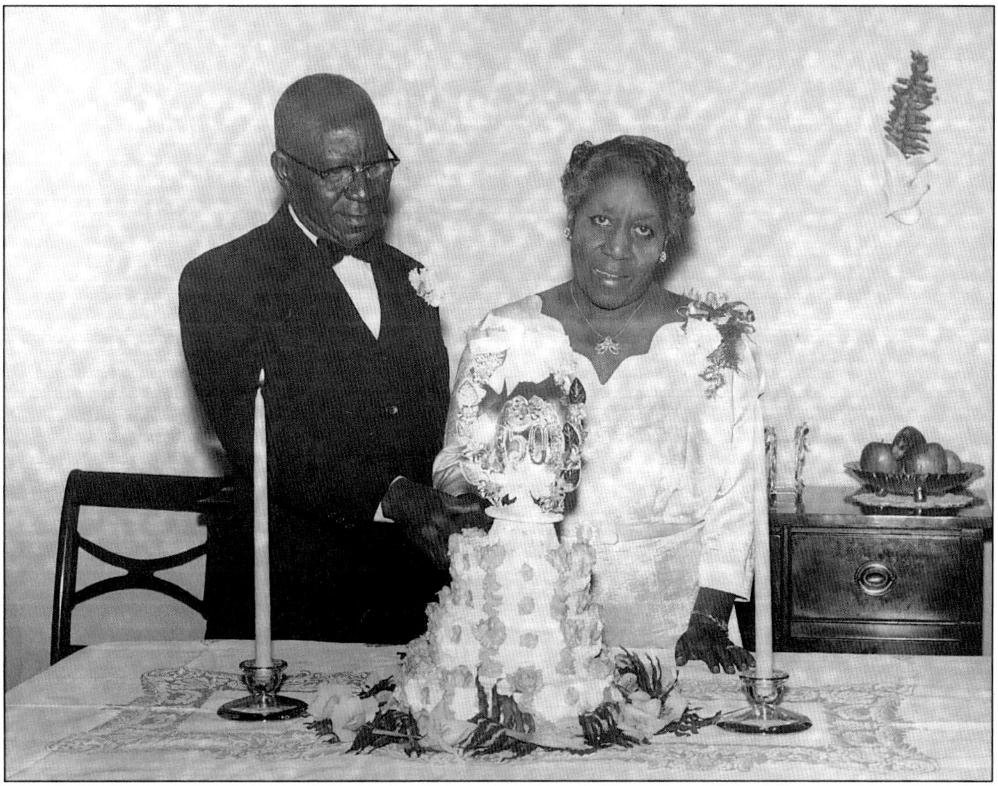

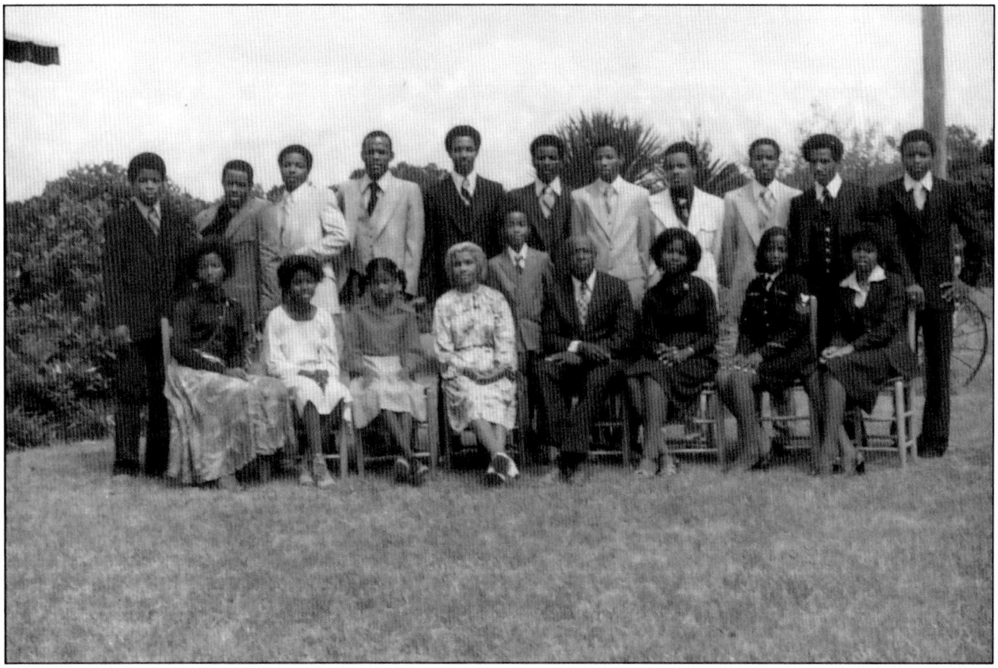

Pictured above is Rev. Walter Morgan Sr., his wife, Annie, and their 18 children. They reared their children on their farm off Highway 73, south of Marianna. Annie Morgan returned to high school while in her early 50s and earned her high school diploma. At age 54, she received an Associates Degree in Applied Science with a speciality in mental retardation from Chipola Junior College. She later worked as an aide at the Hope School for Exceptional Children in Jackson County. One Morgan child graduated from Bethune-Cookman College and another from Bowie State University in Maryland. Others have pursued careers in the military, government, and as entrepreneurs and farmers.

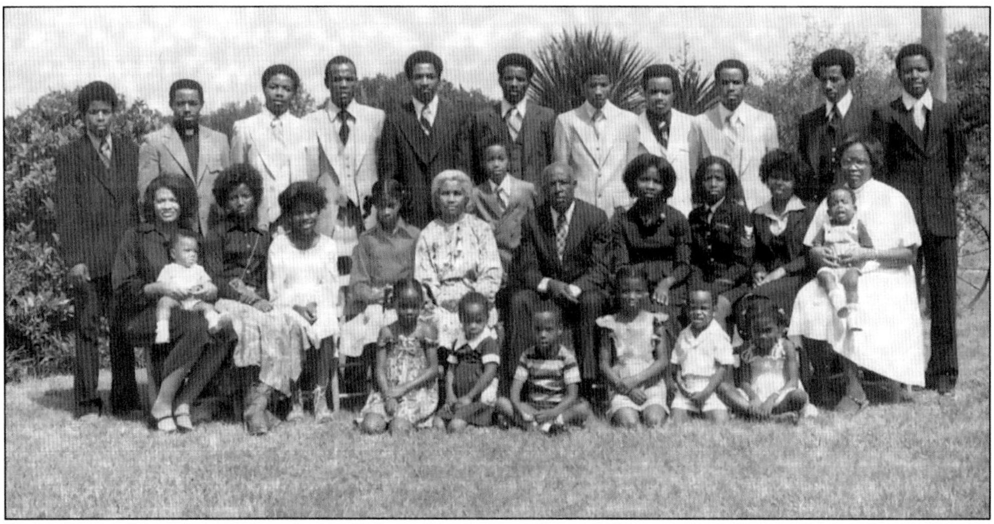

The above picture was taken during a family gathering of Rev. Walter Morgan Sr., his wife Annie, and their children, children's spouses, and grandchildren. Some of the grandchildren have completed college. Others "grands" either attend elementary school, high school, or college.

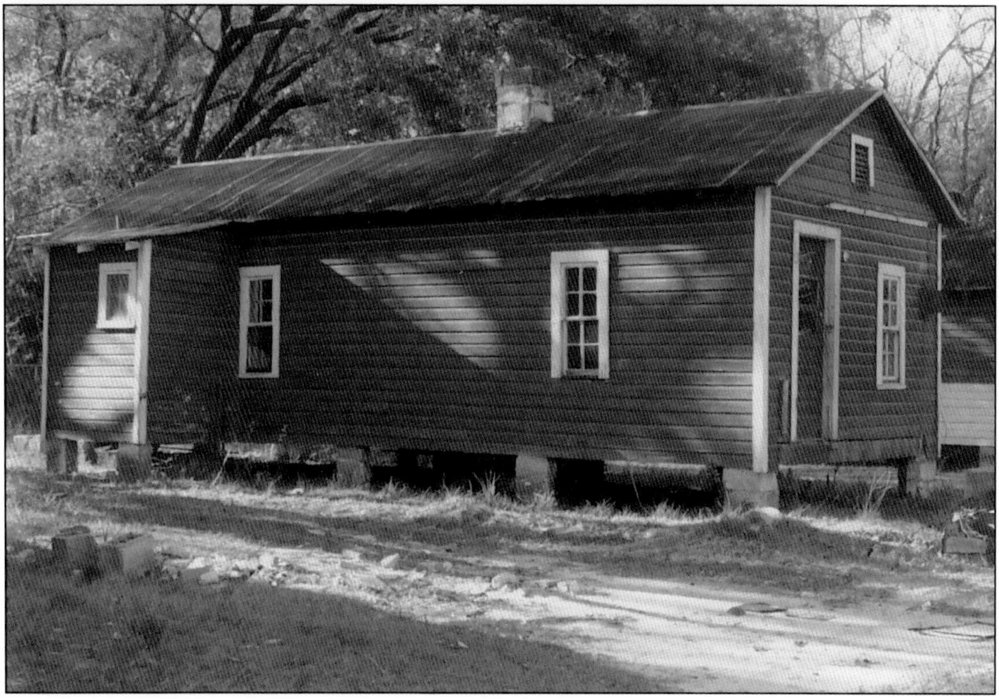

This house was the birthplace of Sarah Speights Pender and one of many located in "Burton Quarters," one of the oldest communities for African Americans in Marianna. These houses were not insulated and were without indoor toilets. The houses were later demolished and have been replaced by modern homes. The area is now known as Chipola Village.

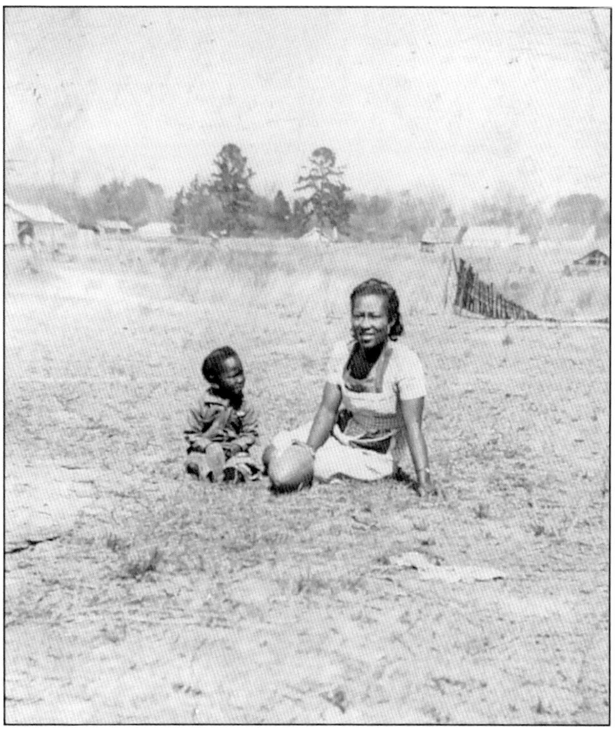

Sarah Speights and "Little Sarah" are seen outside the family home in Burton Quarters, resting after a game of touch football. Sarah Speights and her husband, Cleaster, raised three daughters and were their first and most influential teachers. They instilled in them that a good education is important and that hard work has its rewards.

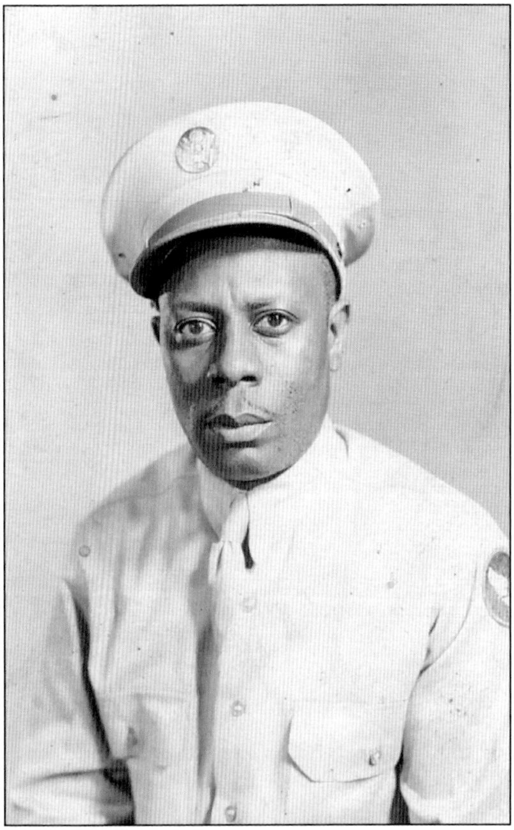

J.Y. Rolack (1907–1986), a descendant of Nero (b. 1805) and Nelly (b. 1811) Roulhac, was raised in the Buckhorn community. He and his wife, GeHazel Gibson Rolack, of the McChapel community, instilled in their children and grandchildren a love of family, self esteem, and trust in God. Rolack served in the Army during World War II, from August 1942 until November 1945. J.Y. lost his eyesight in 1952 but maintained his independence by operating a peanut vending concession in the Jackson County Training School snack bar for several years. J.Y. and GeHazel stressed the importance of education and what it could accomplish for their three children, Willie Hazel, Roy, and Sylvester, and six of their grandchildren, William, James, Freddie, Toney, Jamie, and Derrick, whom they helped raise. In 1965, J.Y. and his family relocated to Miami.

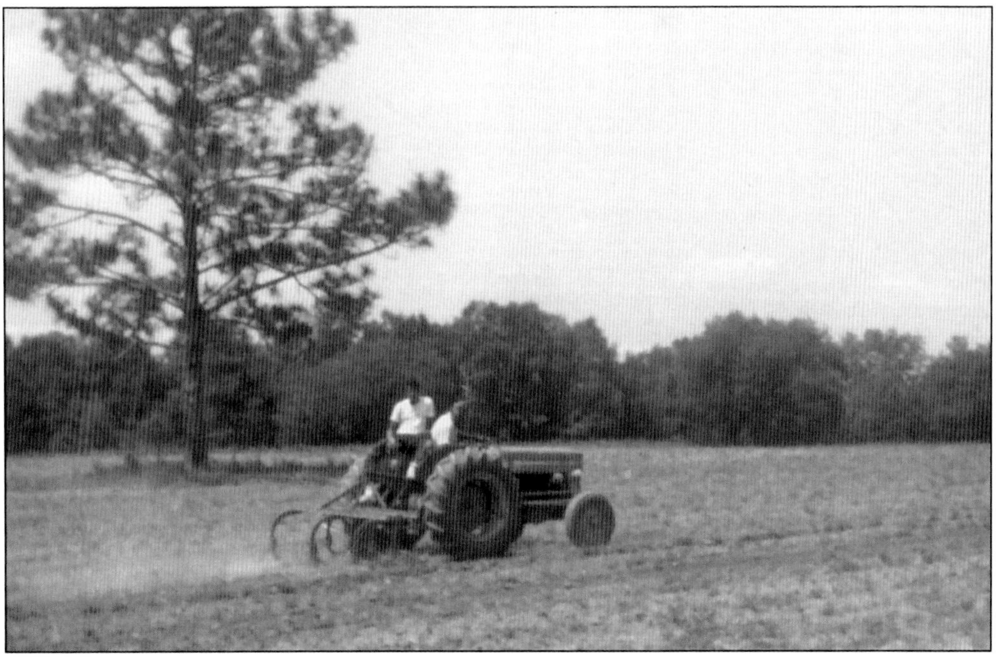

Rev. Walter Morgan Sr. is shown with his son, Randolph. Farm life was the primary livelihood for both large and small families.

Four

Religious Life

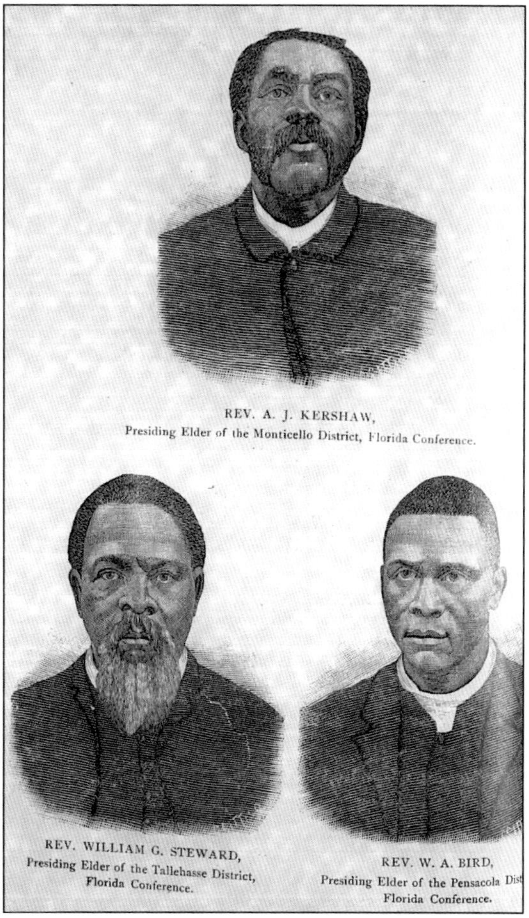

Ministers of the African Methodist Episcopal Church, led by presiding elder Charles H. Pearce, played a leading role in Florida's Reconstruction politics. Pearce believed that "A man in this State cannot do his whole duty as a minister except he looks out for the political interests of his people." During the 1868 constitutional convention, 10 of the 18 black delegates were affiliated with the A.M.E. Church. Four—Charles Pearce, William Bradwell, Robert Meacham, and Major Johnson—were ministers; six—Owen B. Armstrong, Auburn H. Erwin, Emanuel Fortune of Jackson County, Frederick Hill, Anthony Mills, and John W. Wyatt—were A.M.E. laymen. Rev. William G. Stewart of Georgia was sent to Florida to assist Pearce in organizing the A.M.E. Church. The above photo was taken during the Quarto Centennial Conference of the A.M.E. Church in Charleston, South Carolina, May 15-17, 1889. (Florida State Archives Photographic Collection.)

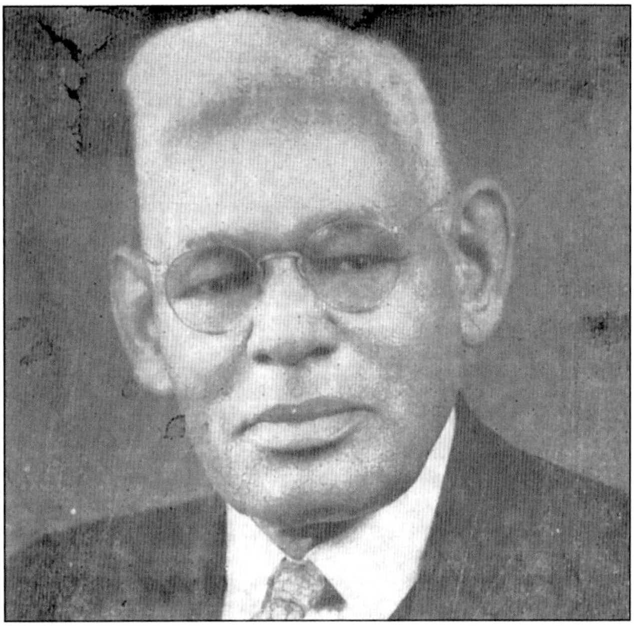

Rev. K.D. Britt was the founder and president of the West Florida Industrial College, also known as the Baptist Academy. The college, founded in 1910 in the Mt. Olive community, was later relocated to Marianna. Among the incorporators were A.H. Hays, G.H. Hill, A.H. Roulhac, J.N. Milton, D. Ellis, and J.D. Dinah. Reverend Britt served as pastor of St. Luke Baptist Church for 17 consecutive years. Under his leadership a new church was built on East Jackson Street. He was born and raised in Jackson County and was a member of St. John Baptist Church.

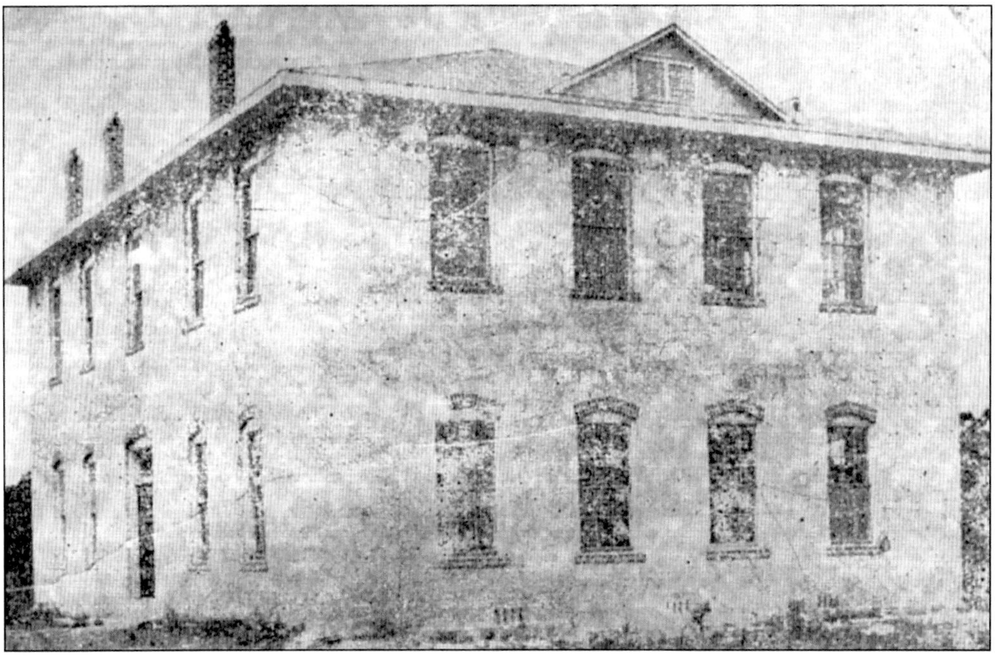

Pictured above is the Baptist Academy. In 1943, this two-story building became the first Jackson County Training Elementary School for students in grades one through six. There was no lunchroom; therefore, teachers and students took a packed lunch, often with peanut butter and jelly or bologna sandwiches. The structure was sub-standard in other ways—there were no indoor bathrooms or screens on the windows, and the building was heated with wood and coal. The school closed in 1952s, when for the first time, the county constructed a school for blacks. During its existence, the school was led by the following principals, respectively: L.C. Herring, Reola M. Bryan, William H. Harley, and George A. Bradley. The old elementary school site is now occupied by a one-story building owned by the 2nd West Florida Baptist Association.

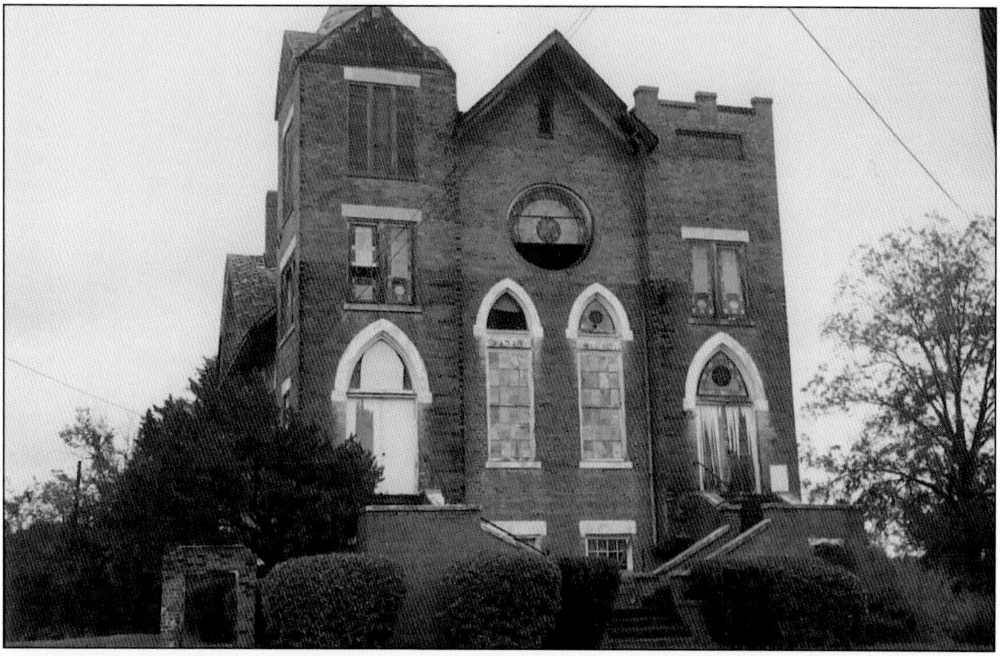

The old St. Luke Missionary Baptist Church was erected in 1921, under the leadership of Rev. K.D. Britt. Organized in 1867, St. Luke is one of the oldest black churches in Jackson County. In 1984, a new church was constructed on Orange Street, in the West End, on the original site of Gilmore Academy.

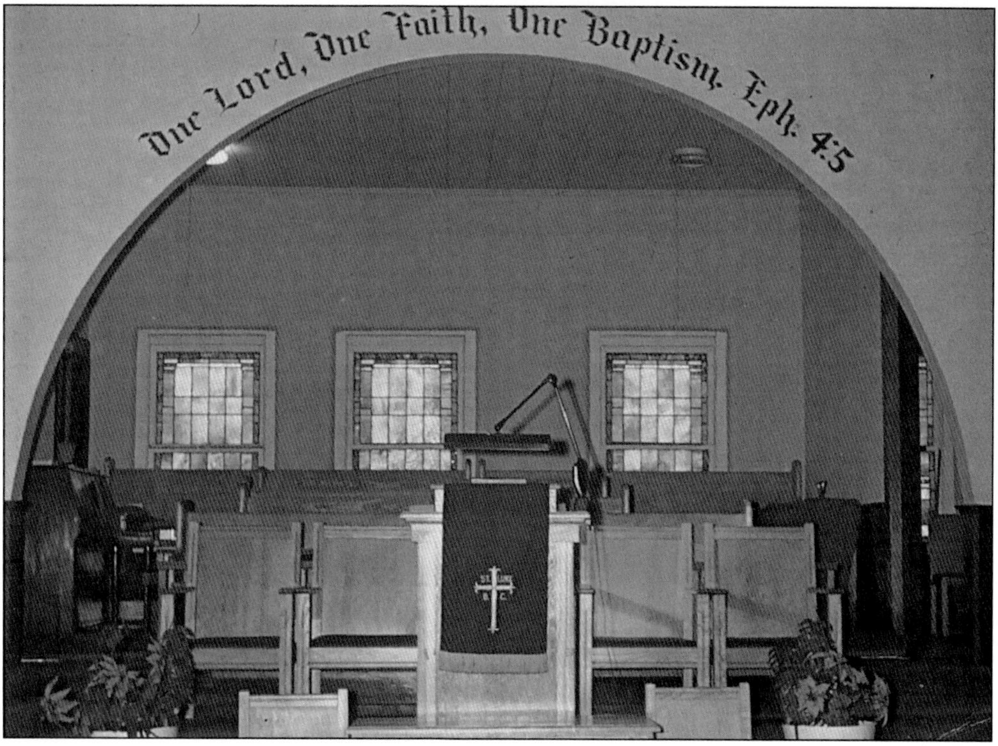

Shown here is the pulpit and choir stand of old St. Luke.

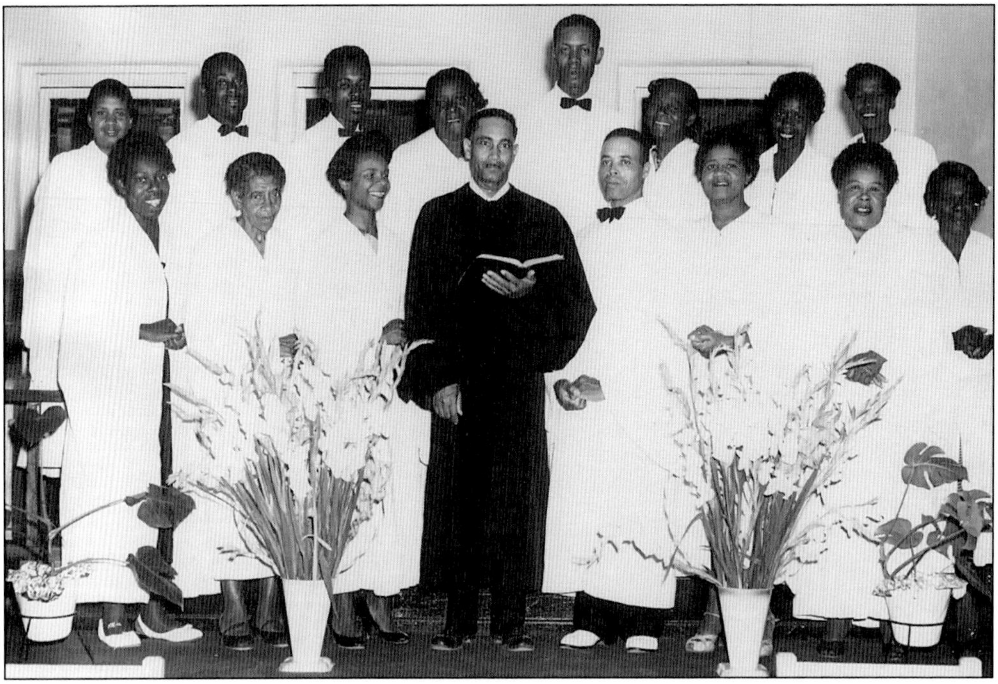

Pictured here is the St Luke Missionary Baptist Church Senior Choir. Rev. A.H. Parker, pastor, is in the center. Pianist and director of music, Ruth W. Glenn, is third from the right.

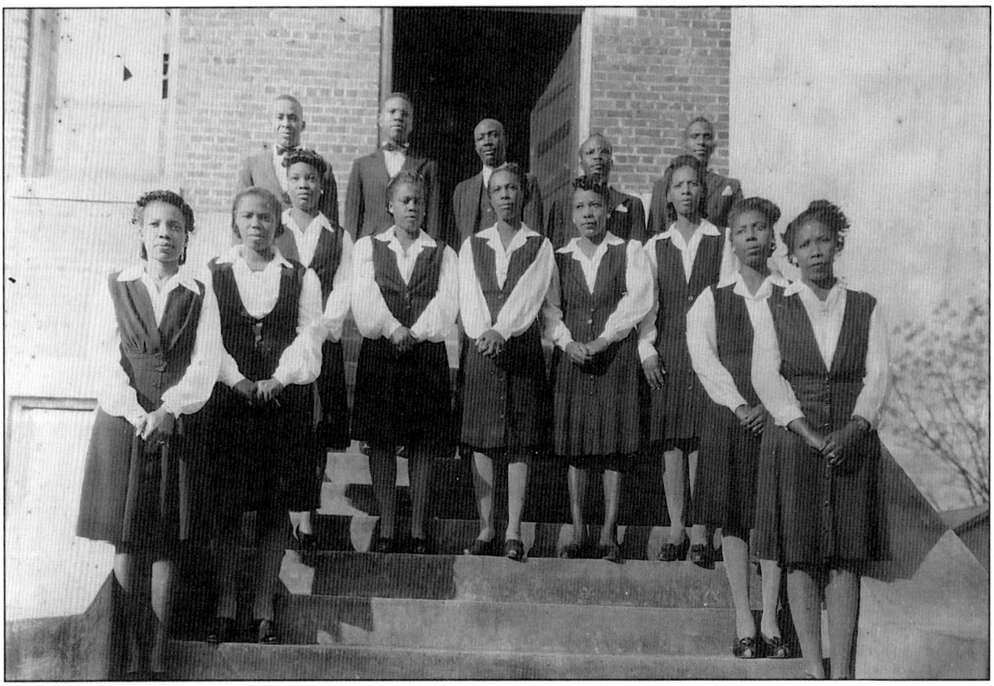

Seen here is the Senior Usher Board of St. Luke Baptist Church. Pictured are Myrtle Robinson (first on left); Christine Anderson (second from left); Annie Lee Wynn (second from right); and Paul Edwards (back row, second from left). These ushers have been devoted servants for more than 50 years.

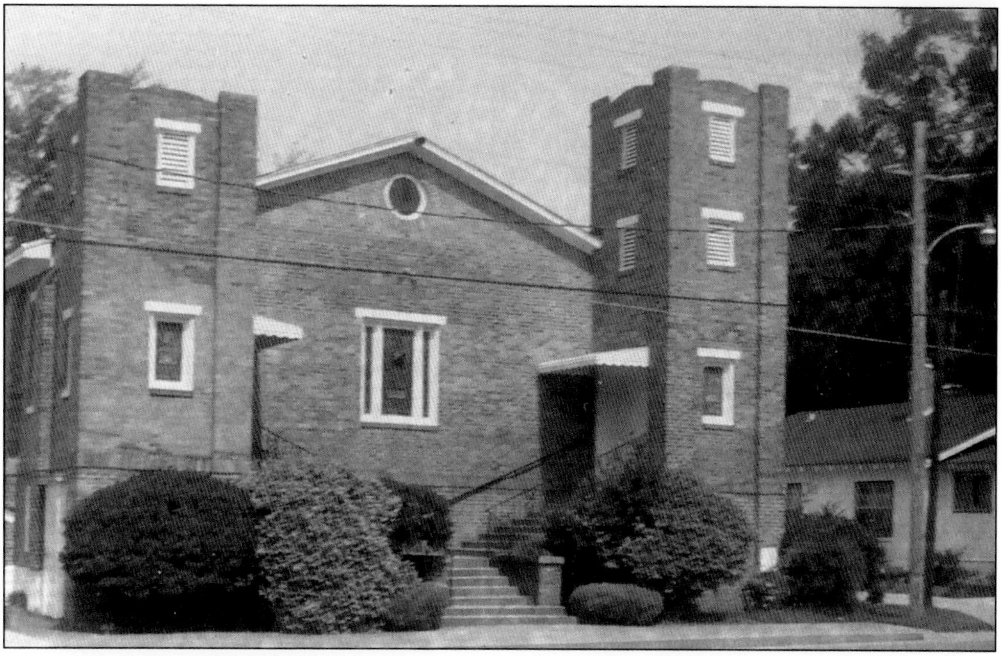

The African Methodist Episcopal Church is one of the oldest black religious denominations in Florida. It was founded by Rev. Henry Call, who established the first A.M.E. Church in Jackson County in the Bethlehem community, near Cottondale. St. James, established in February 1866, was located on Clinton Street in downtown Marianna. The present structure, located at the intersection of Orange and St. Andrews Streets, was built in the late 1930s under the leadership of Rev. E. Harley. The sanctuary was completed during Rev. N.H. Leath's pastorage. Francis Epton, a faithful member, helped to lay the foundation. Presently, Rev. F.C. Griffin is the current pastor.

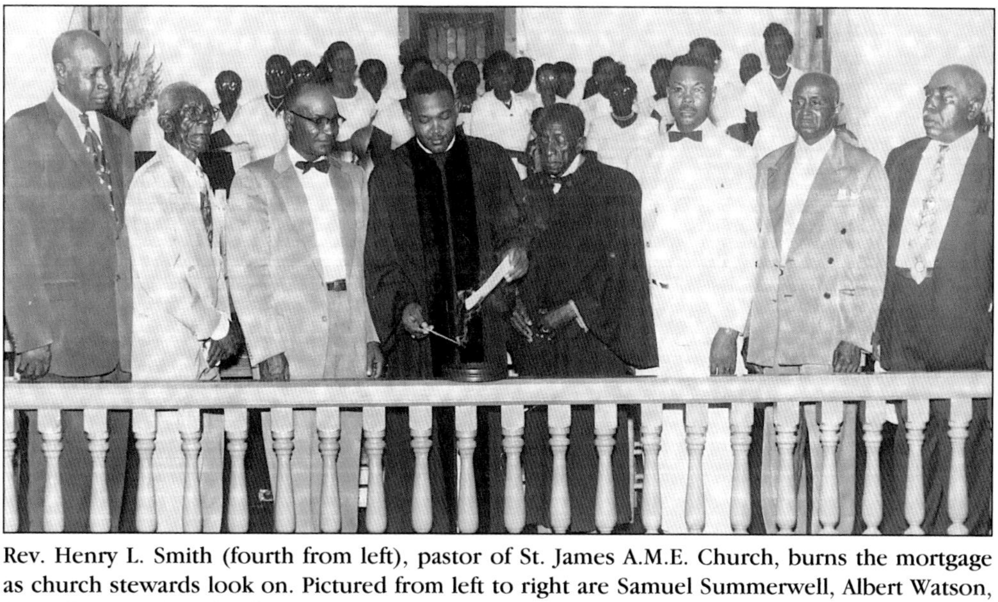

Rev. Henry L. Smith (fourth from left), pastor of St. James A.M.E. Church, burns the mortgage as church stewards look on. Pictured from left to right are Samuel Summerwell, Albert Watson, Major Pittman, Rev. Smith, Rev. R.A. Martin, Oscar Long, Robert Summerwell, and Lemon Harvey. The senior choir is in the background.

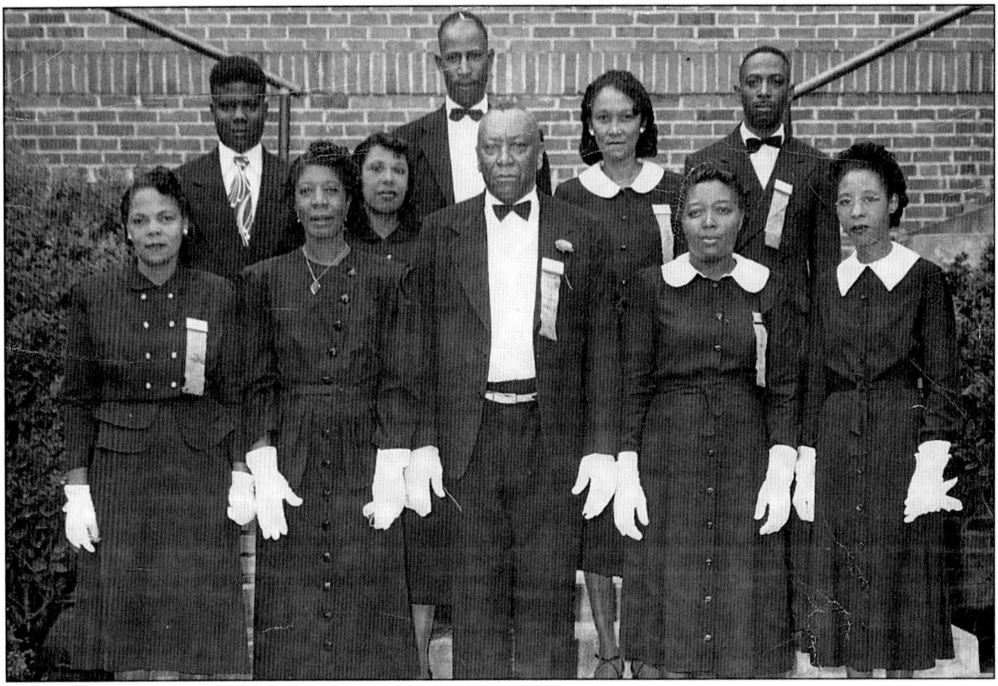

Pictured is the St. James A.M.E. Church Senior Usher Board. Lillie M. Martin, fourth from left, and Thomasena Briggs, fifth from left, are still members, with more than 50 years of dedicated service.

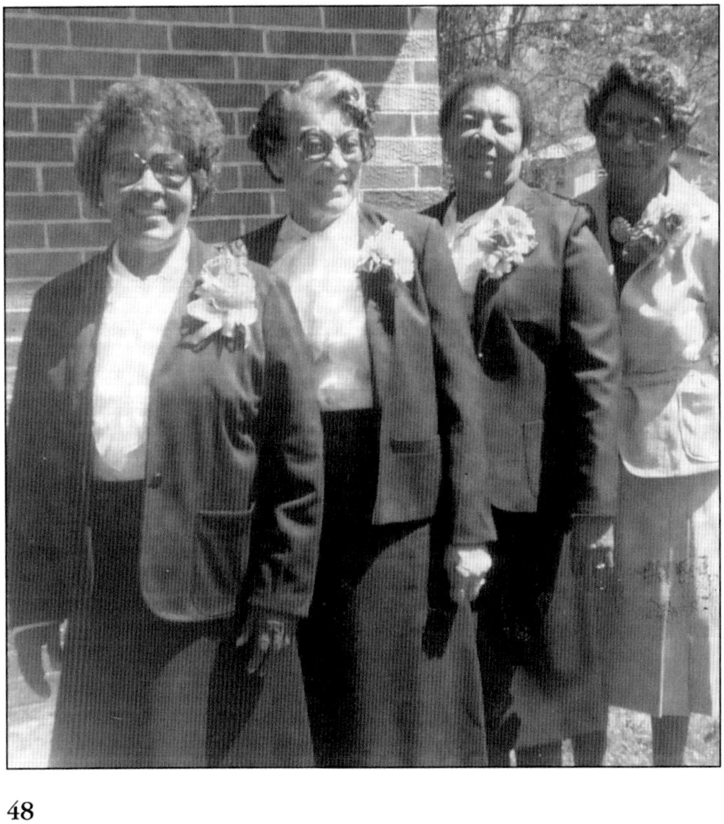

These women were loyal members of the local, district, and conference A.M.E. Missionary Society, Lay Organization, and Youth Department. From left to right are Ruth Bess and Maggie P. Atwater, conference youth directors; Roberta E. Pressley, area lay district president; and Willie J. Hutchinson, conference youth director and lay president. They devoted their time and talents to their church and community. Their combined teaching experience in Jackson County schools exceeded 120 years.

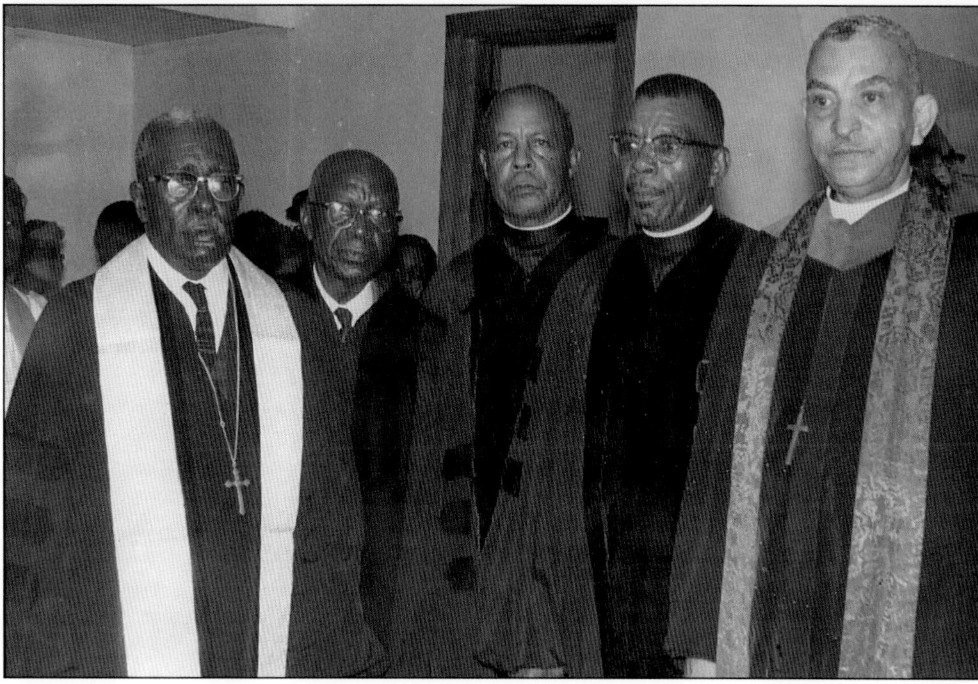

Pictured above are presiding elders of the West Florida Conference of the A.M.E. Church. From left to right, they are Rev. J.W. Walker, Rev. Elijah Harley, Rev. C.H. Coosby, Rev. ? Ash, and Bishop Eugene Hatcher.

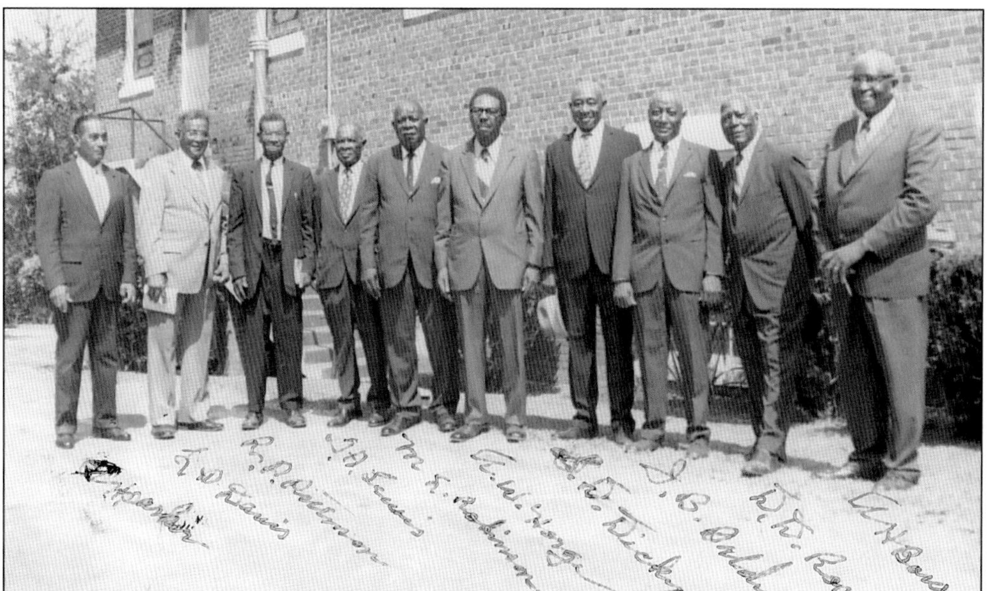

This photo depicts ministers and officers of 2nd West Baptist Association. Several held local as well as state offices. This and the following series of photographs were taken for a special occasion at Mt. Tabor Missionary Baptist Church. From left to right are Rev. Alonzo Parker, Rev. L.P. Davis, Rev. George B. Baker, Rev. T.A. Lewis, Rev. Milous L. Robinson, Rev. Andrew W. Hodge, Rev. S.D. Dickens, Rev. J.B. Baldwin, Deacon David D. Rose, and Rev. Andrew H. Bowers.

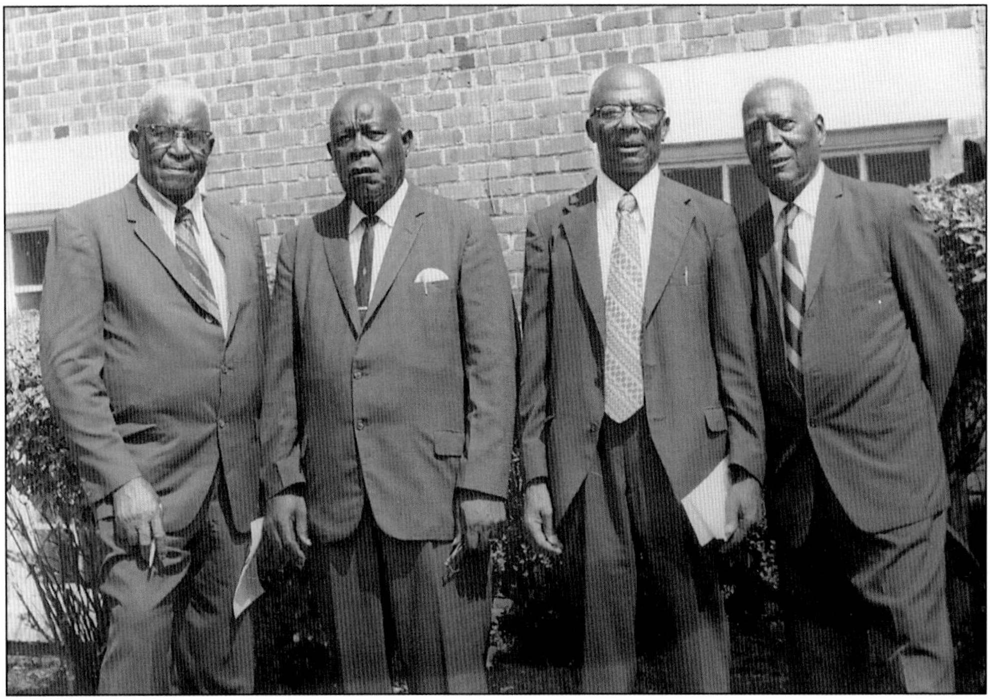

Pictured above are officers of the 2nd West Florida Baptist Association. From left to right are Rev. Andrew H. Bowers, Rev. Milous L. Robinson, Deacon Alfred Wooten, and Deacon David D. Rose.

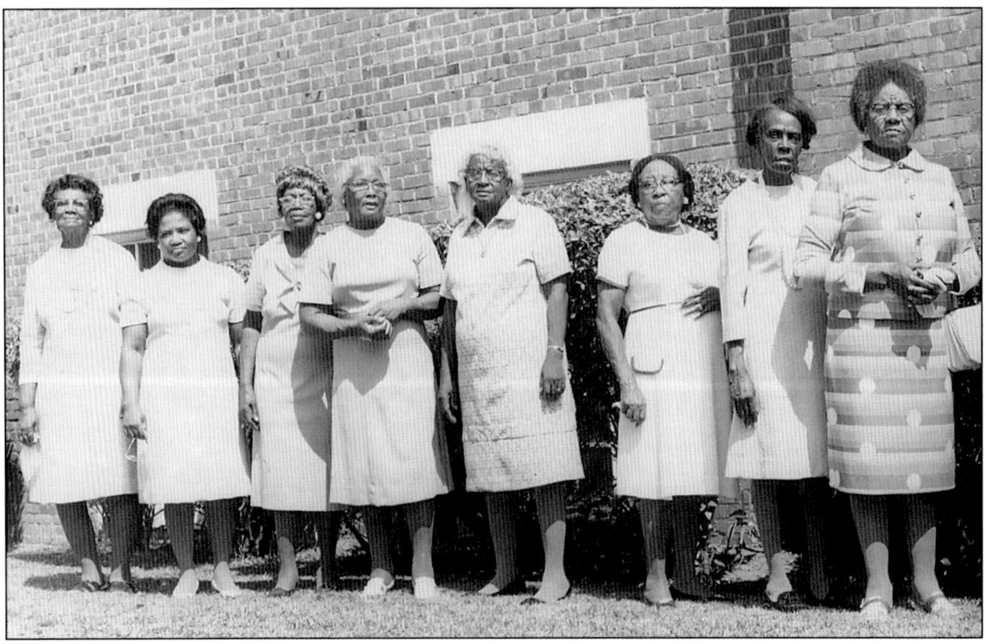

These women played a major role in the Association's affairs. From left to right are Callie Granberry, Mary Waddell, unidentified, unidentified, Mary Washington, Maude Wynn, Alice Dickens, and Gladys Parker (wife of Rev. Alonzo H. Parker, the moderator of the Association.) Callie Granberry served as president of the Missionary Society for more than 50 years.

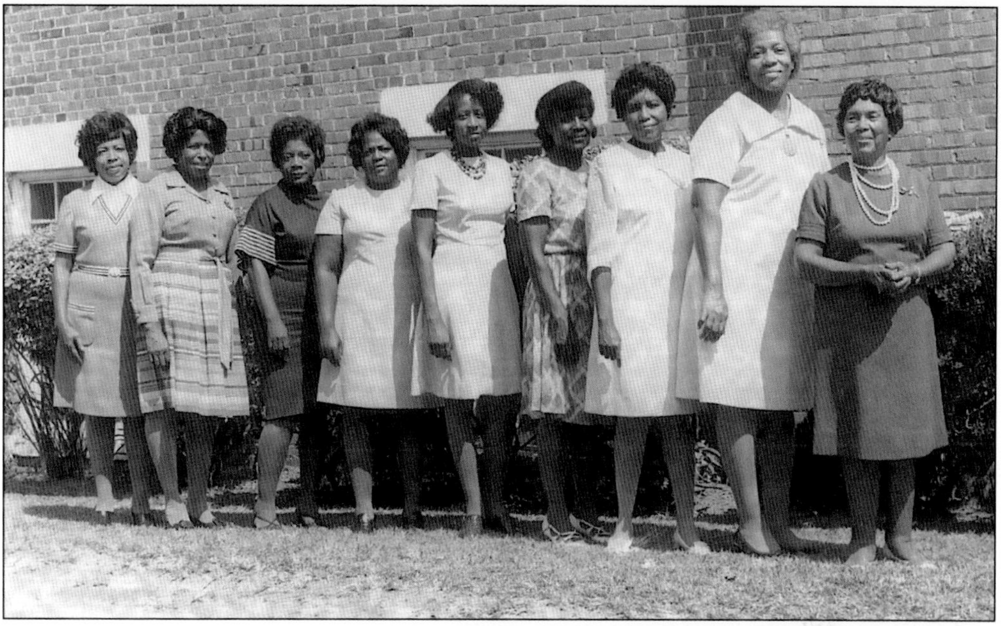

Pictured on this page and at the top of the next page are the missionaries and dedicated workers of the 2nd West Florida Baptist Association. Their roles included training and teaching young adults leadership skills, public speaking, Biblical knowledge, and how to use their skills in the local churches. These women were outstanding role models. In the above photo, from left to right, are Myrtle Robinson, Mary G. Jones, Ida Spires, Frances Hodge, Angeline Bowles, unidentified, Willie Dickens, Alice Spears, and unidentified.

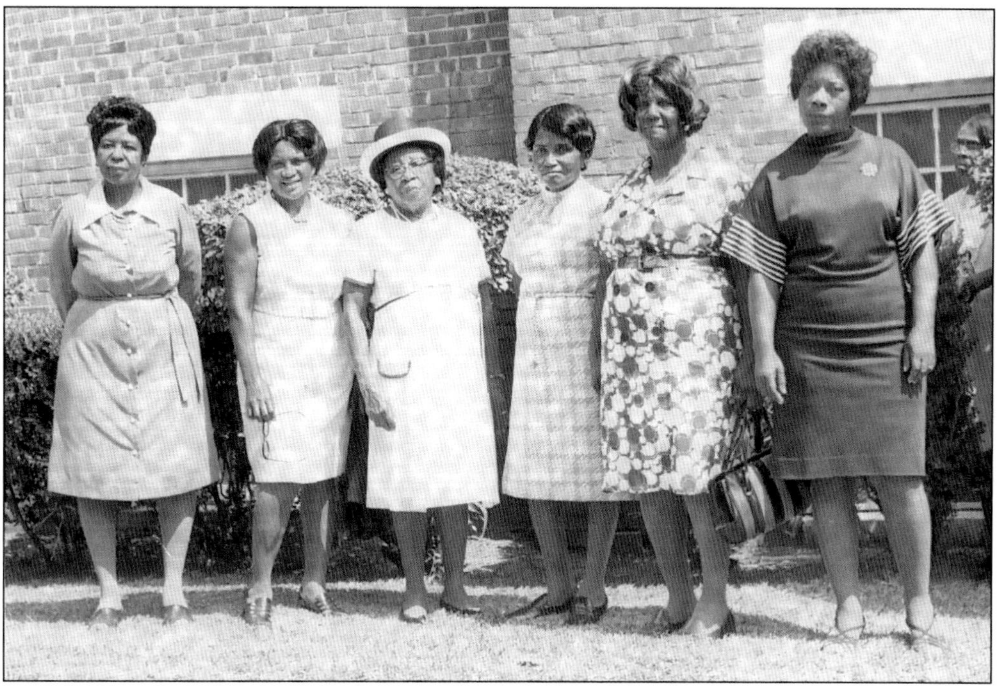

Shown here, from left to right, are Reola M. Bryan, unidentified, Maude Wynn, Irene Hodge, unidentified, and Ida Spires.

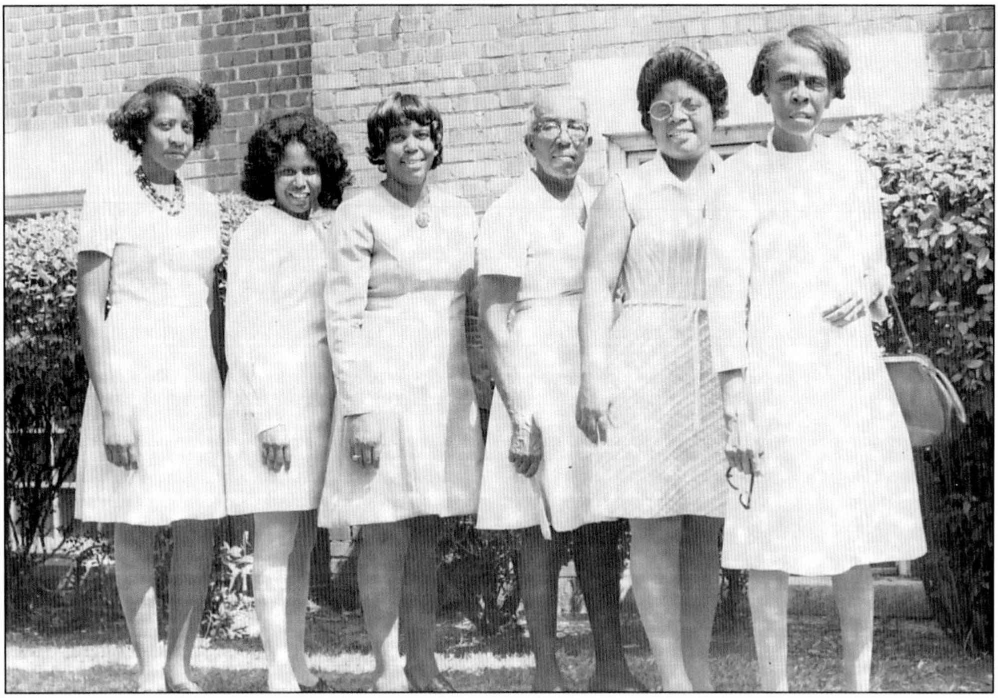

Pictured from left to right are Angeline Bowles, Geraldine Boyd, Cora Hunter, Nancy Glynn, Annie Bradwell, and Alice Dickens.

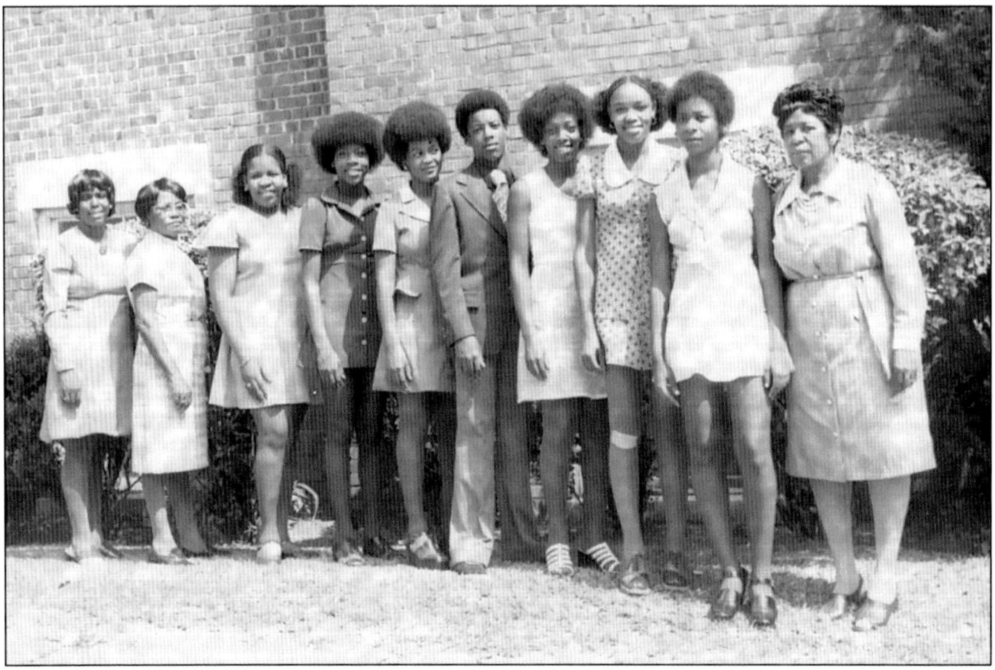

Young people were a valued part of the 2nd West Florida Baptist Association. Pictured here, from left to right, are Cora Hunter, unidentified, Sharron Dickens, unidentified, Yvette Crawford, Anthony Granberry, Lois Pinkard, unidentified, Gwen Reed, and Reola M. Bryan.

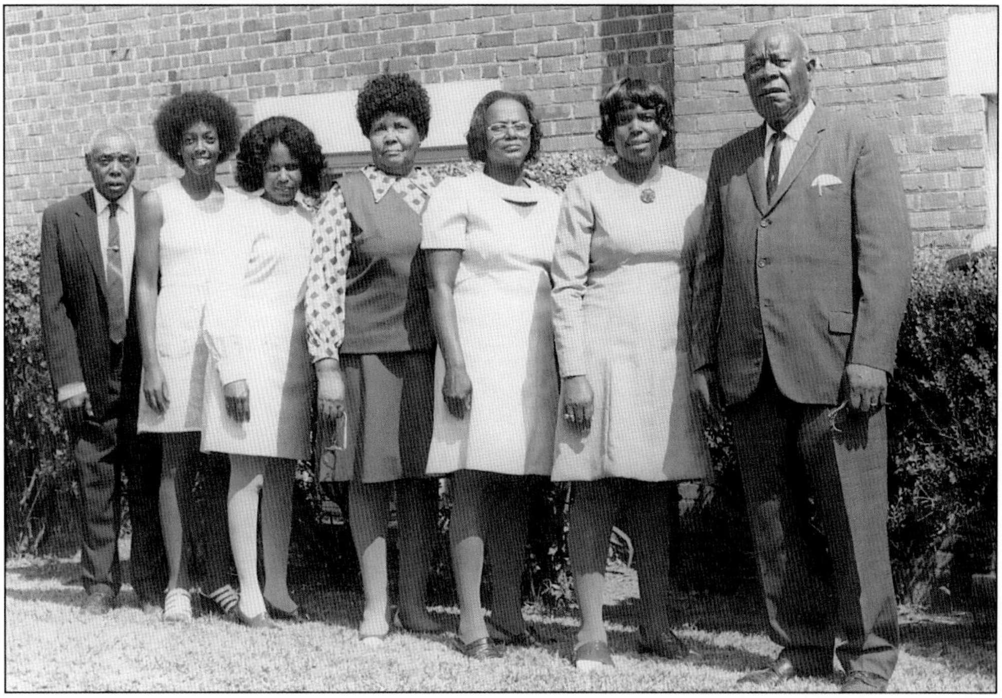

The Association's youth and adult officers are seen here. They are, from left to right, unidentified, Lois Pinkard, Geraldine McGriff, Mary Wilson, Elizabeth Mack, Cora Hunter, and Rev. Milous L. Robinson.

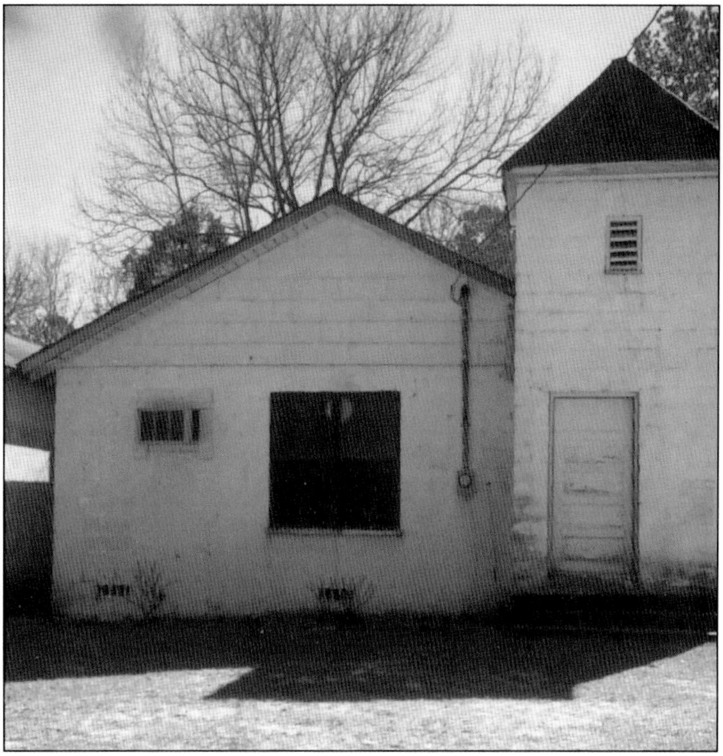

Antioch A.M.E. Church, located on Highway 90 West, once housed a church-based elementary school, grades one through eight.

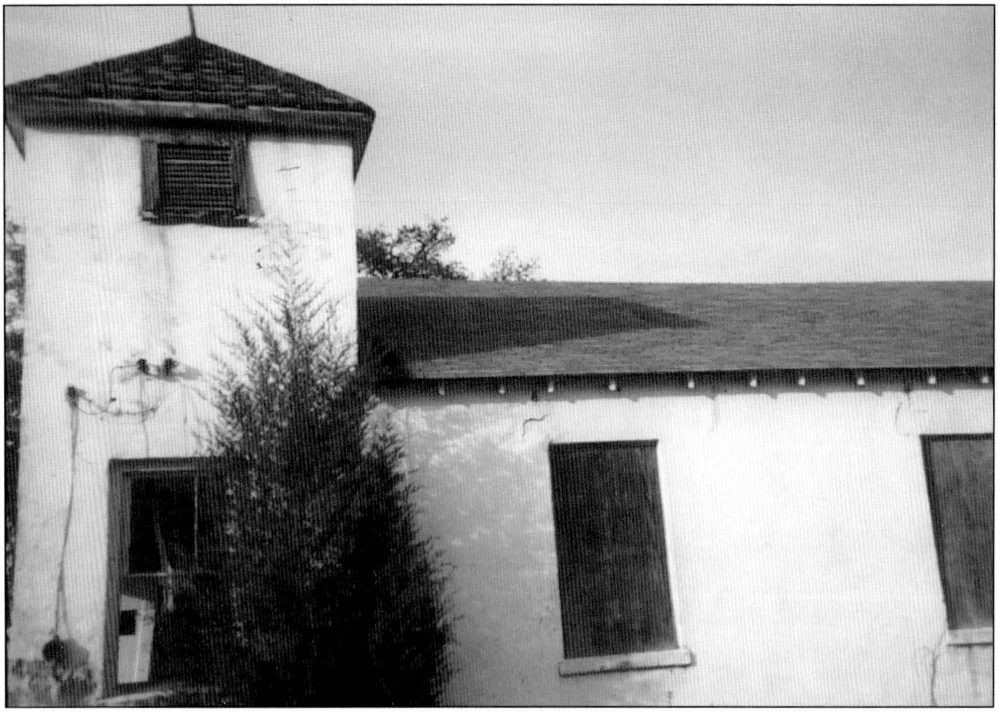

St. John Missionary Baptist Church, located in the St. John community, also had a church-based elementary school, grades one through eight.

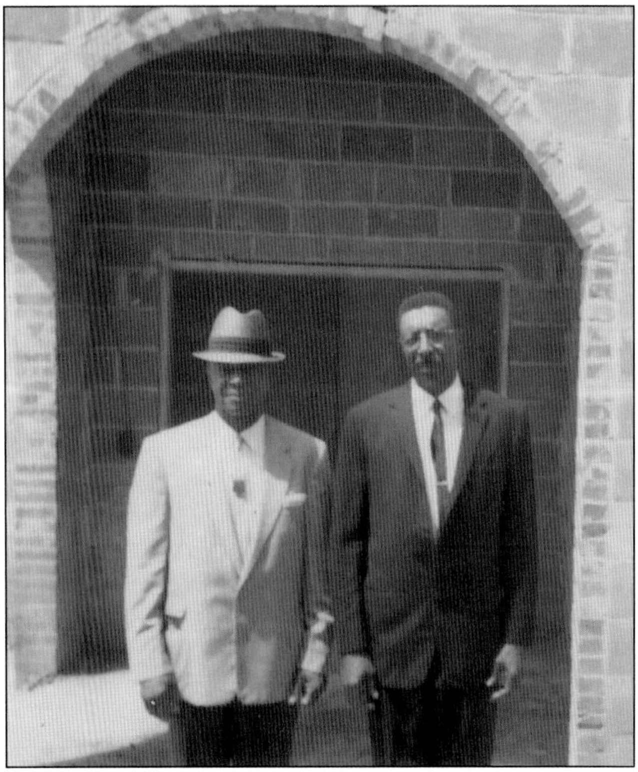

Old Union Hill Missionary Baptist Church, located on Union Hill Road, served the Blue Hole community. From left to right are C. Speights and Jack Golden.

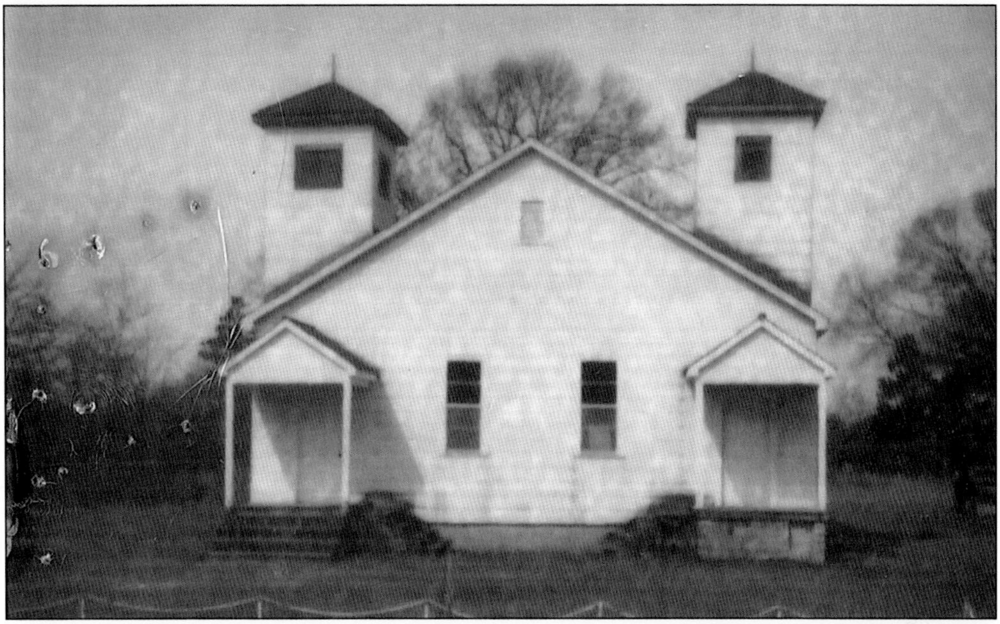

Little Zion Missionary Baptist Church, located in the Little Zion community, had a church-based elementary school, grades one through eight. Most church-based schools closed in the 1950s.

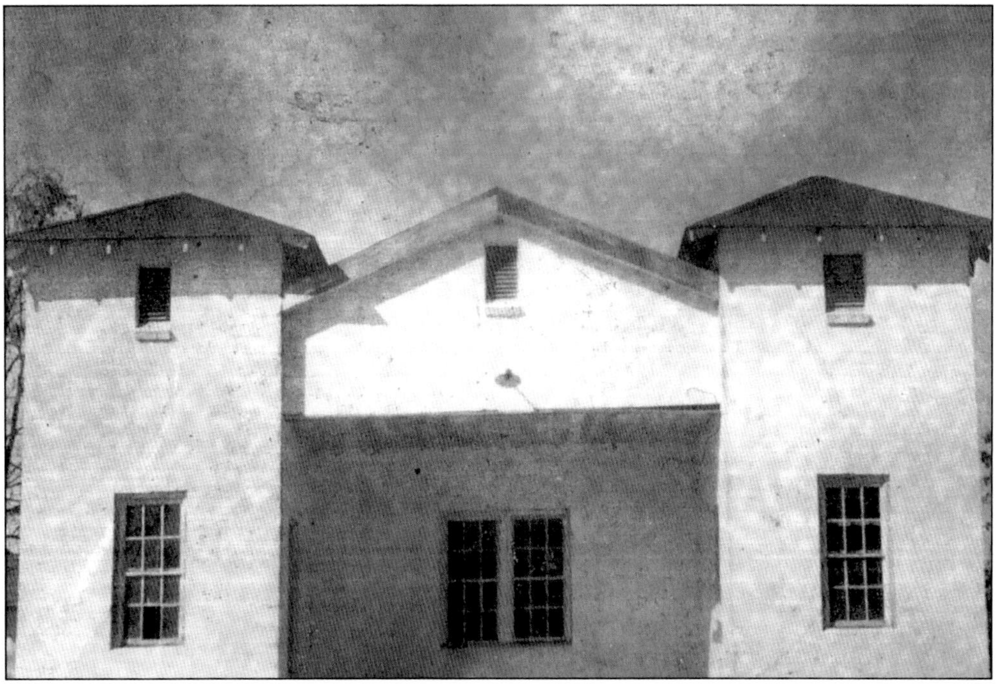

Mt. Zion Missionary Baptist Church, is pictured in Malone, Florida, in 1972. Rev. A.H. Bowers Sr. was pastor when this photograph was taken.

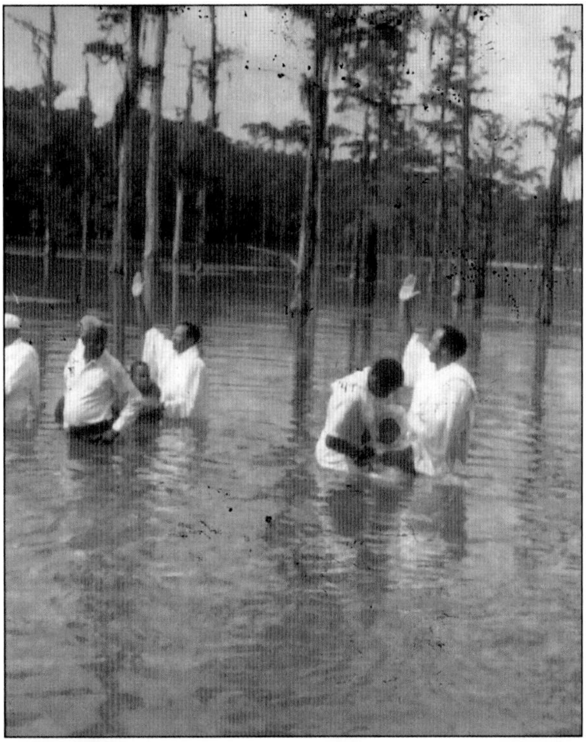

For many years, Mt. Tabor, New Hope, and Poplar Springs Baptist Churches held joint baptisms at Blue Springs on the third Sunday in August, after weeks of "revivals." People came from far and near for this celebration. Mt. Tabor was established in 1866 by African Americans who, since 1845, had been members of the white Union Academy, which later became Greenwood Baptist Church. Rev. George W. Martin, Mt. Tabor's first pastor, served for 43 years and helped establish Popular Springs, Buckhorn, Mt. Zion, and Little Zion Baptist Churches.

Ministers and deacons offer prayers at the conclusion of a baptism.

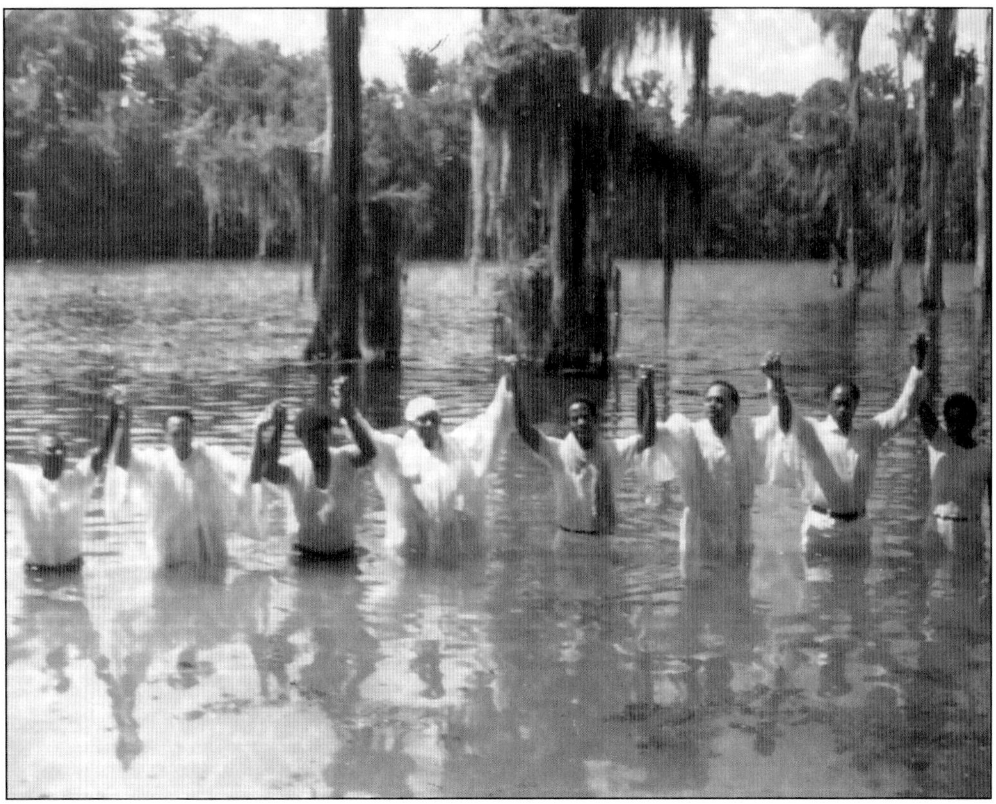

Five

Places of Work

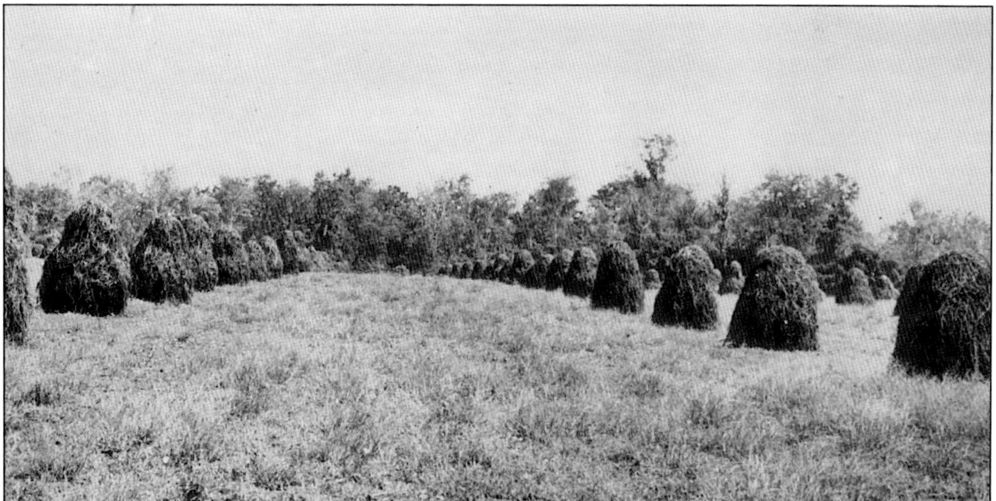

Peanuts were and continue to be a key industry in the area. Before mechanization, peanuts were harvested by hand, primarily by African Americans. Pictured here are stacks of peanuts. (Florida State Archives Photographic Collection.)

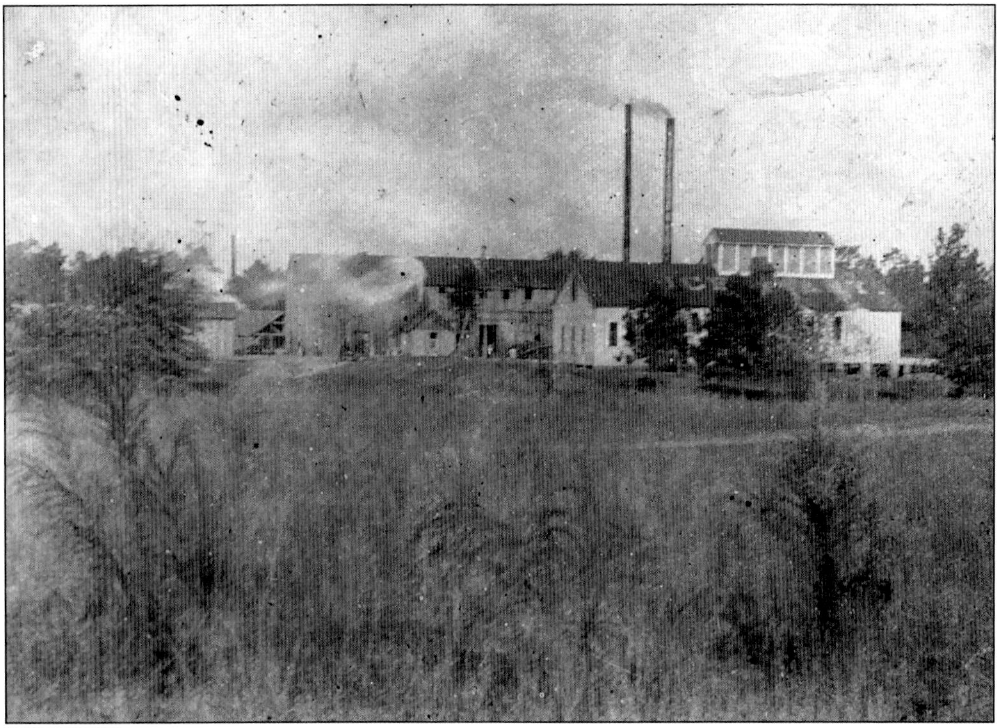

A peanut mill at Malone is pictured *c.* 1895. Many blacks worked in the peanut industry. (Florida State Archives Photographic Collection.)

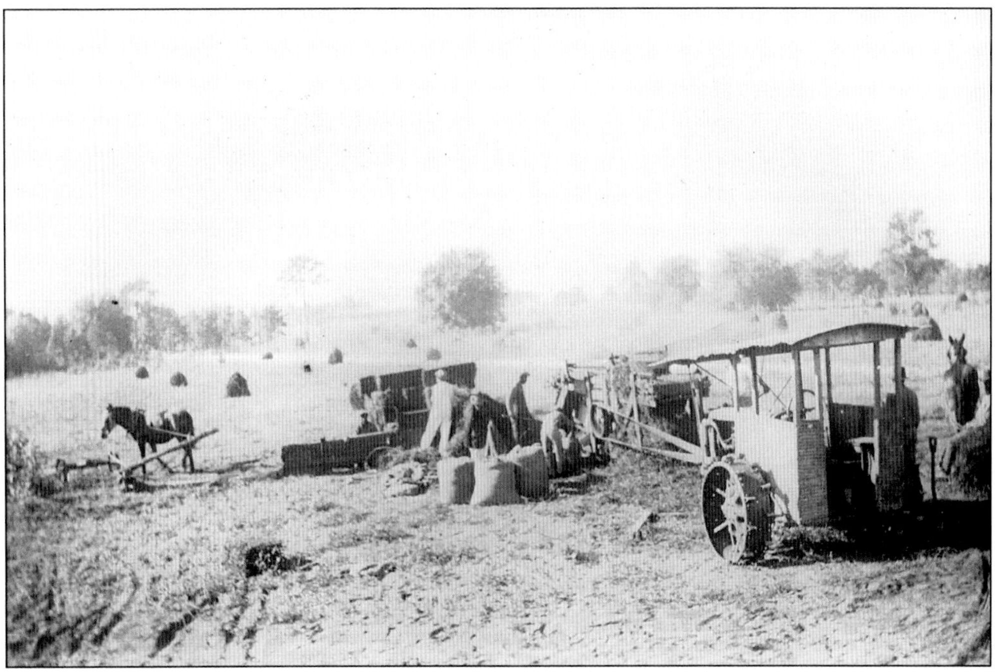

This type of horse-driven peanut thrashing machine moved from farm to farm in the African-American farming community. (Brewer's Studio.)

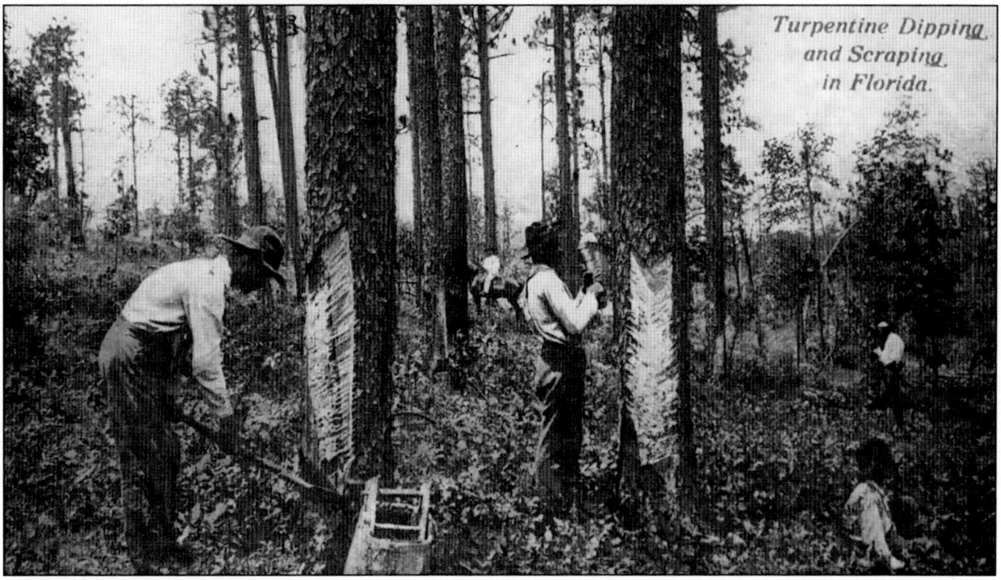

The turpentine industry was another place where African Americans were employed. Trees were prepared for harvesting gum to make spirits of turpentine. (Florida State Archives Photographic Collection.)

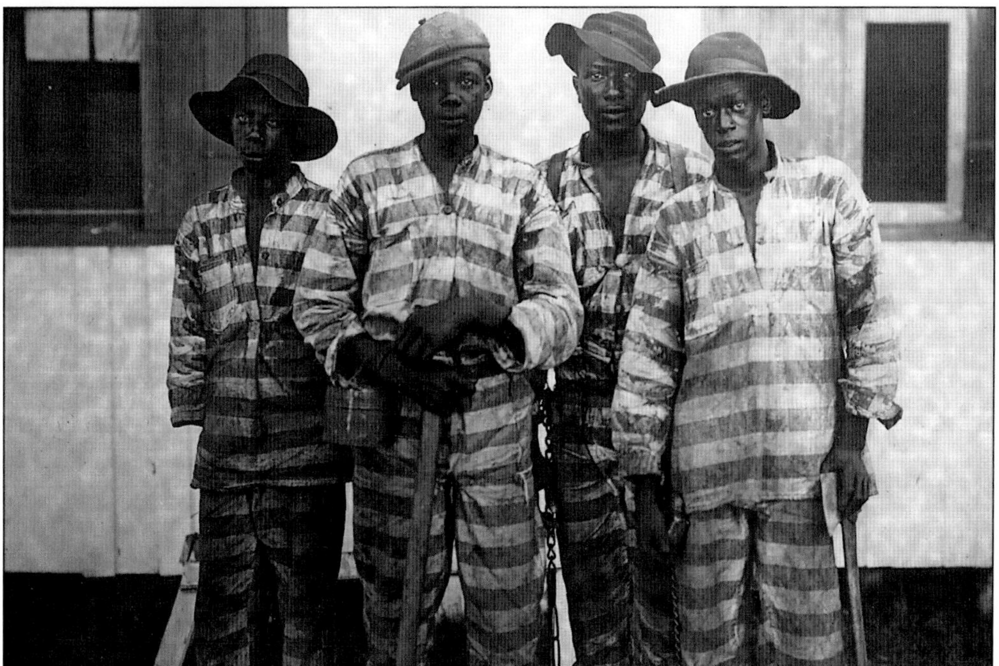

In the early 20th century, convicts were leased to private companies. This practice provided a cheap labor source for the companies and saved the government the expense of maintenance. In November 1905, several leased prisoners were burned to death at a large turpentine camp near Alford in Jackson County. Despite the tragedy and the near-slavery conditions under which prisoners labored, the practice continued until 1923. Convicts "on the chain gang" engaged in hard physical work building roads, bridges, etc.

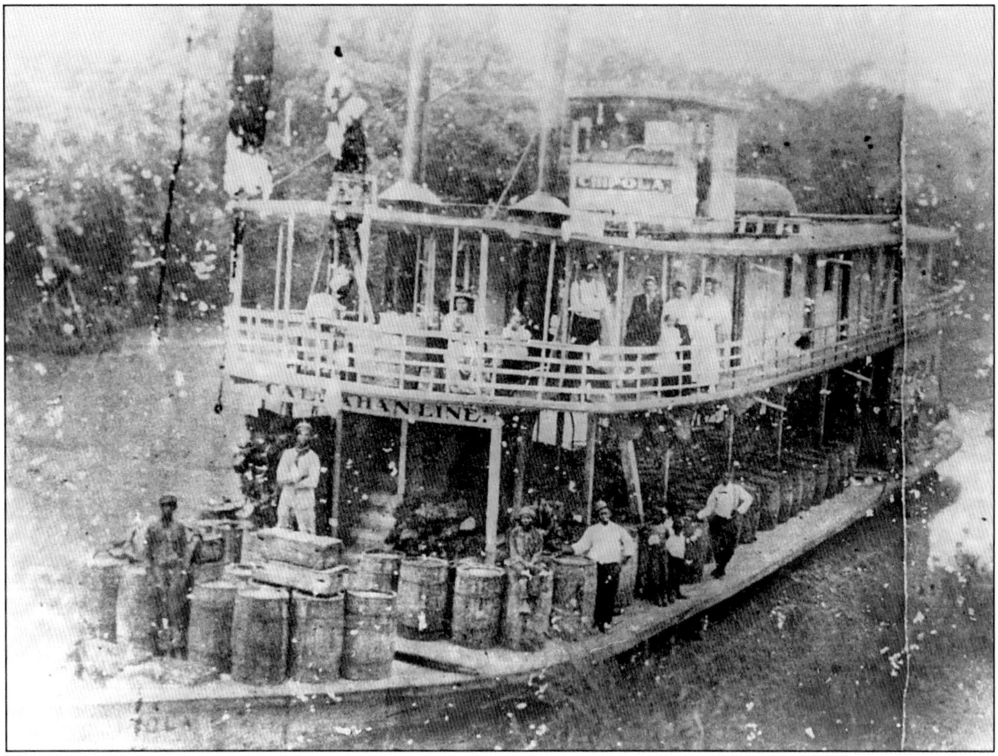

Steamboats navigated the Apalachicola and other area rivers. Slaves and later freedmen worked on these steamboats. In 1867, Elijah Williams, a former slave, was granted a patent for inventing a propeller which allowed boats to navigate shallow waters such as those in the Apalachicola River.

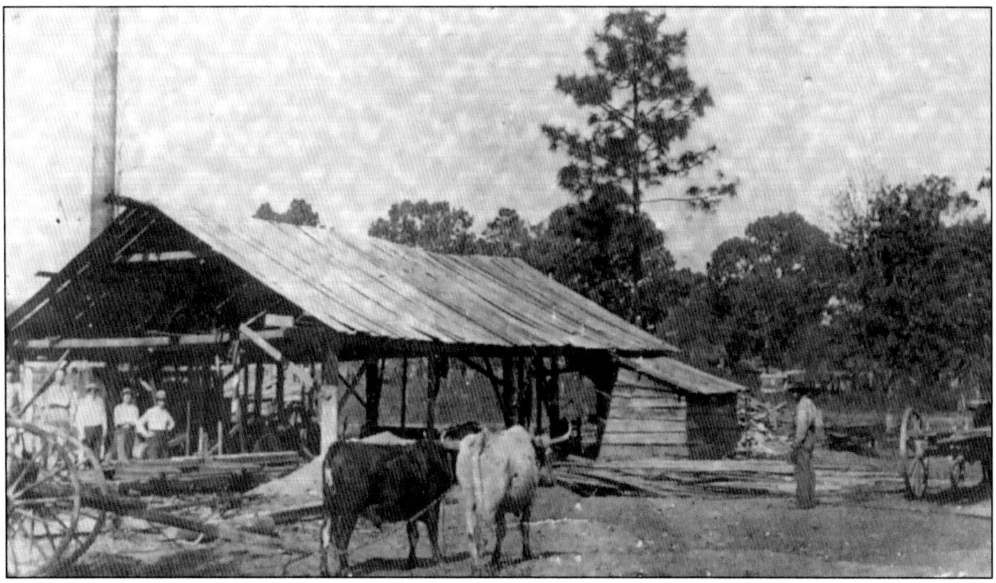

Many blacks were employed at various saw mills. Hodges Mill was once a large sawmill on Hodges Mill Road, now Pennsylvania Avenue. Several members of the Hayes family were employed at the mill.

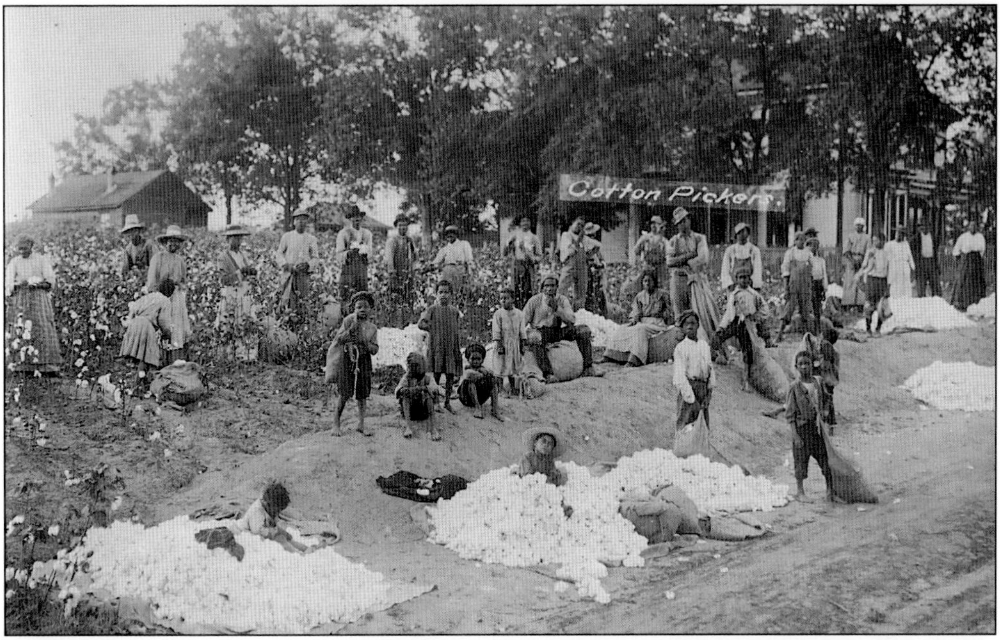

Cotton was a major industry in Jackson County and fueled the plantation system.

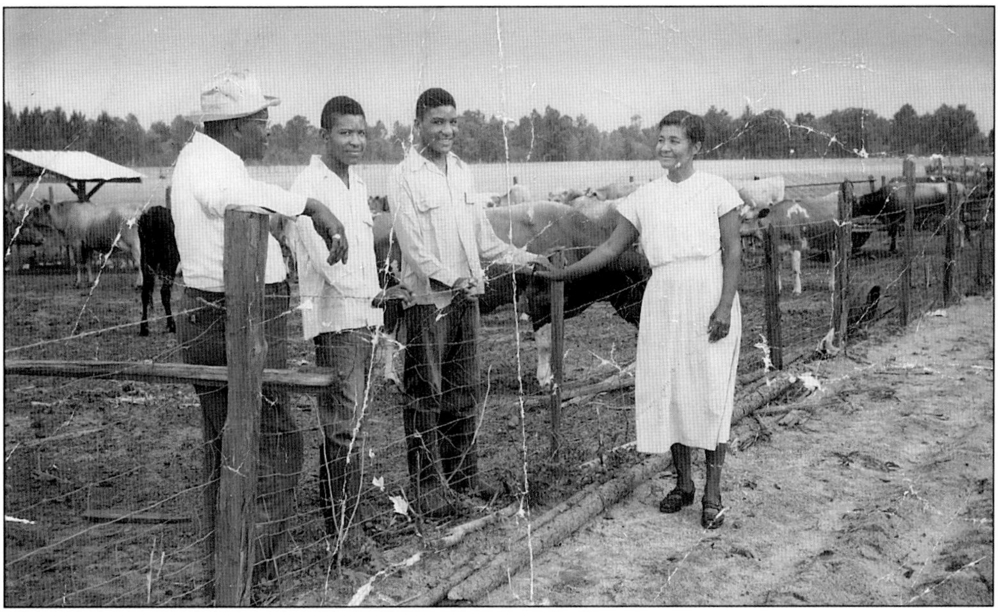

Pictured standing, as they observe the cows and prepare to begin milking, are Rev. Andrew H. Bowers; his wife, Gertrude; son Mirion, now a physician; and son Nehemiah (deceased), who was an agriculture teacher and pastor. Reverend Bowers began operating his dairy in 1945 with the assistance of his six sons and a few employees. The dairy expanded from 20 cows, which were milked manually, to 60 cows that were milked by electric milkers. In addition to operating the dairy, Reverend Bowers was successful in producing cotton, peanuts, hogs, and vegetables on the farm. In later years, he invested in growing and harvesting pine trees. Today, his 270-acre pine tree farm and peanut quota remains a Bowers' family business, owned and operated by the Bowers children.

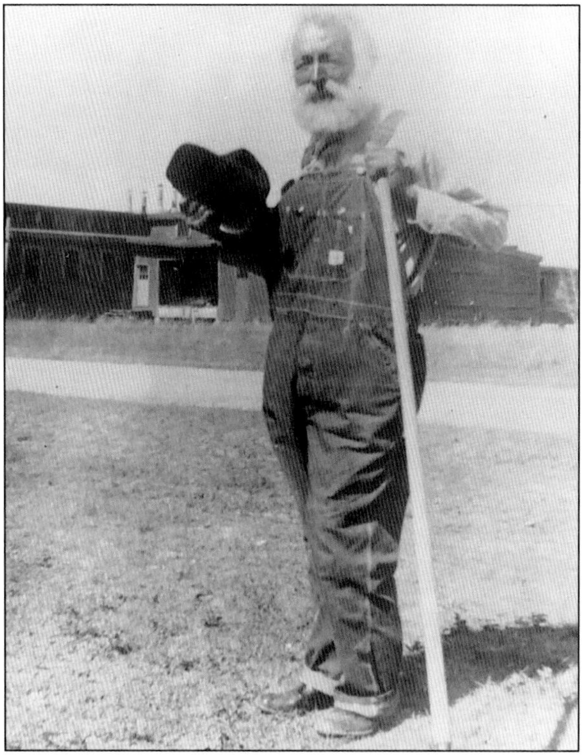

Richmond Hartsfield was born in Marianna and grew up in Jackson County. He began farming as a sharecropper but soon realized that that was not going to "cut it." He received a loan and bought 440 acres of land just outside of Marianna. The land contained a lime pit from which rocks were used to build his tobacco barn, homes, and Vann's Florist in Greenwood. Hartsfield also owned and operated Hartsfield Grocery, now demolished, at Highway 73 and Hartsfield Road. The land remains in the family. His son, Idus, owns and operates Hartsfield Mini-mart.

Nizy Gainer, a farm wife, is pictured in Sunday attire. In the background are pieces of equipment and the barn located on the family farm.

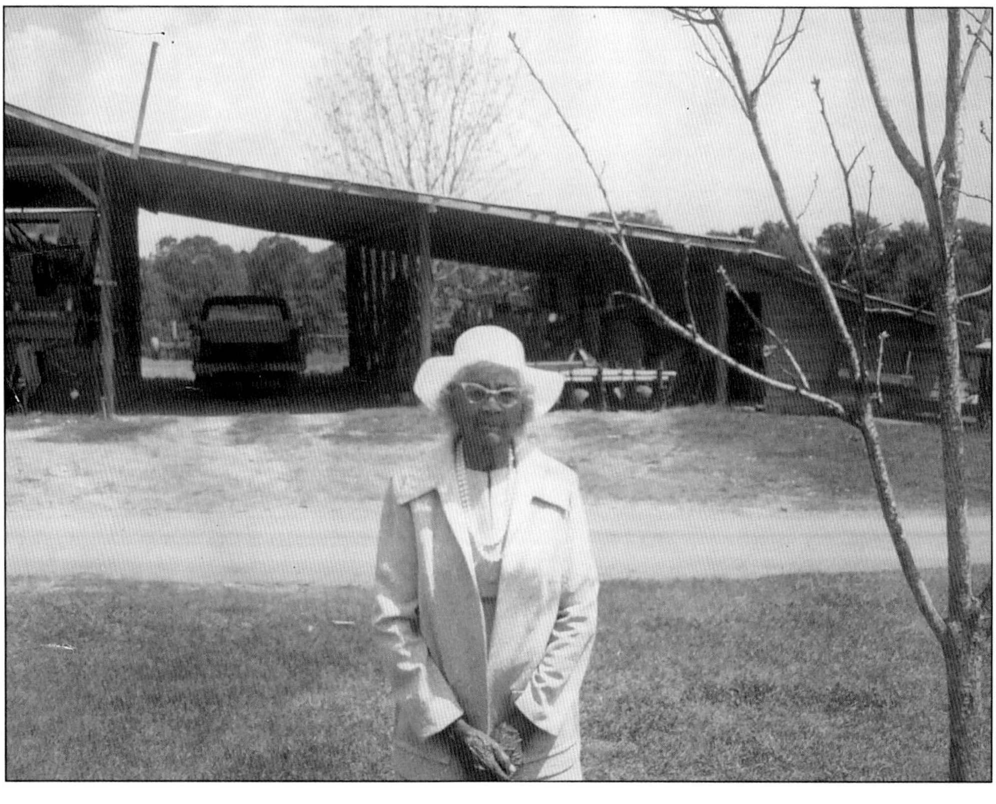

Chester Johnson and his wife, Pellie Lucille Myrick, owned 80 acres of land in the Pope Chapel Community east-northeast of Marianna. He cultivated 40 acres for farming and raised cows and hogs on the other half. A typical area farmer, Johnson used horses and mules for cultivating his crops long before tractors and other equipment were affordable to him. His mule, Emma, is shown here after a hard day in the field.

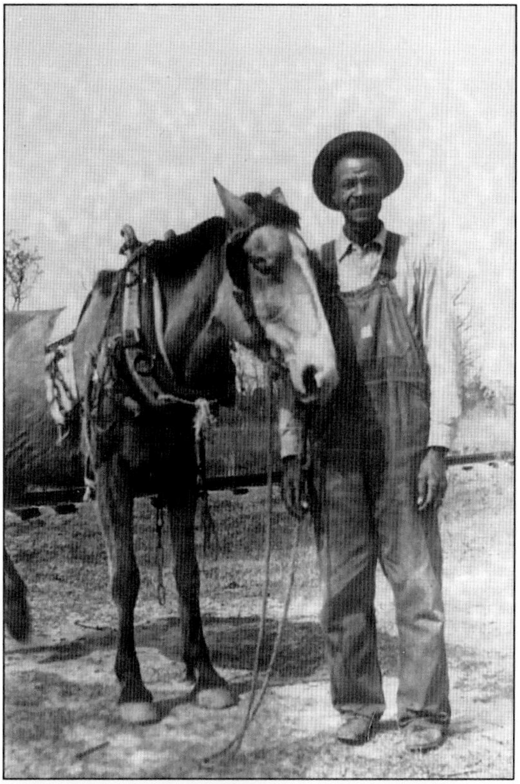

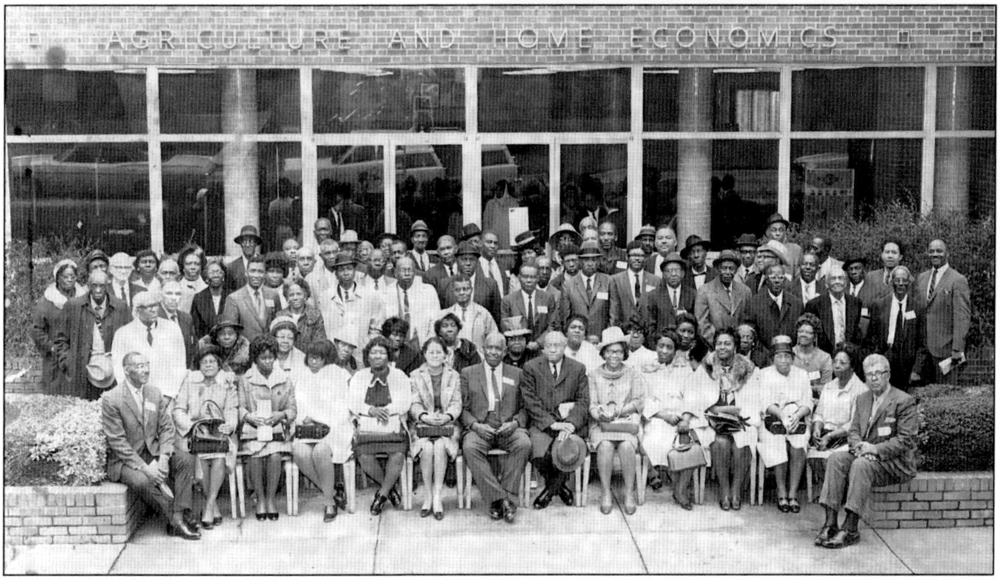

This picture includes several Jackson County farm families who frequently met with other farm families from across the state at Florida A&M University. There they received technical assistance and learned innovative ways to improve production on their farms. Rev. A.H. Bowers, first row at center left, was president of the Farmers Association. Virgil Elkins Sr. (last row, extreme right, holding paper) was the statewide area program director and the Jackson County home extension agent. Dr. C.W. Walker, first row at center right, was the dean of FAMU's School of Agriculture.

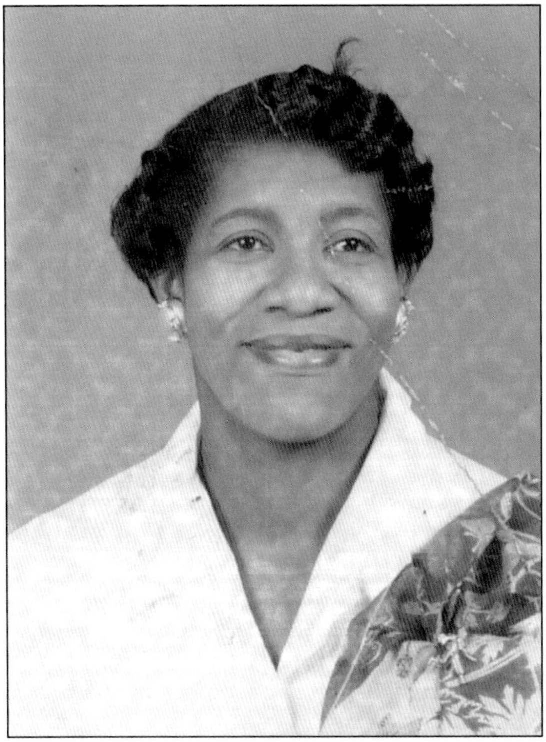

For more than three decades, Alice Spears was supervisor of the Jackson County Training School lunchroom. She planned nutritious meals for students and staff during the school day and for athletes, coaches, and cheerleaders following night sports events. Spears also catered all school banquets prior to 1966.

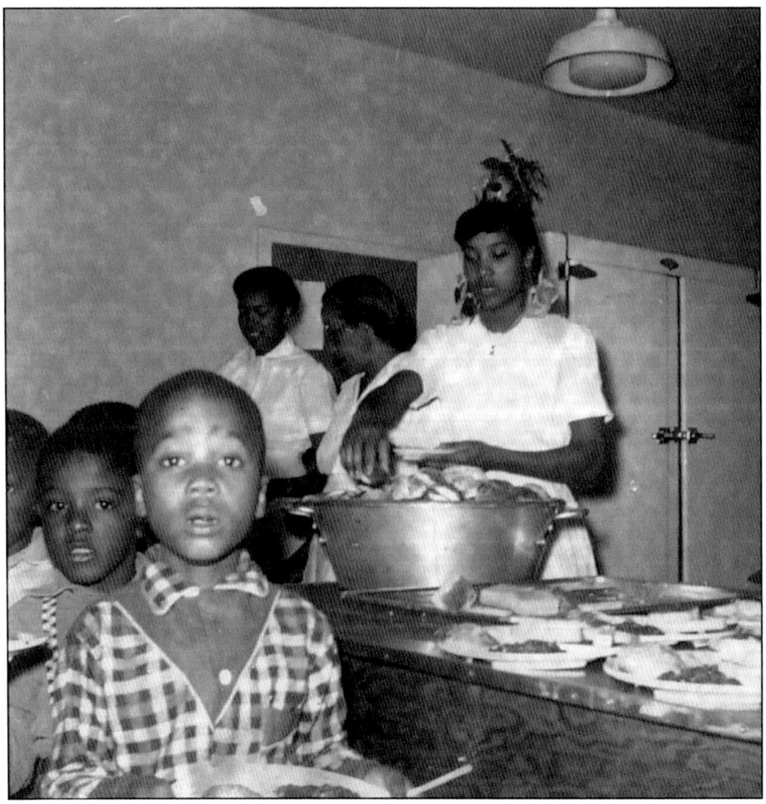

Jackson County Training School lunchroom employees are pictured serving students in 1956. Employees, shown from left to right, are Mary People, Frozena Porter, and Lucy Speights Hawthorne. The average salary was $48 per month.

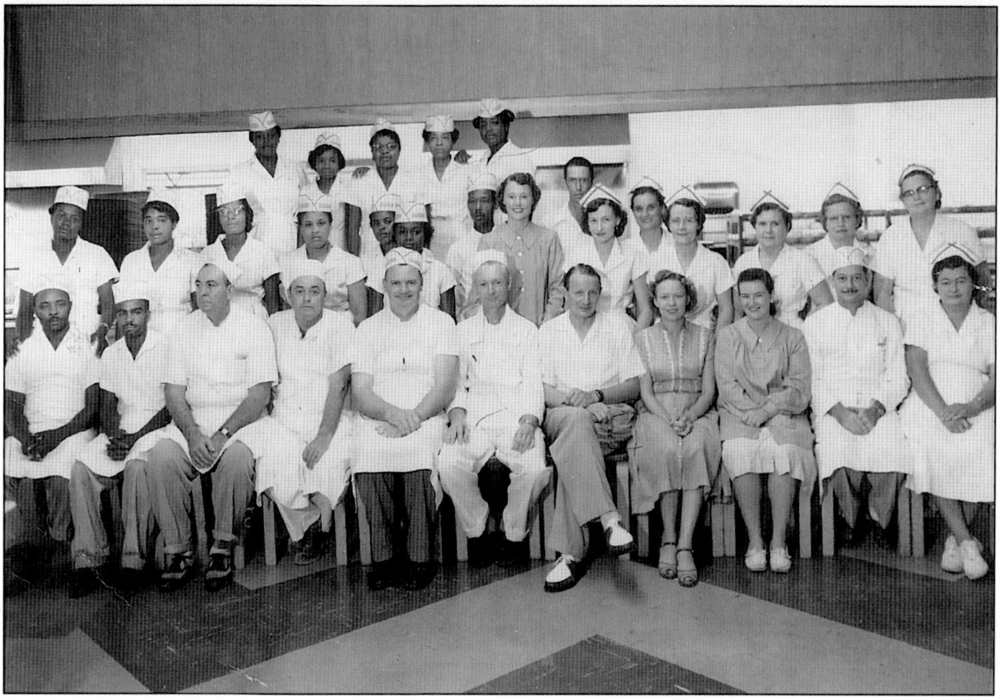

Graham Air Base was used to train air force pilots from 1951 to the late 1960s, when it closed. Many Jackson County African Americans were employed at the base in various civilian roles, such as food service, janitorial, canteen, etc.

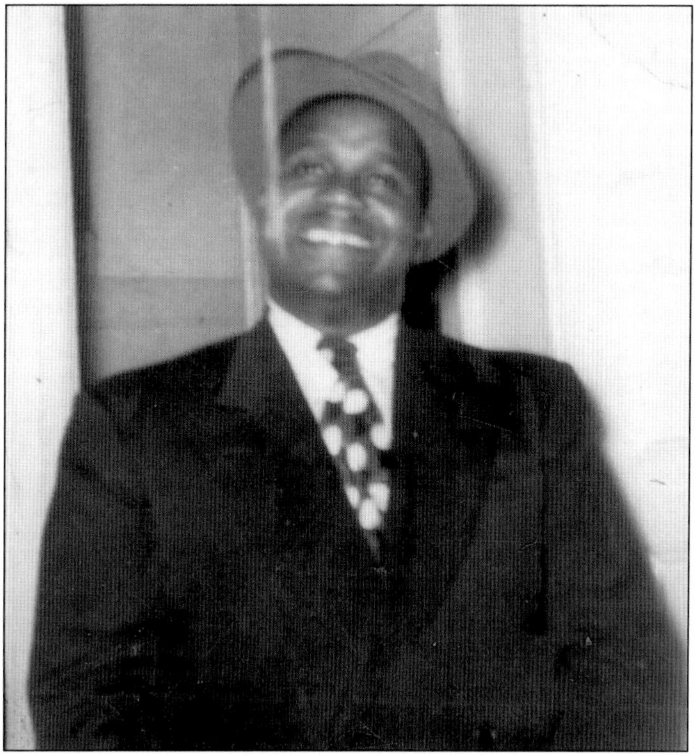

Henry Keith, right, became a deputy with the Jackson County Sheriff's Department in the mid-1950s. He served subsequent to Lynwood Watson, the first black law enforcement officer in Jackson County since Reconstruction. Sergeant Keith's duties included delivering civil papers, serving warrants, and routine patrol in the African-American community. He was an active member of St. James A.M.E. Church where he served as a class leader and steward. He currently resides at a veteran's home.

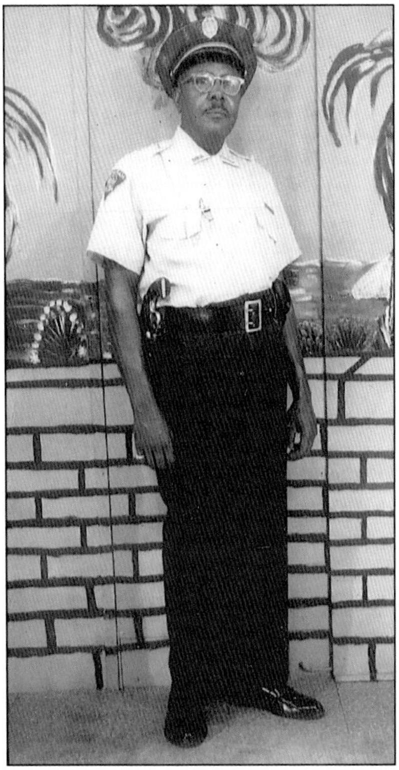

When Rufus Ford Speights was appointed to the Marianna Police Department in 1969, he became its first African-American member. Initially, he was assigned to perform security checks for downtown businesses and the industrial park. Later, he was a familiar figure at Riverside Elementary School were he served as a crossing guard. He also patrolled the black neighborhoods on the West End. He is fondly remembered for his position at the corner of Orange and St. Andrews Streets. Speights served on the police force until the early 1990s.

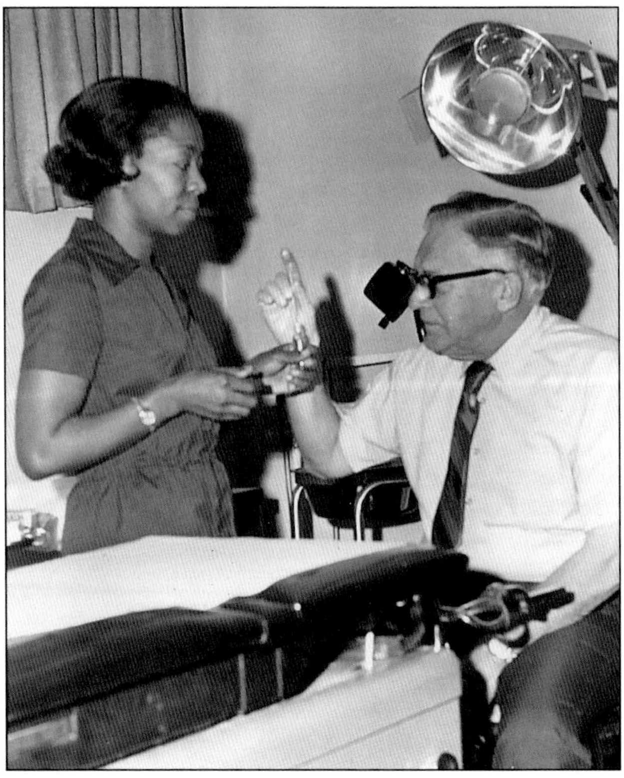

Sarah S. Pender is shown with health officer Dr. Howard Krigler. In August 1971, she became the first black professional employed by the Jackson County Health Department, when she was hired as a public health nurse. Nora McCall worked at the clinic as a nurse's aide in the 1940s and 1950s.

Six

Black Businesses

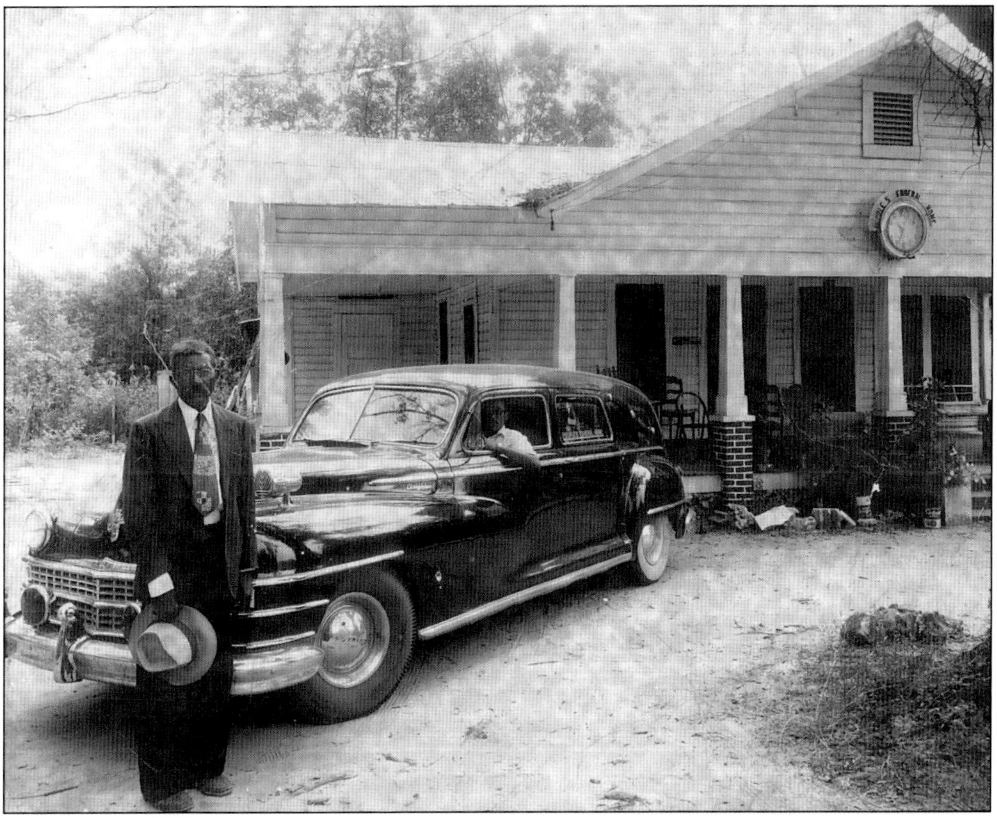

People's Funeral Home on Orange Street, one of the longest continuously operated black businesses in Jackson County, was established by Lemon Granberry. In the foreground is Tom Hart, funeral director. Seated in the newly acquired Cadillac hearse is Egbert C. McLean, mortician. The funeral home is presently owned and operated by Aaron Granberry III.

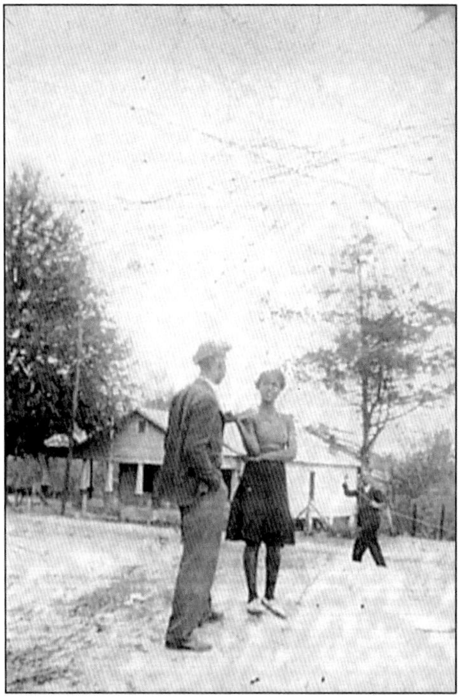

The original People's Funeral Home, pictured in the background, was located across the street from Gilmore Academy on Orange Street. It has been remodeled several times.

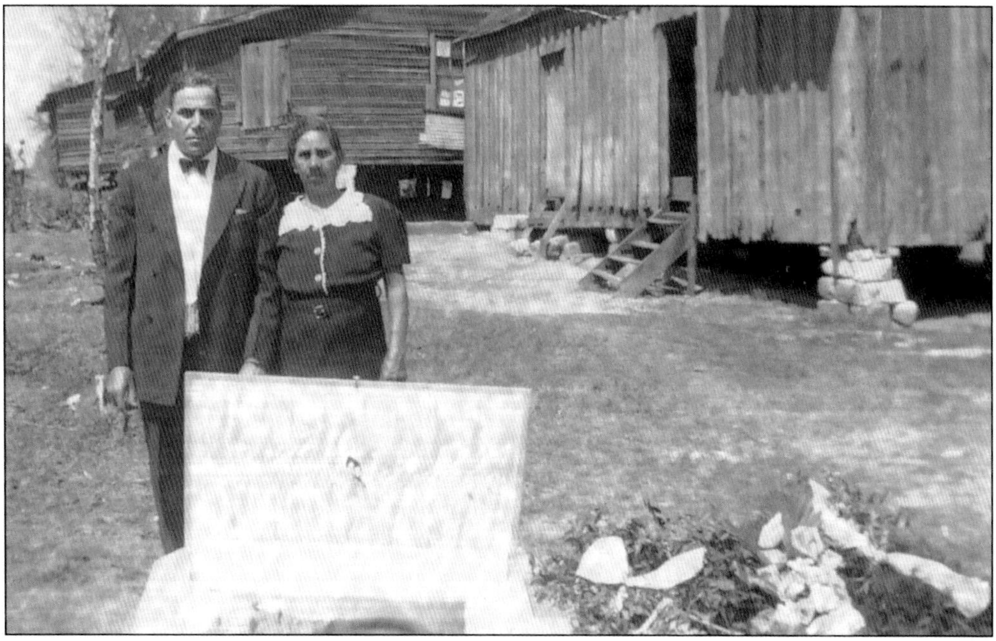

Some families buried relatives on their property in family plots. Most African Americans, however, were interred in church cemeteries or in one of Marianna's two public cemeteries. Orange Hill Cemetery, located on the West End, is all black, and Riverside, near downtown, has separate sections for blacks and whites. Pictured above are Green Samsome and his wife after a loved one was buried behind their home. The Orange Hill, Carter's Mill Road, Union Hill, and Friendship cemeteries have been surveyed and are posted on Jackson County's USGEN website at http://members.aol.com/BettyMae/index.html.

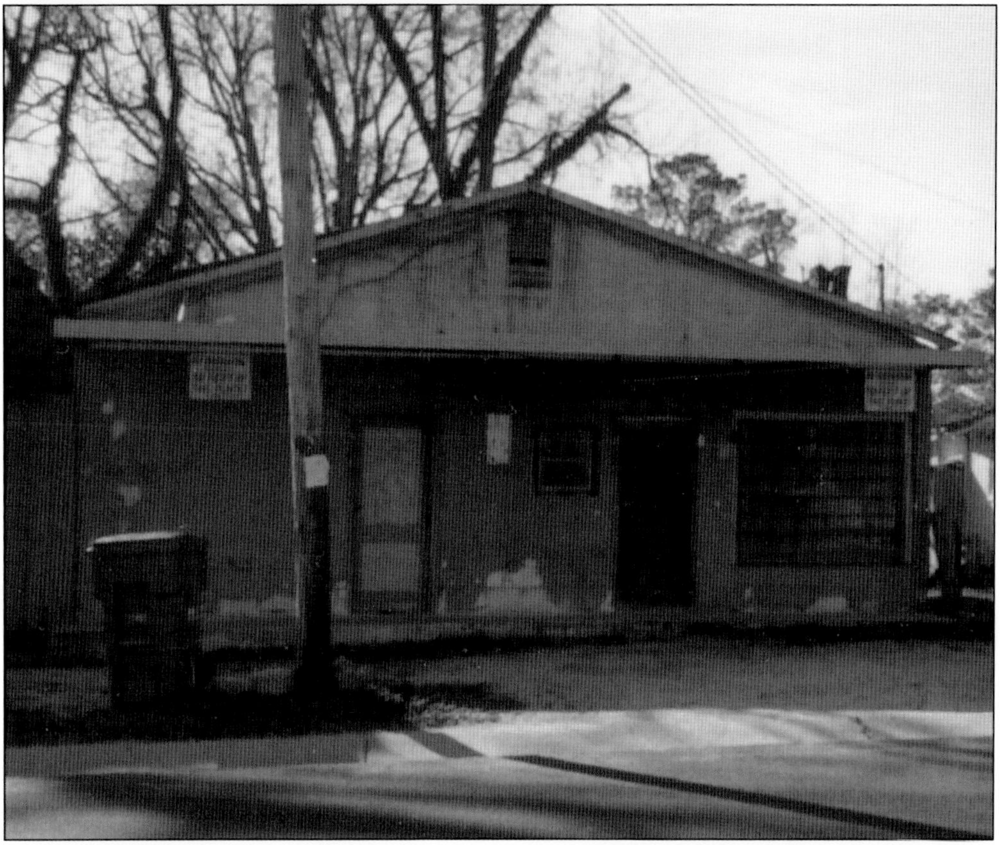

Lindsey Hadley's Café, located on Orange Street, was a favorite gathering place for area citizens to "chew and chat."

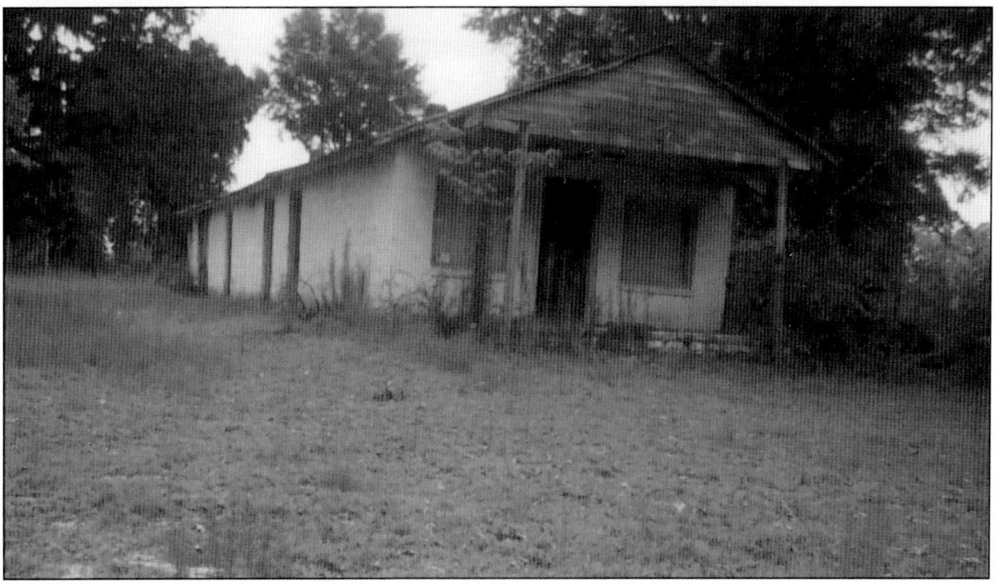

Pete's Store, located in the Mt. Tabor Community, was owned and operated by Elijah Pete Sr. A variety of groceries and merchandise was always available.

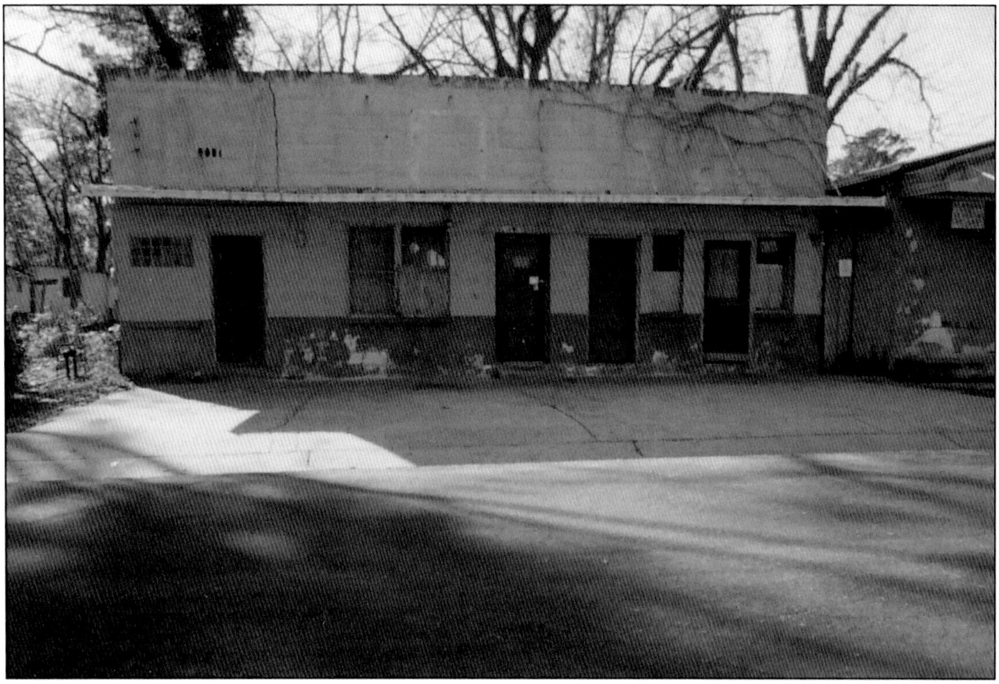

West End Sweet Shop, owned and operated by Paul and Bessie Harrison and their children, was located on Orange Street, next door to Odell Pittman's barber shop. The Sweet Shop was a popular hangout for teenagers and provided employment for a few high school students, including Bonzell Harrison and Robert "Coon" Smith.

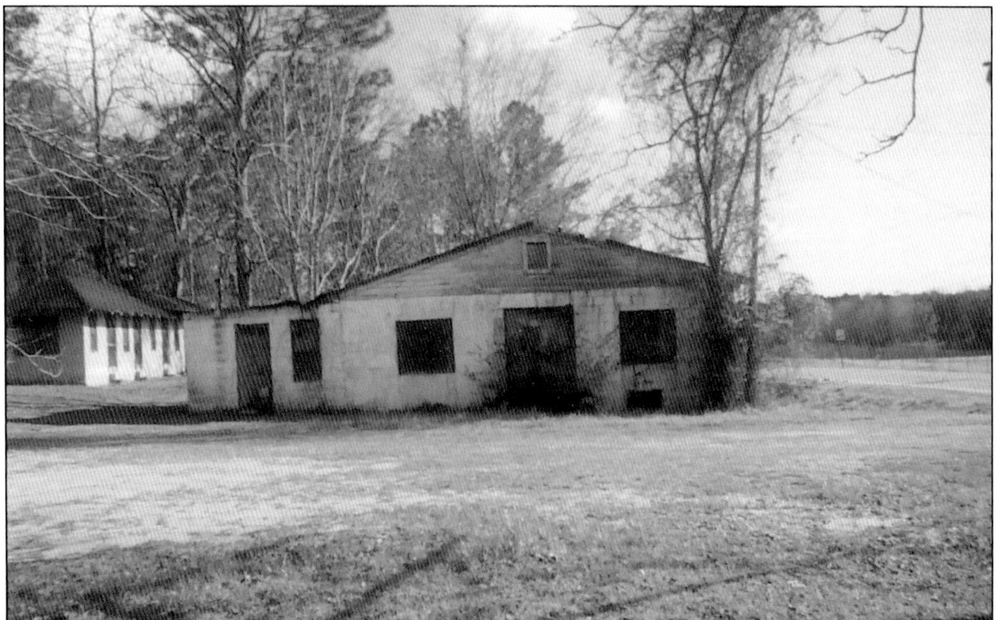

River's Inn, located on Old Hodges Mill Road (now Pennsylvania Avenue), was owned and operated by Allen Rivers. He provided delicious food, spirits, and entertainment for a broad spectrum of clientele for many years.

Johnny's Gulf Station was located on Orange Street and built in the 1950 by Johnny Sansome, contractor. Workers included Johnny Speights, Elijah Gilbert, and "Bunion" Long. It is now Bryant Enterprises, owned by Elmore Bryant.

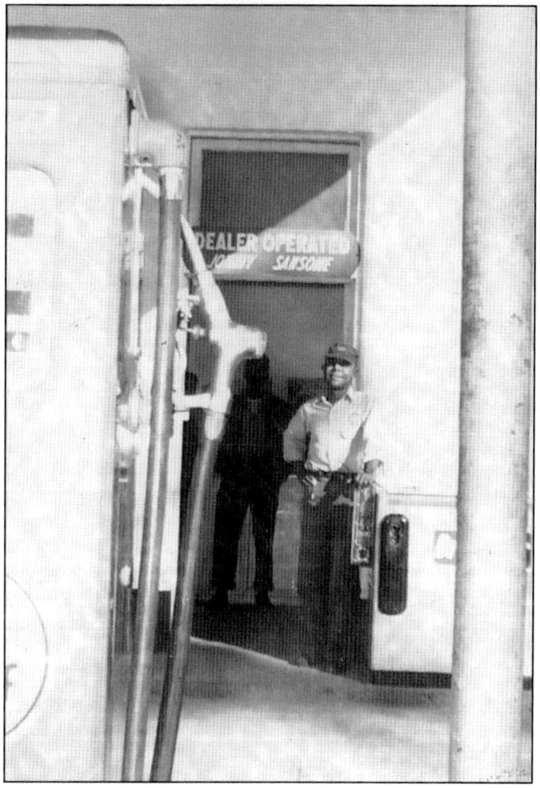

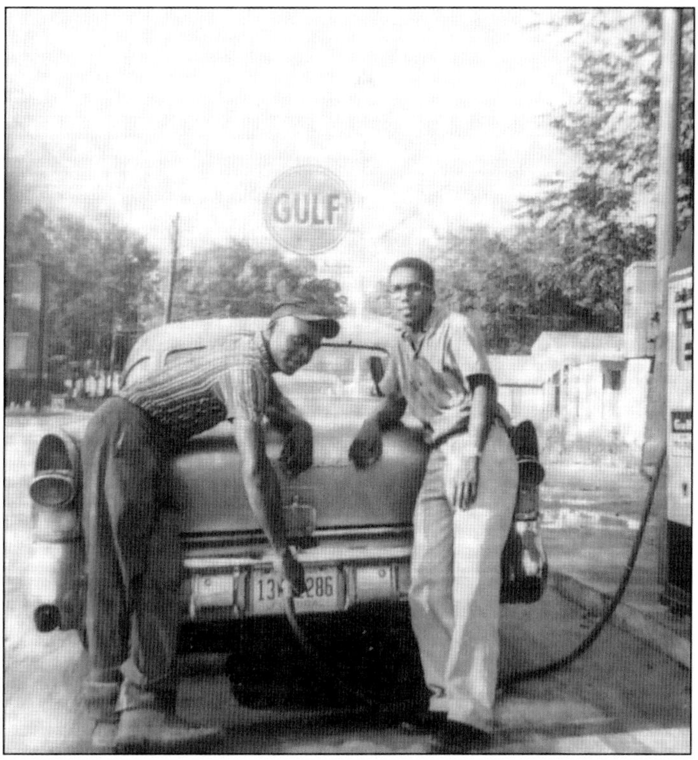

Johnny's Gulf Station was "a full service station." "Bish," a longtime employee, is shown here pumping gas. He was and remains a "full service provider."

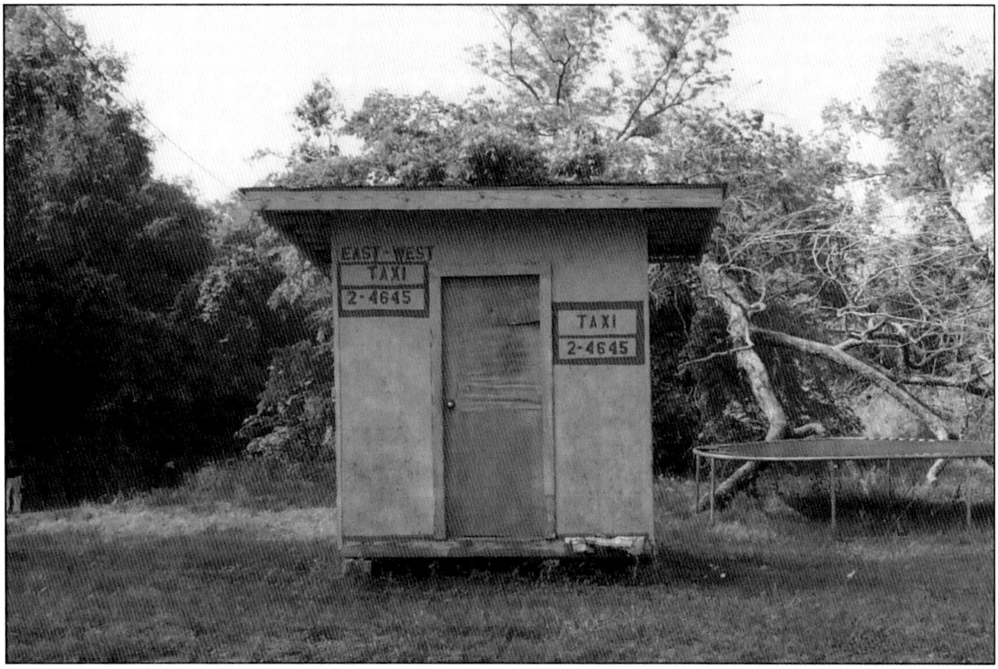

The East/West Taxi Stand, originally located on East Lafayette Street, provided employment for drivers, and transportation, primarily for African Americans. Taxi drivers and owners included William "Bunk" Wynn, Grant Price, Henry Keith, C.W. Pittman, William "Tookie" Bryant, and Andrew Swails. Pearlie Speights and Linzey Summerwell were among the first telephone dispatchers for the business.

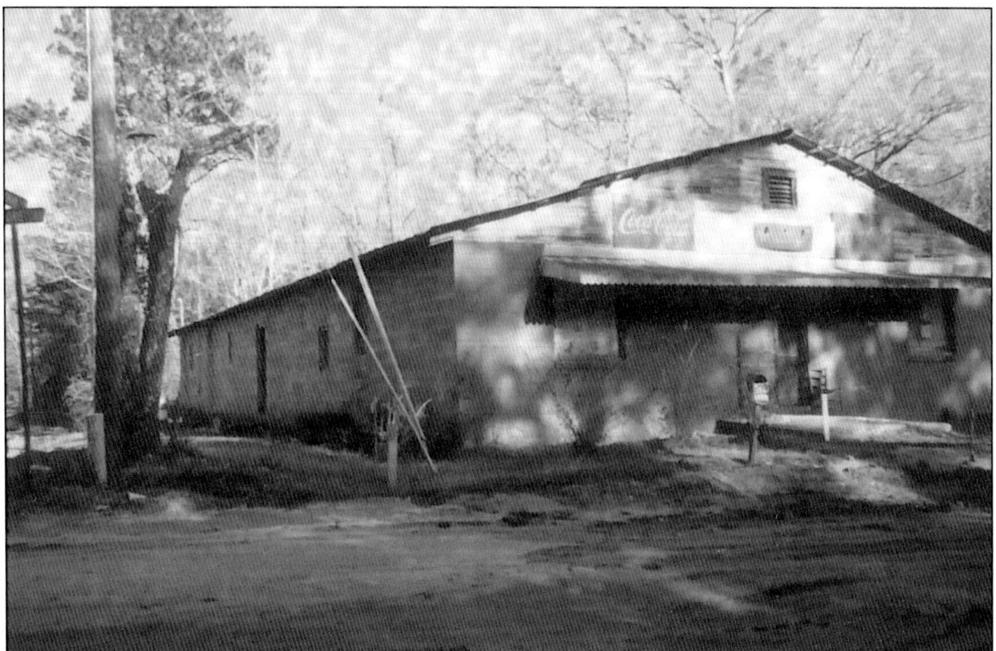

Mae's Supper Club, or "Monk's Place," located in the Blue Hole, was another favorite gathering spot for food, spirits, and entertainment, such as dancing and card playing.

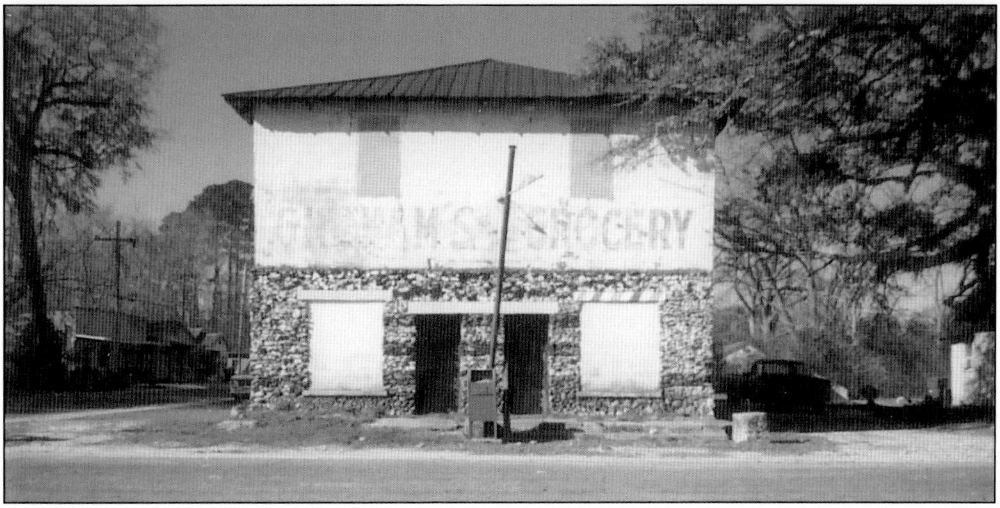

Graham's Place, better known as the "Honey Dripper," located on the corner of Orange and St. Andrews Streets, was established by Arthur Graham Sr. The business was later operated by his son, Arthur Graham Jr. The huge upstairs dance area provided a setting for many generations of couples and individuals to enjoy the jitterbug, cha-cha-cha, and other popular steps of the day. The first floor housed an original "fast food" store, poolroom, and grocery store. Many high school proms were held here.

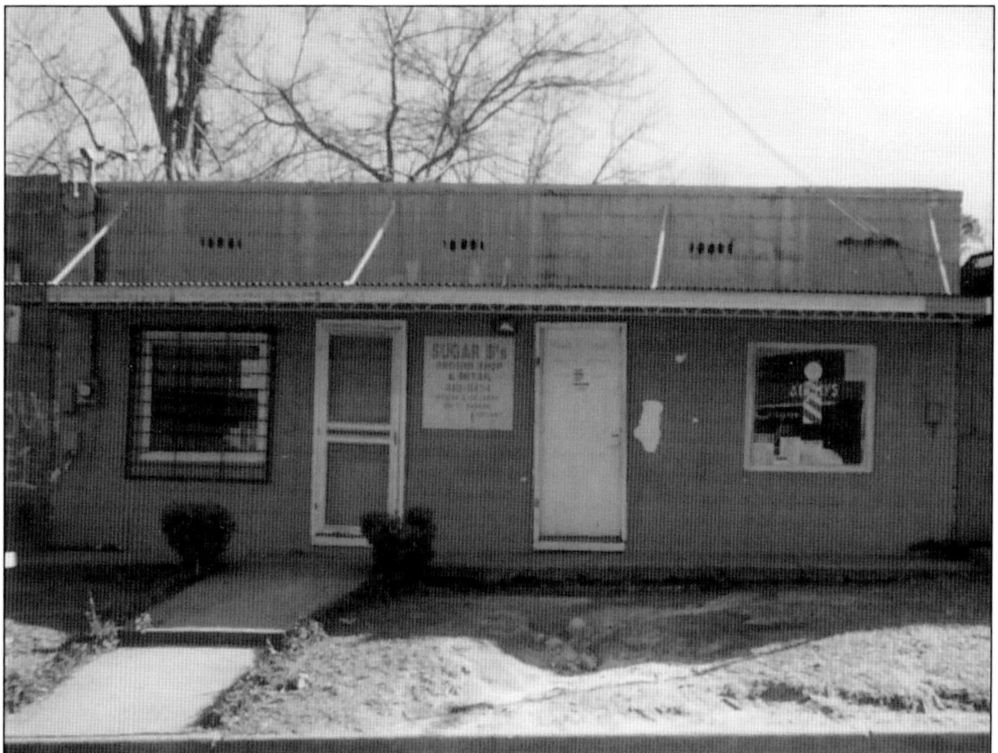

Willie Pender's Barber Shop and Sweet Shop, located on St. Andrews Street, operated at this location for more than 40 years, providing expert service to men, boys, and women. The sweet shop closed long before the barbershop.

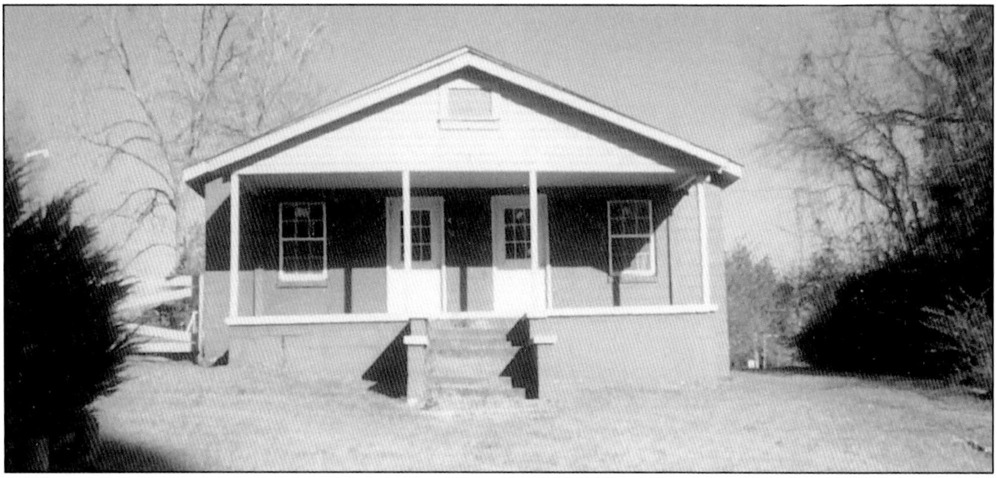

The Redbird Café, located on South Madison Street in downtown Marianna, was owned and operated by Plassie Hadley Cook. Her menu included stew beef, chitterlings, collard greens, cornbread, her famous sweet potato pies, and a wide assortment of refreshing drinks. Her clientele included both whites and blacks. The Redbird's location on Madison continued a long tradition of African-American business ownership in downtown Marianna. In the early 1900s, blacks owned several downtown businesses. Such early businessmen included James Speights; Willie Horne; Robert Livingston, who operated a fruit market; and Frank White, Larkin Gilbert, and Zannie Garret, barbers. William Holden's fish market, Richard Baker's cleaners, and Armstrong Purdee's law office were also located downtown. The last of the black-owned downtown businesses were located in the "Blue Front" section of Lafayette Street, just west of the courthouse. Included were Reverend Robinson's barbershop, Claudia Gant's and Lula Williams's beauty shop, and Cleve Roulhac's poolroom. They all closed in the 1970s. Today, most black businesses are concentrated on the "West End."

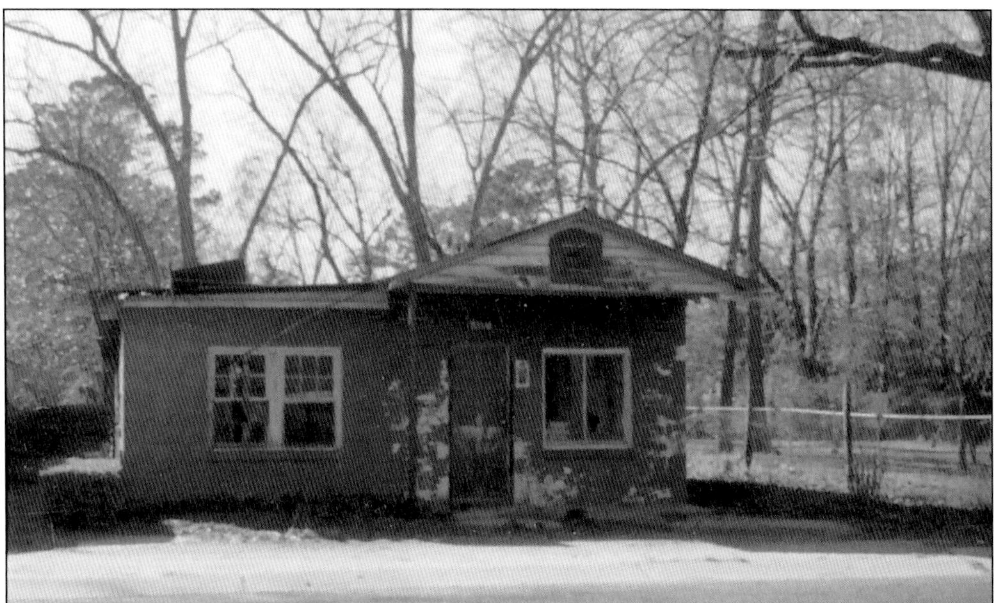

Bryant's Grocery Store on Orange Street was operated by Eddie Mae Bryant. She sold most grocery and miscellaneous items, except meat.

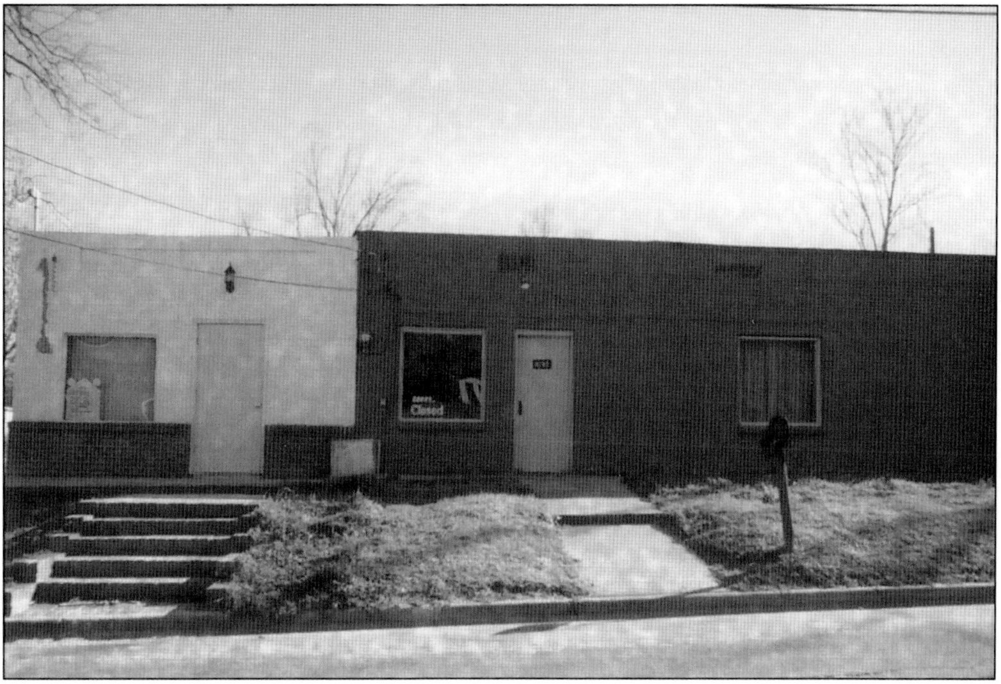

West End Cleaners and Pressley's Shoe Shop were located on St. Andrews Street. The cleaners was operated by the Washington brothers. Leo cleaned and pressed while Eddie provided expert tailoring service. David Pressley was one of two "shoe doctors" on St. Andrews Street. The other shop was operated by Robert Summerwell.

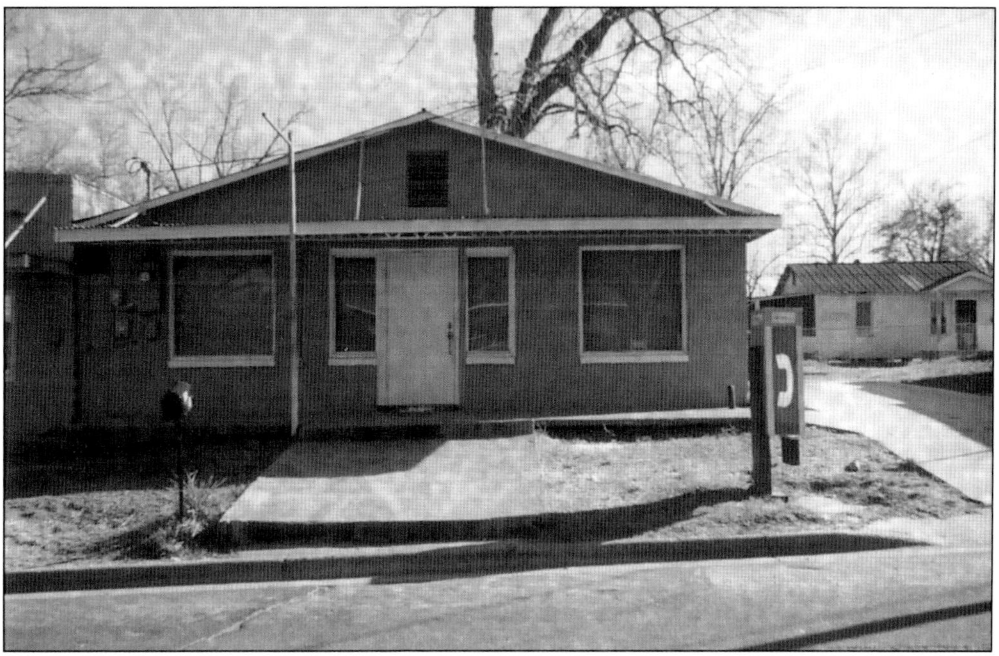

Mildred's Café was owned and operated by Mildred Long for many years. Her menu included a variety of "soul foods." Speciality items included an assortment of cakes, pies, and other baked goods. This business was originally owed and operated as a café by the Luke Coleman family.

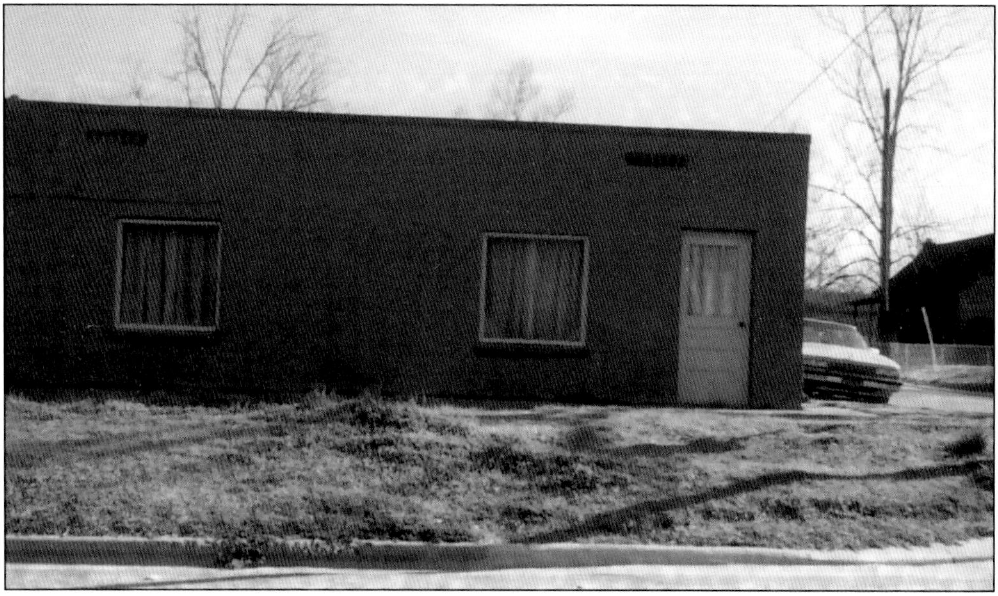

Cozy Corner, also known as Leo's Place, was operated by Leo and Earnestine Washington. It provided another place for relaxation. Bonnie Peace was employed as a cashier.

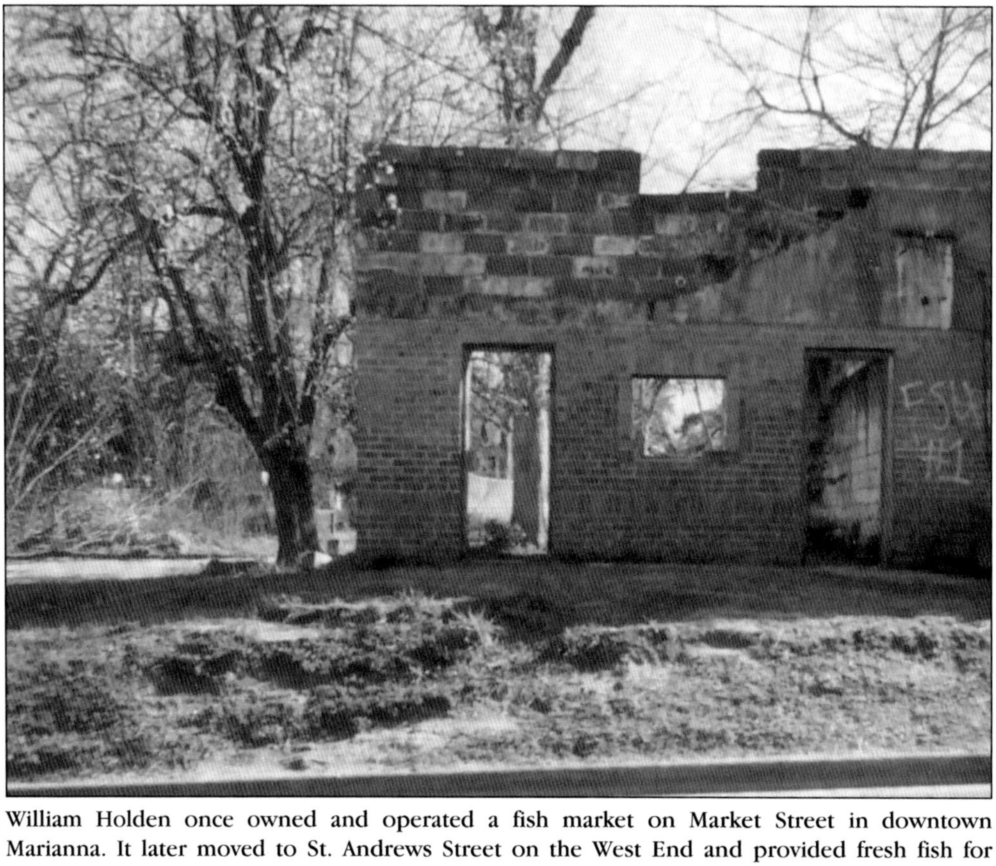

William Holden once owned and operated a fish market on Market Street in downtown Marianna. It later moved to St. Andrews Street on the West End and provided fresh fish for the community.

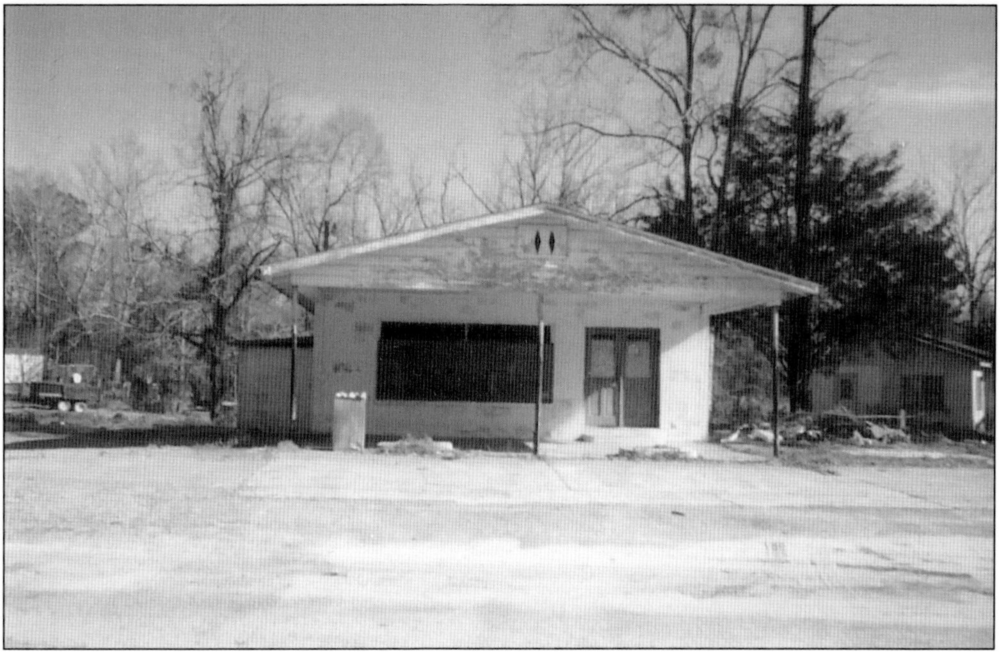

Long's Grocery Store and Gas Station provided part-time employment for several students, one adult (as a meat cutter), and a mechanic. Long's Grocery was the only black-owned store that offered a full line of groceries. This was also a hangout for checkers players and observers.

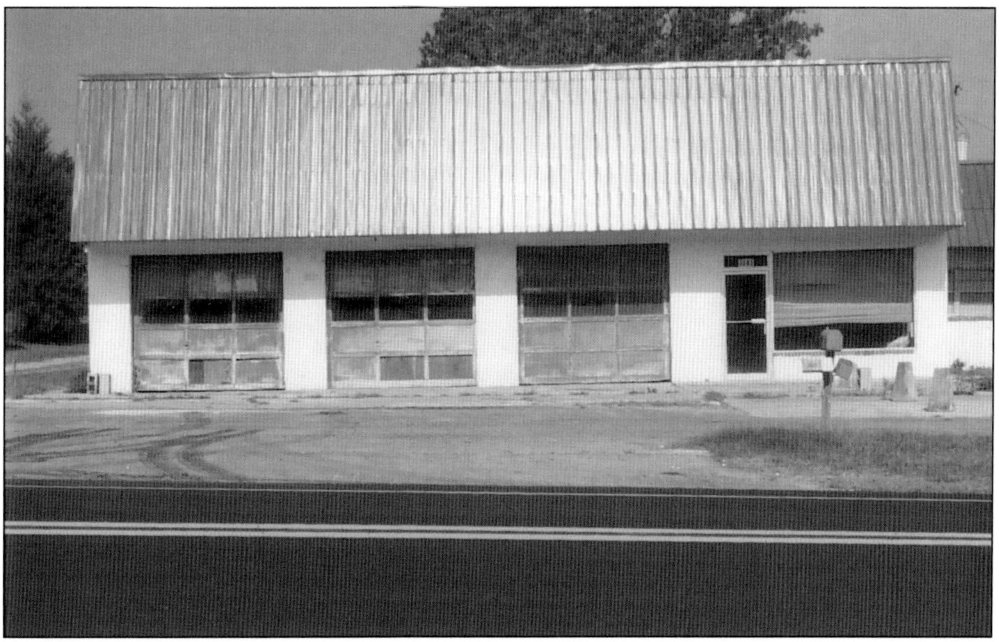

Ephriam's Garage, owned and operated by Thomas Ephriam Sr., a self-taught mechanic, began as a home-based business in the Jerusalem Community. Later, it was relocated to Highway 73, south of Marianna. Ephriam was known as an excellent mechanic.

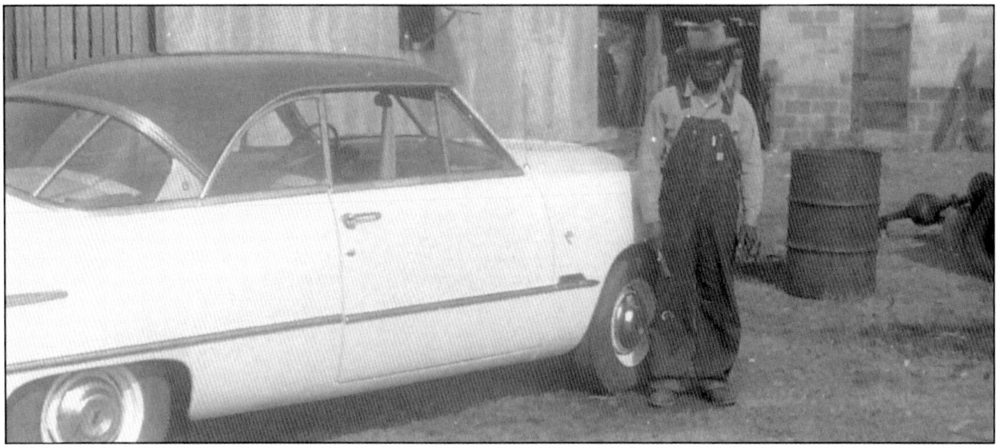

Yank Speights Garage, owned by Cleaster "Yank" Speights, another self-taught mechanic and farmer, once had a contract with the City of Marianna to repair its vehicles. His businesses enabled him to provide for his family and afford a good education for his three daughters. He owned and operated his garage on Cedar Street in Marianna and was considered an outstanding mechanic and provided services for many area citizens. In addition to his mechanic services, he raised hogs, cows, chickens, cane, and sweet potatoes on Cedar Street until the city ordinance changed. Later he produced cotton, peanuts, corn, and peas on the Baker-Speights farm and operated a wood business, selling and delivering wood to the people in the community.

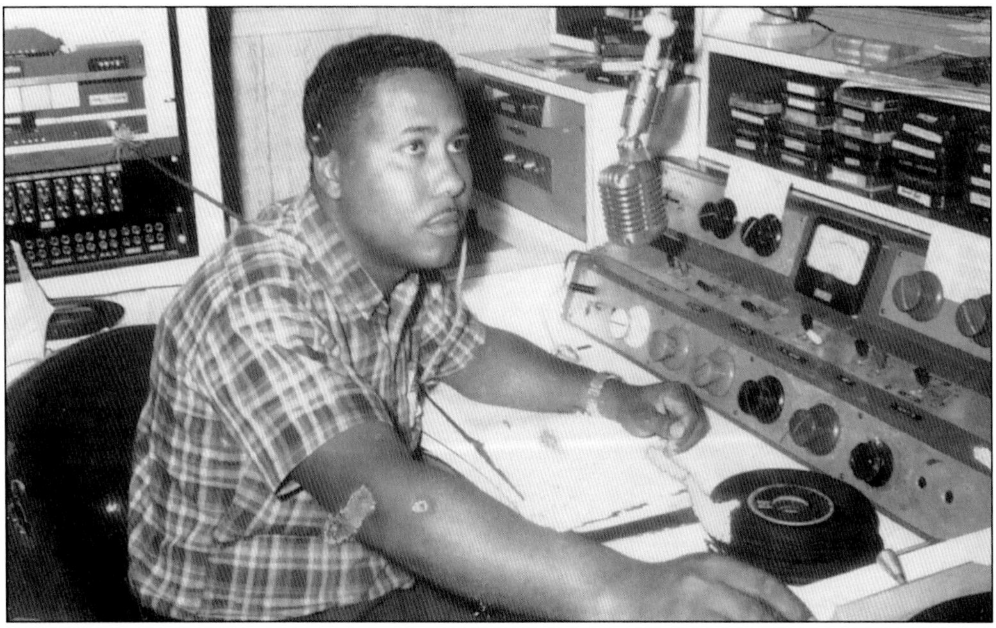

The "Spiritual Echoes" program was founded and hosted on WTYS for many years by Virgil Elkins. When Elkins relocated to Tallahassee, James Garris hosted the program. In 1964, Johnny Speights, pictured above, became the host of the one-and-a-half-hour program that airs each Sunday morning. His first broadcast was on the first Sunday in February. The original theme song, "It's a Highway to Heaven," was later changed to "Touch Me Lord Jesus." Speights's program, sponsored by many area businesses in the surrounding area, has been enjoyed by area citizens for the past 35 years.

Seven

Pre-School Education

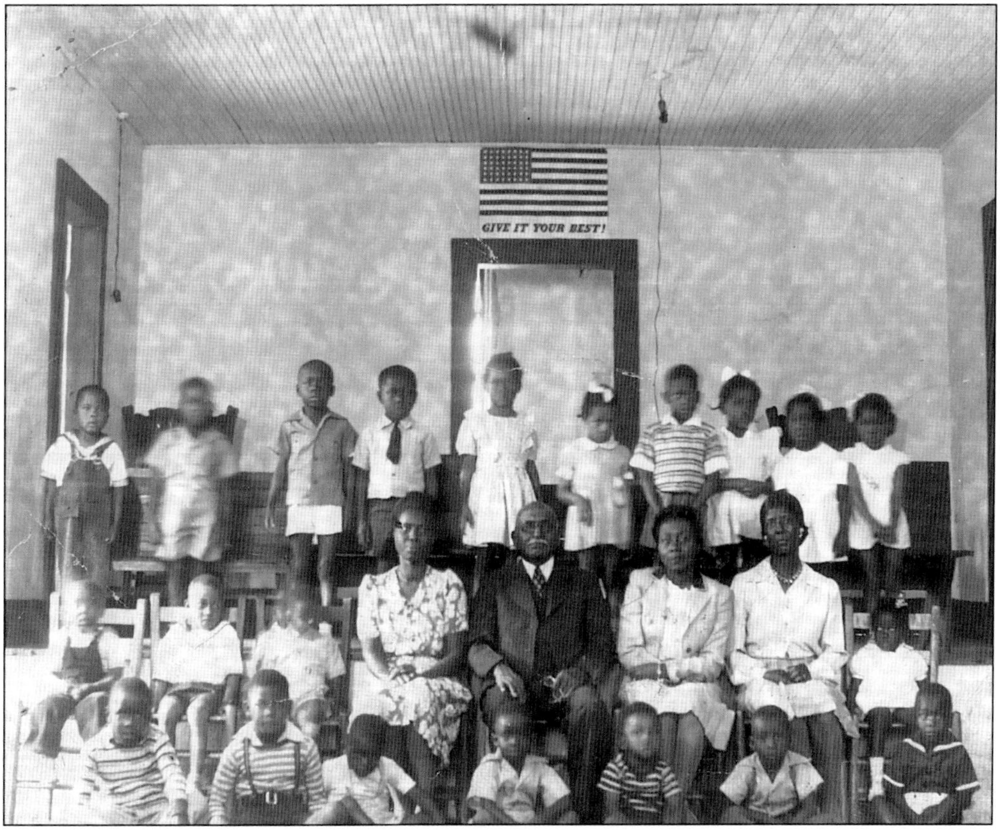

This a group of three-to-five-year olds who attended a private kindergarten at the JCTS building in the early 1940s, according to Thelma L. Ellis Alexander (second row, left of R.T. Gilmore, center) who taught at the school. The kindergarten was attended by children whose parents were working and assisting in the war effort. The attendance fee was $1.25 per week.

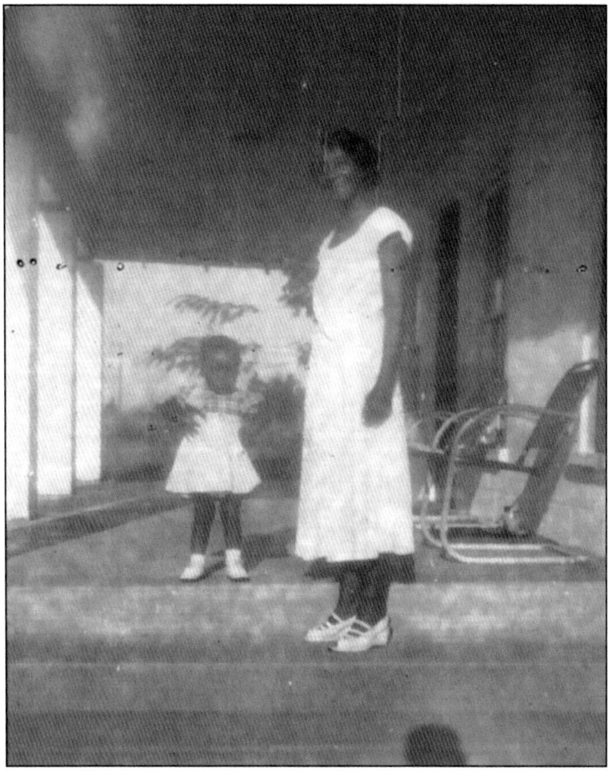

Ester Livingston Watson stands on the front porch of her Pinecrest Kindergarten on South Street with student Harriet P. Brown, now an attorney in Orange County. Watson lent her talents and expertise to nurture children and to provide the only pre-school for African-American children in the community. When her students entered first grade, the difference was obvious. Mrs. Watson owned and operated this fine school and graduated about 20 classes. Prior to opening the kindergarten, Mrs. Watson taught at J.C.T.S. Elementary School and worked as a canning club demonstrator for black women under a federal grant to encourage interest in agriculture and home economics. Mrs. Watson and her husband, Albert, owned the entire block on which the school was located.

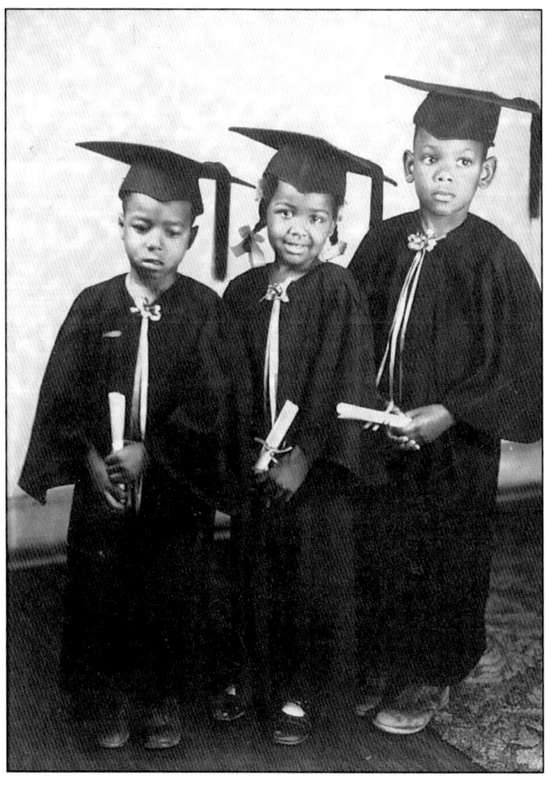

Pictured are, from left to right, Gary Harrison, Brenda Page, and Donnie Roulhac. They were members of the Class of 1948, the first class to graduate from Pinecrest. The education these young students received gave them a strong foundation for future learning. Gary and Donnie, both college graduates, continue to reside in Florida. Brenda, who relocated to California with her parents, died at an early age while undergoing a tonsillectomy.

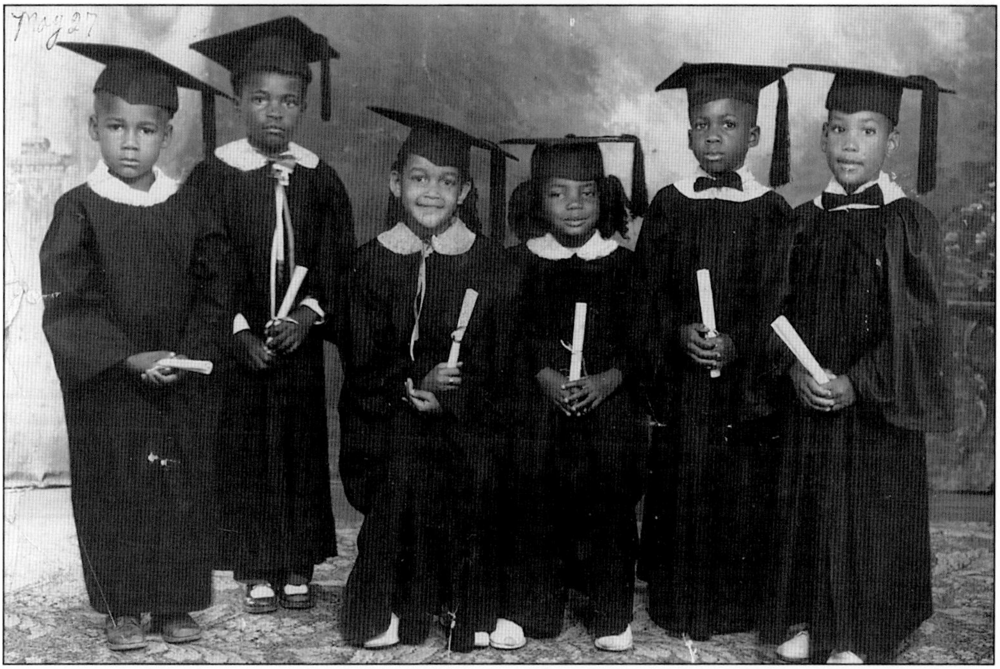

The Pinecrest Kindergarten Class of 1950 consisted of, from left to right, Rufus Jones, Jimmy Council, Sharrod Black, unidentified, Stanley Wilson, and Jimmie Bryant.

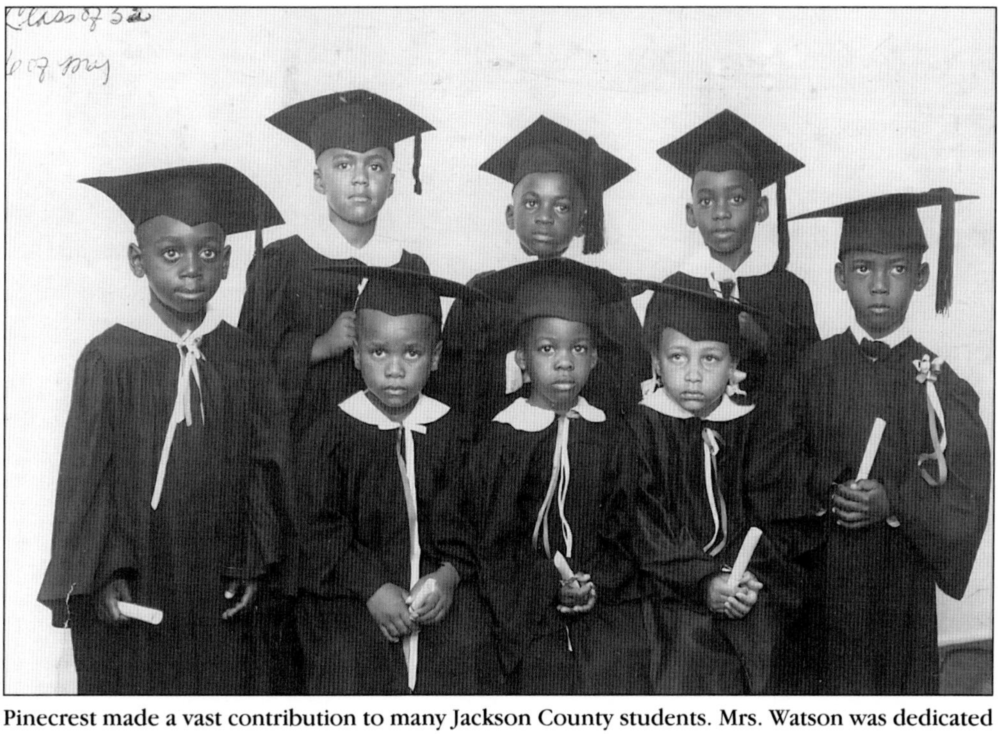

Pinecrest made a vast contribution to many Jackson County students. Mrs. Watson was dedicated to bringing out the best in each child. Pictured above is the Class of 1952. From left to right are (seated) Gerald Myrick, unidentified, and Joan White; (standing) William Harley Jr., Stanley Whitehurst, Chambers Wilson, Freddie Spires, and William Clay.

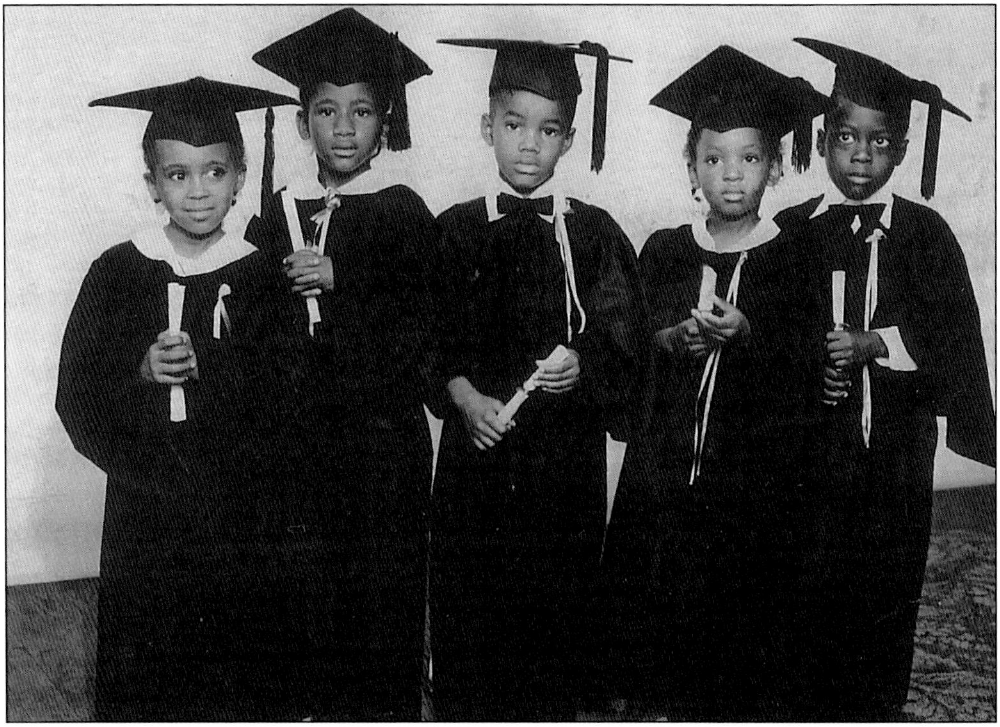

Most parents who could afford to sent their children to Pinecrest. Pictured above is the Class of 1953. From left to right are Dayatra Baker, Anna Spears, Willie Pender Jr., Connie Speights, and Bernard Clay.

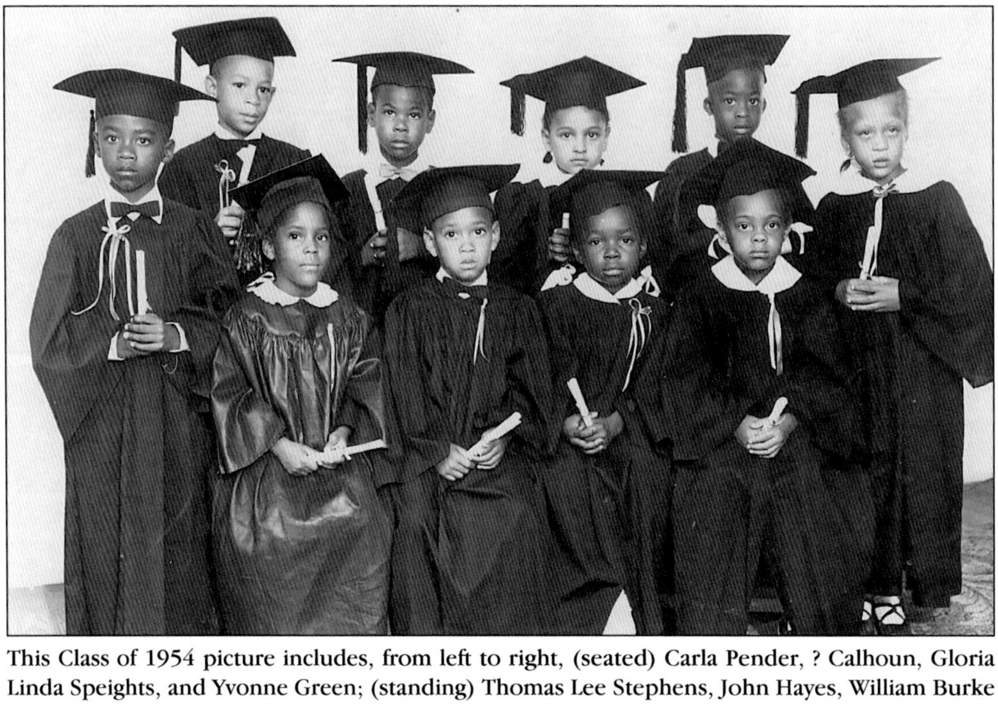

This Class of 1954 picture includes, from left to right, (seated) Carla Pender, ? Calhoun, Gloria Linda Speights, and Yvonne Green; (standing) Thomas Lee Stephens, John Hayes, William Burke Jr., Sandra Borders, George Howard, and Cheryl K. Woods.

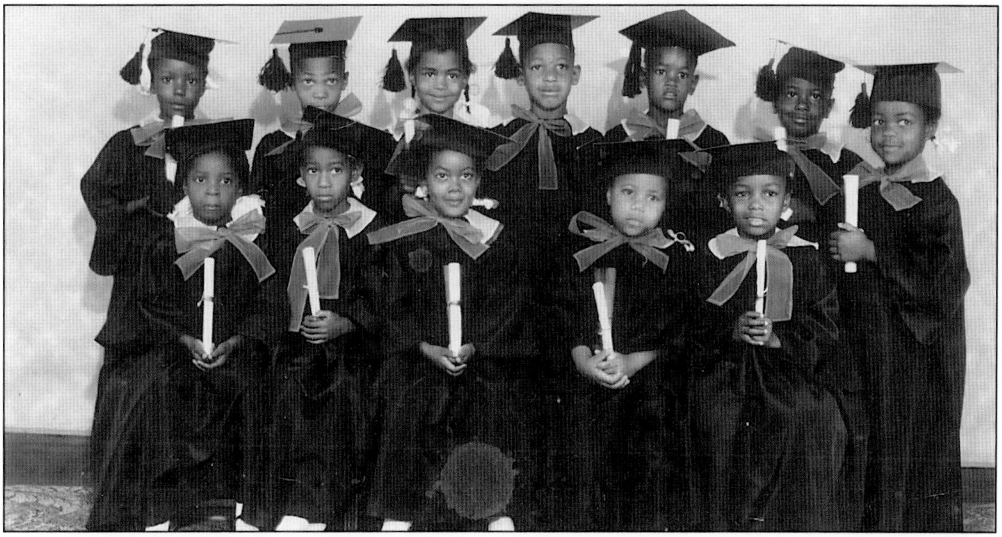

Graduation Day was a day of excitement for Pinecrest Kindergarten students. On this special day, each child received their first diploma and was required to stand and make a presentation before the audience. Two students from each class were selected to greet the audience with a long speech or to sing a special solo that was always performed without mistakes. What a day it was for these students to remember. Pictured above is the Class of 1955. From left to right are (seated) Louise Speights, Essie Mae Smith, unidentified, Yvonne Swilley, and unidentified; (standing) Jeanette Bowles, Charlie Holden Jr., Griselda Swilley, Cornelius Leslie, James Blackshear, Earnest Swilley Jr., and Harriet Brown.

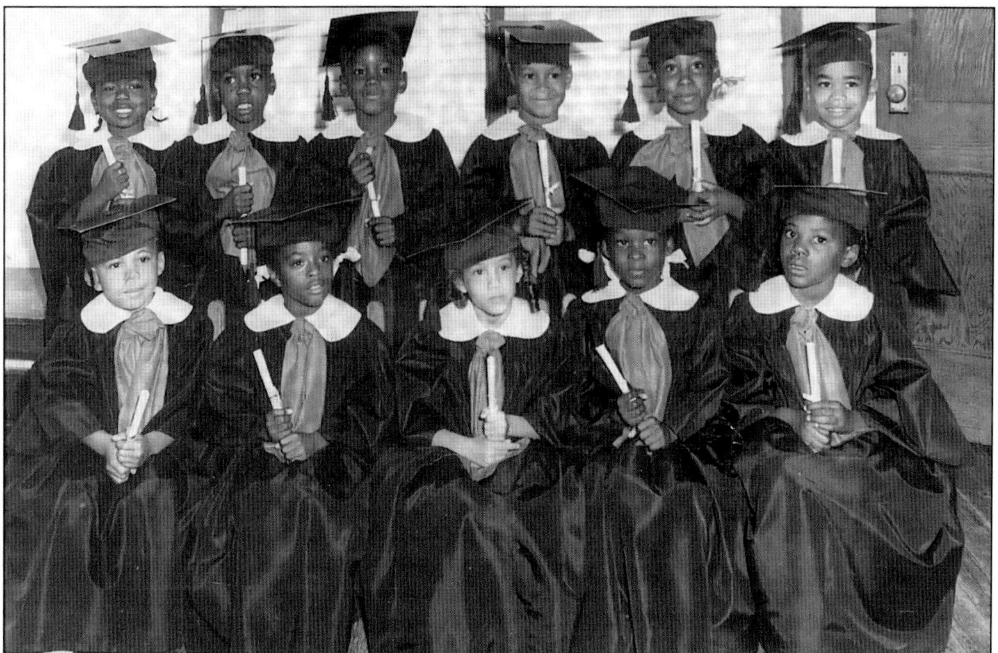

The Class of 1958 includes, from left to right, (seated) unidentified, Katrina Warren, Sonja White, Gwenette Elkins, and Barbara Koonce; (standing) Cheryl Milton, unidentified, William Long, Bruce Bellamy, unidentified, and Reginald Swilley.

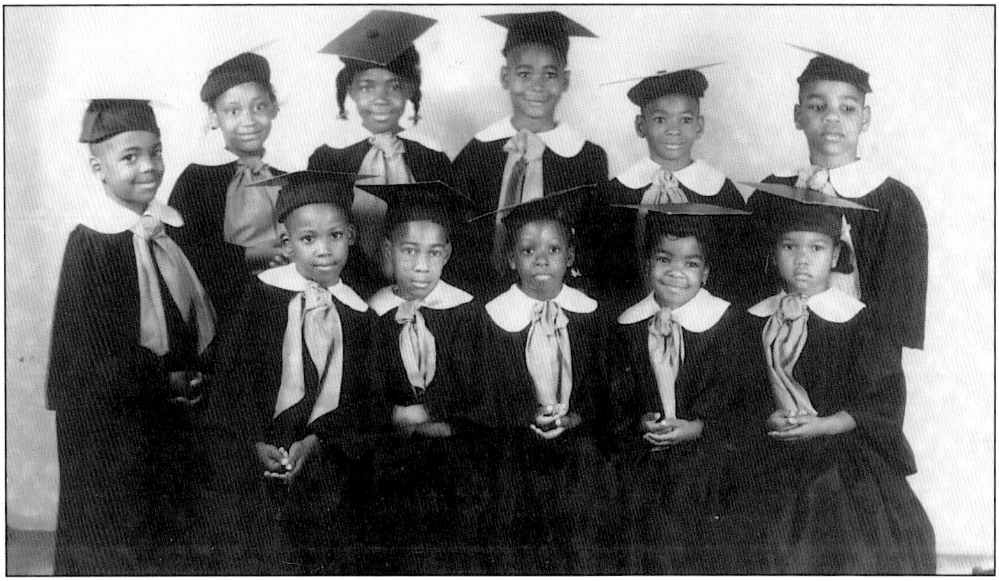

Most students who graduated from Pinecrest became top students and leaders when they entered elementary school. Under the watchful eye of Ester Livingston Watson, the children were disciplined, respectful, and eager to learn. Many are making outstanding contributions in their communities. From left to right are (seated) Laron Robinson, William Al Hayes, Patrice Bradley, Patricia Mitchell, and Natalie Harvey; (standing) Patrick Brown, Genetta Boykins, unidentified, Melvin Shack, unidentified, and Gilbert Porter.

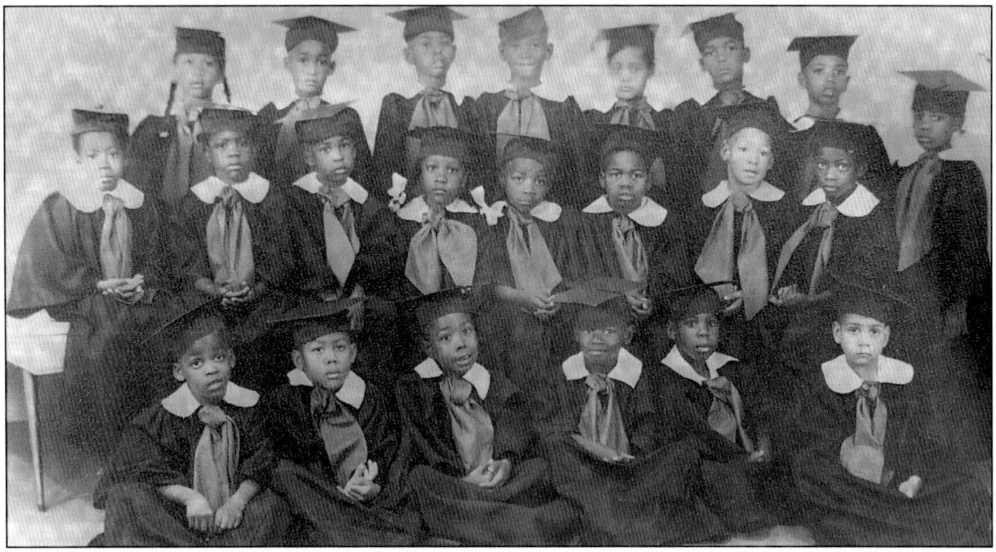

The Class of 1967 was the last to graduate from Pinecrest Kindergarten. It closed after 20 years of service when the county, for the first time, allocated funds for the pre-school education of African-American children. Pictured, from left to right, are (front row) Andre Branton, Dexter Hawthorne, Eric Speights, Elijah Gilbert, Shelley Mitchell, and Ronald Fagan; (second row) Angerine Bowles, Carla Menchion, Jerome Robinson, Gloria Sims, Gregory McNeil, Arthur Wynn, Douglas Jones, Cassandra Cooper, and Vanessa Robinson; (back row) Marcietta Swilley, Granville Harvey, Reginald Harrison, Rodney Summerwell, Stephanie Barkley, Toney Hayes, and Randall Scott.

Eight

Jackson County Training School: Sports and Classes

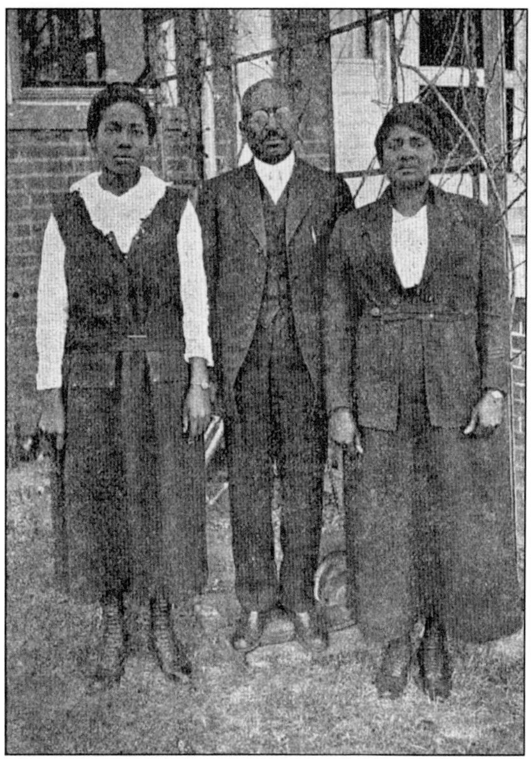

Pictured are R.T. Gilmore, his adopted daughter Girlinda (left), and his wife, Selena. According to the 1920 Jackson County Census, Gilmore, age 40, was a high school teacher and his wife, age 39, and their 19-year-old daughter taught grammar school. Gilmore was also employed as the principal in the "colored" section of the Florida Industrial School for Boys, which in 1920 had 220 black inmates and 104 whites. In 1922, Professor Gilmore established the Gilmore Academy on Orange Street. In 1931, the Academy was replaced by the Jackson County Training School, the first publicly supported school for African Americans in the county. The site is now the home of St. Luke Baptist Church. (Florida State Archives Photographic Collection.)

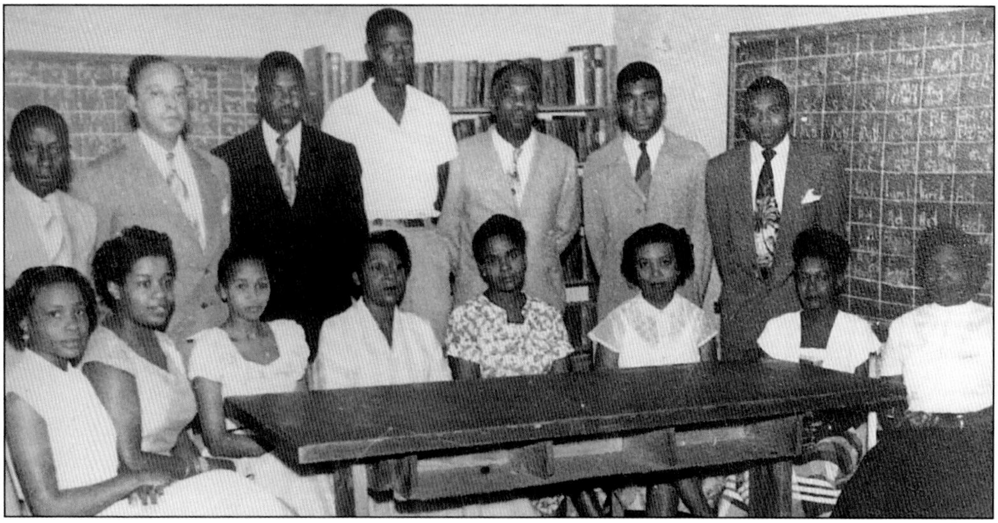

Faculty members of Jackson County Training School in the early 1950s are, from left to right, (seated) Mildred McMullen, Bessie Willis, Mamie Cooper, unidentified, Annie Mae Bryant, Erin Weatherspoon, ? Haywood, and Mrs. Susie Baker; (standing) William H. Harley Sr., Mosely Baker, Amos P. Brown, King David Wilson, Morris McDuffie, Isaac Pittman, and Alvin Pearsall.

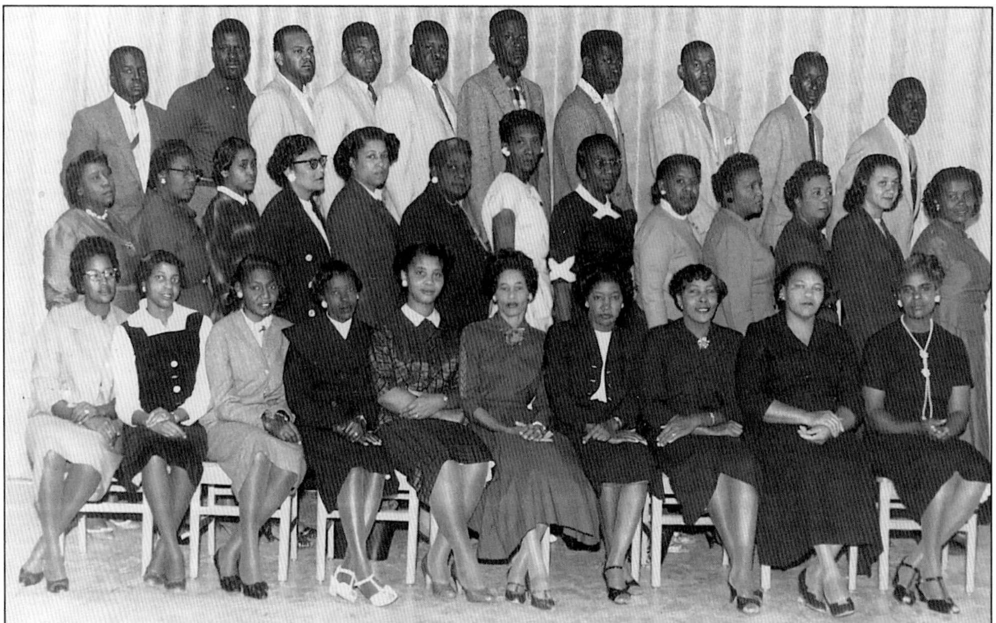

The combined faculty of JCT Elementary and High School is seen here *c.* 1958. From left to right are (seated) Theresa Bryant, Rosie B. Bryant, Viola Dixon, Ollie Pender, unidentified, Florice Garrett, Mamie Blackshear, Elrea Daniels, Thelma Swilley, and Annie Mae Bryant; (second row) Ethel Watson, Susie Baker, Mamie Cooper, Maggie P. Keith Atwater, Francis Brown, Lola Harley, Vivian Koonce, Willie J. Hutchinson, Reola Bryan, Sallie Harley, Erin Weatherspoon, Nellie Wilson, and Mary Milton; (back row) Ben Bowles, Willie Cooper, Joseph Fagan, Isaac Pittman, Amos P. Brown, King David Wilson, Lindsay Summerwell, Labert Hawthorne, George A. Bradley (assistant principal), and William Harley Sr. (principal).

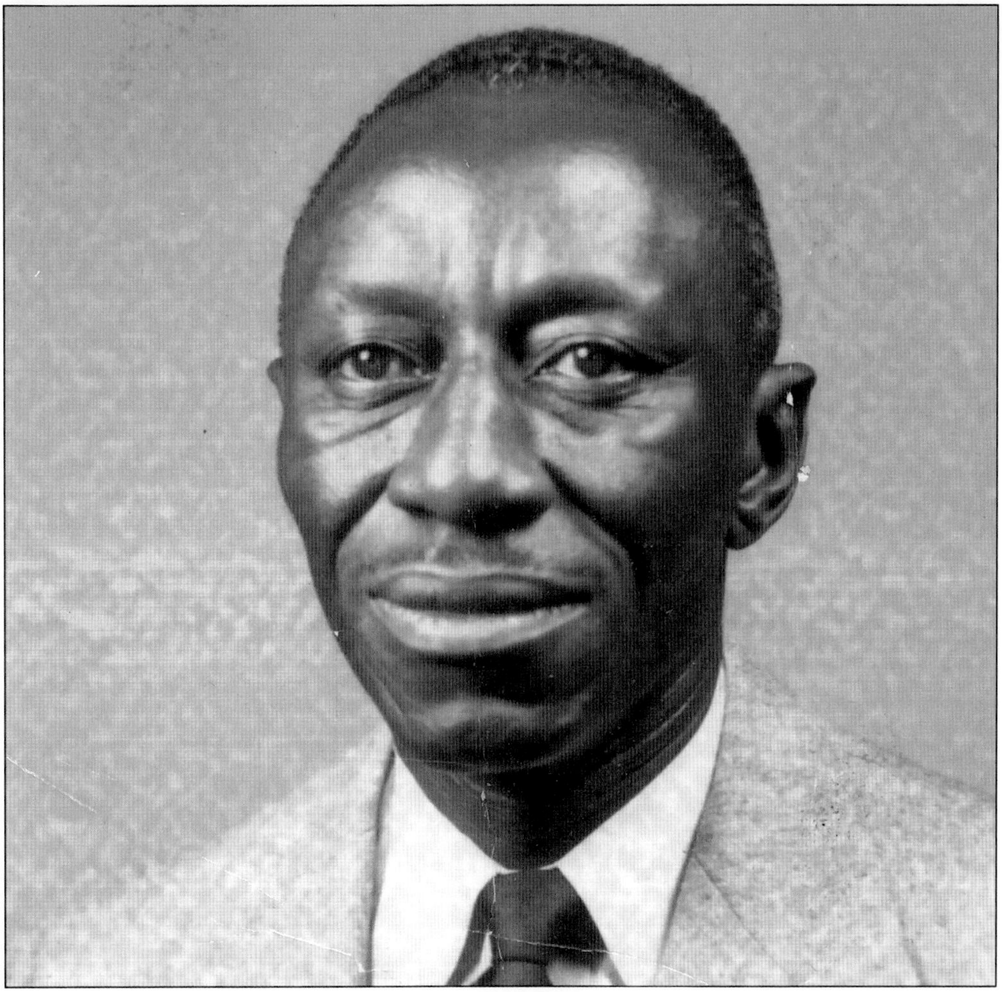

William H. Harley was born and reared in Jackson County. He was the son of Presiding Elder Elijah Harley and Annie B. Harley. He was an active member of St. James A.M.E. church, where he served as a steward and class leader. Harley received his early education in the Jackson County School system. Later, he attended Florida Normal College in St. Augustine and transferred to Florida A&M University, where he received BS and MS degrees. He was a veteran of World War II. Harley was employed by the Jackson County School Board for more than 37 years, and he served as principal and teacher at St. Mary's and Buckhorn Elementary Schools, principal of Jackson County Training School, and president of Jackson Junior College. Under his leadership as principal of JCTS, several innovative programs were initiated. He was known as a strict disciplinarian who was firm in his decisions, yet compassionate in his feelings. In 1961, while serving as principal, Harley was appointed president of Jackson Junior College. He was its only president for the five years of its existence. Harley was married to Sallie S. Harley who was a Jackson County teacher. They had one son, William Harley Jr., who is an educator. In 1989, a street in West End Marianna, Harley Drive, was named for him. On July 20, 1993, the Chipola Junior College District Board of Trustees placed a framed resolution and photo on the walls of the college board room in recognition of his accomplishments as founding president of the Post-Secondary Education Foundation of Jackson County. He died on July 12, 1976. He is remembered and highly respected for his outstanding educational leadership and service to his community.

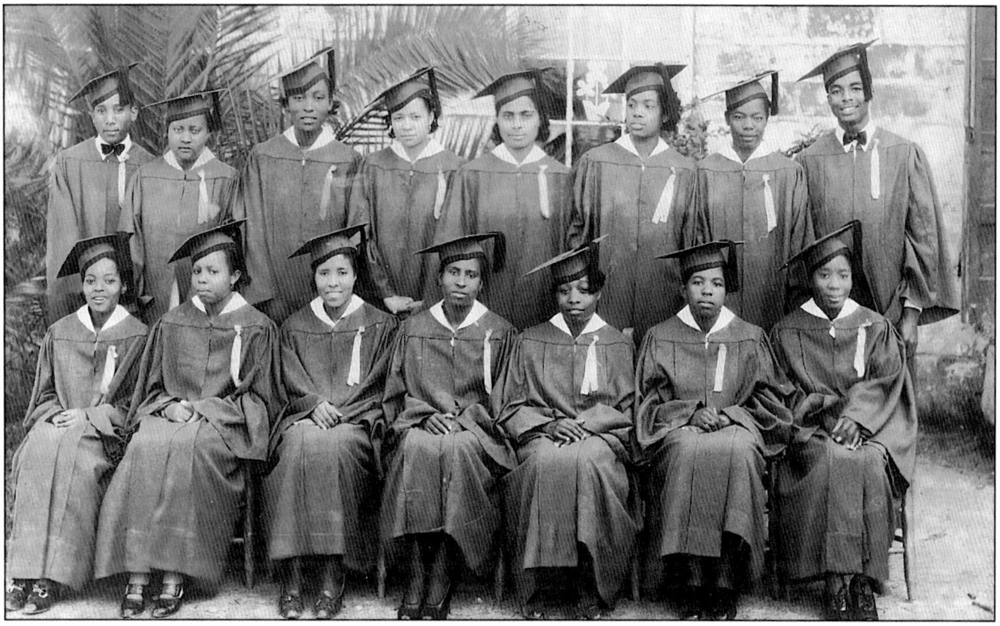

Pictured above is the Jackson County Training School Class of 1937. The class sponsor was Gertrude E. Cotton, and the principal was Roy A. Allen.

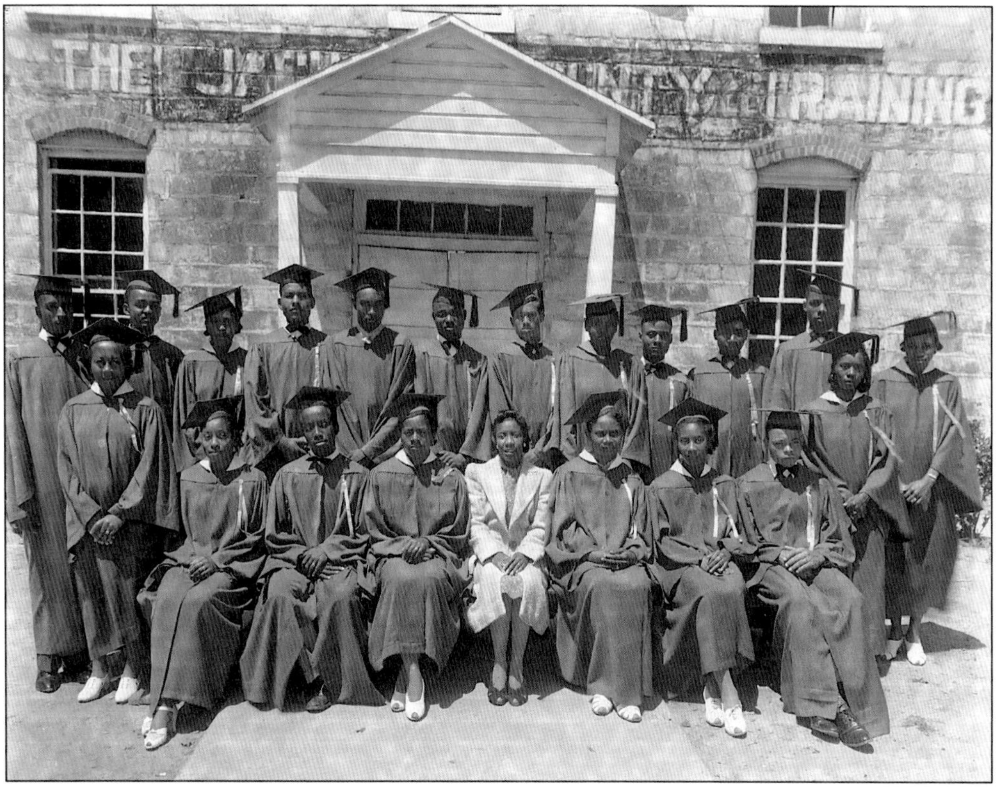

In this photograph of the Jackson County Training School Class of 1940 is Gertrude E. Cotton (front row, center), class sponsor, who was recruited by R.T. Gilmore and was a distinguished English teacher.

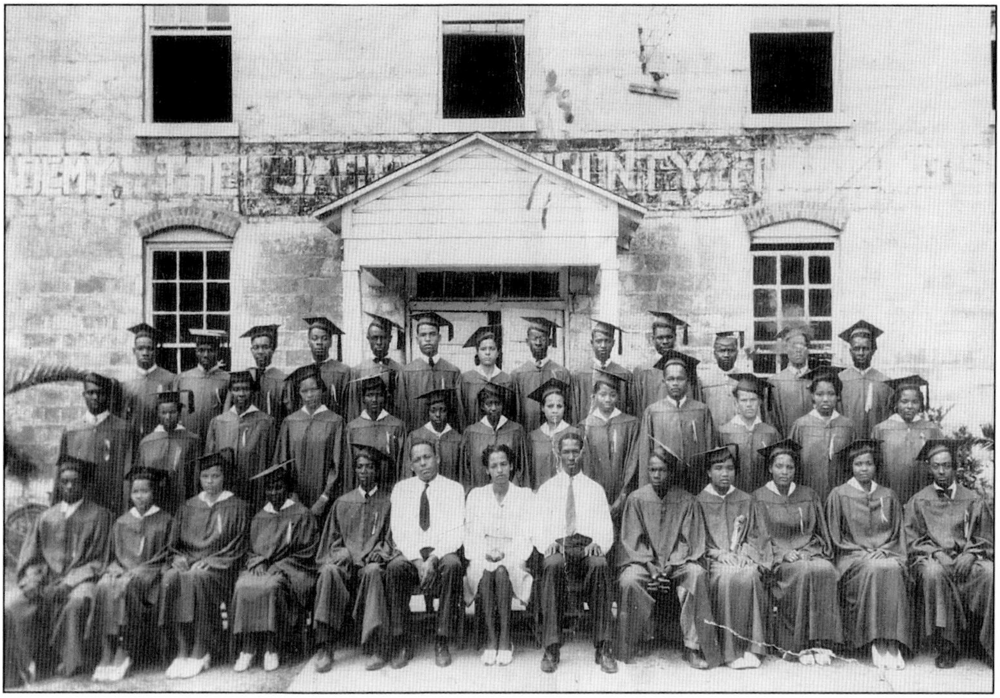

Seen here is the Jackson County Training School Class of 1941 with sponsors seated on the first row (center). They are, from left to right, Colbert Britt; Hiawatha Long; and ? Williams, principal.

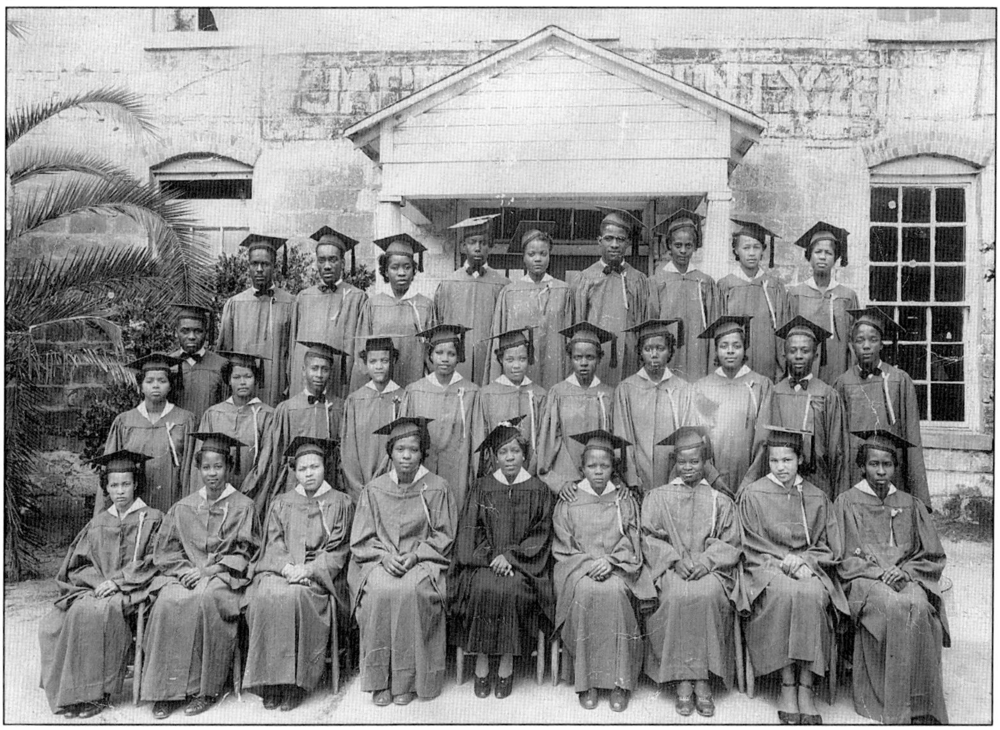

The Jackson County Training School Class of 1944 had as its sponsor Gertrude E. Cotton.

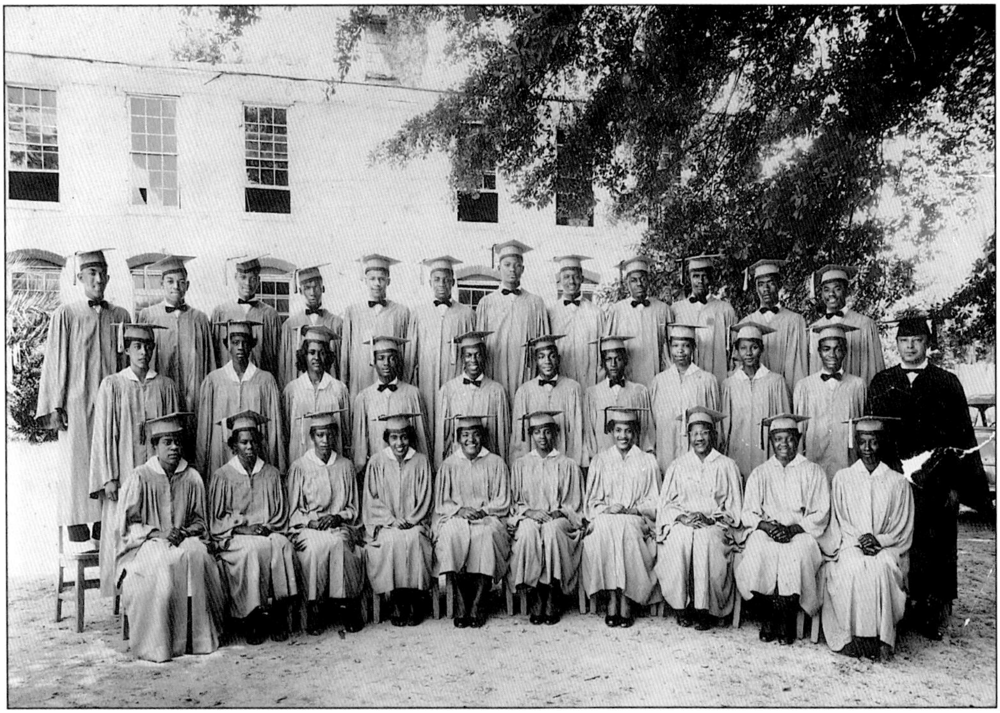

Class sponsor Mosely H. Baker, of the Class of 1954, is seen standing at right, wearing a black robe.

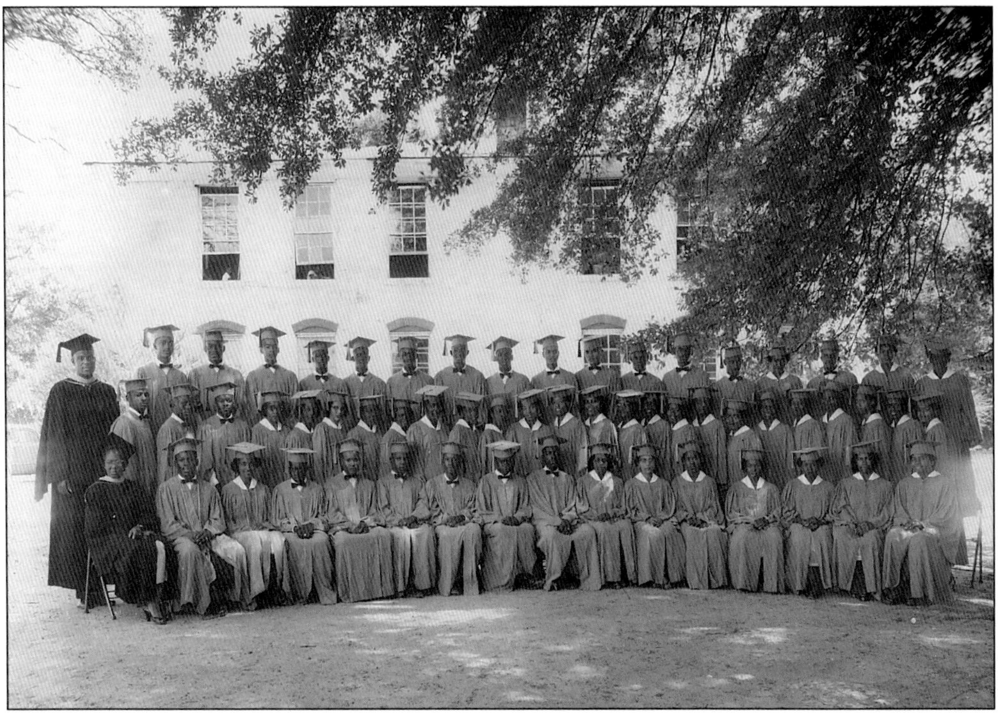

The class sponsors of the Class of 1955 were Susie L. Baker, first row on the left, and King David Wilson, second row on the left.

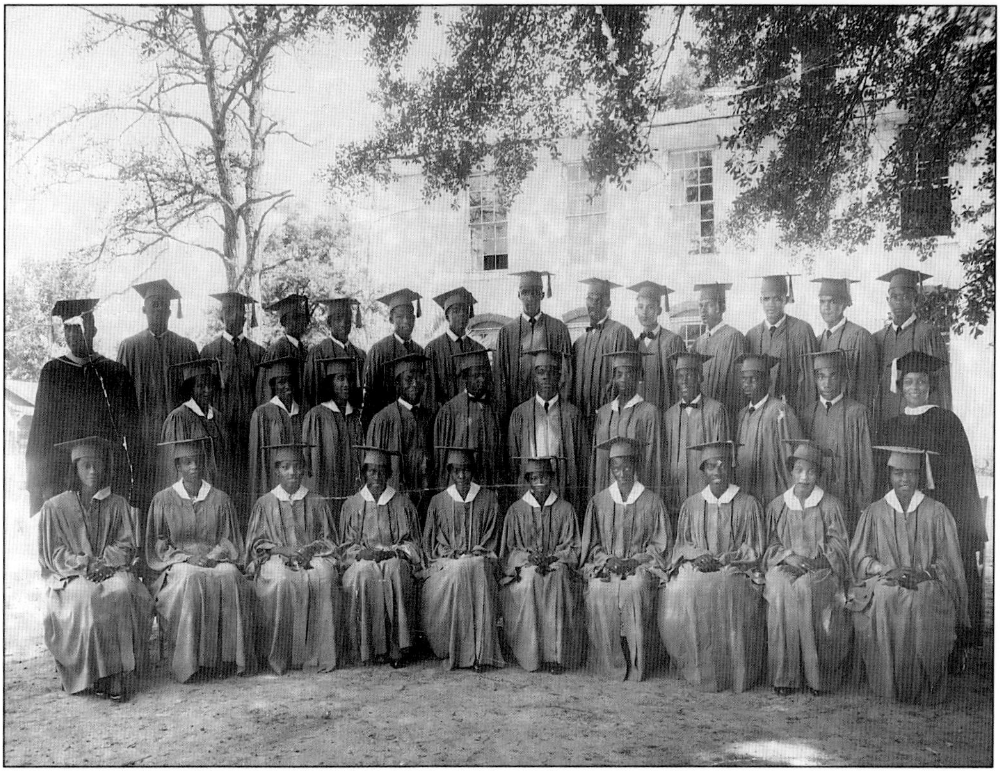

Anna N. Granberry, second row on the right, and King David Wilson, second row on the left, were the sponsors for the Class of 1956. Granberry passed away in September 1999.

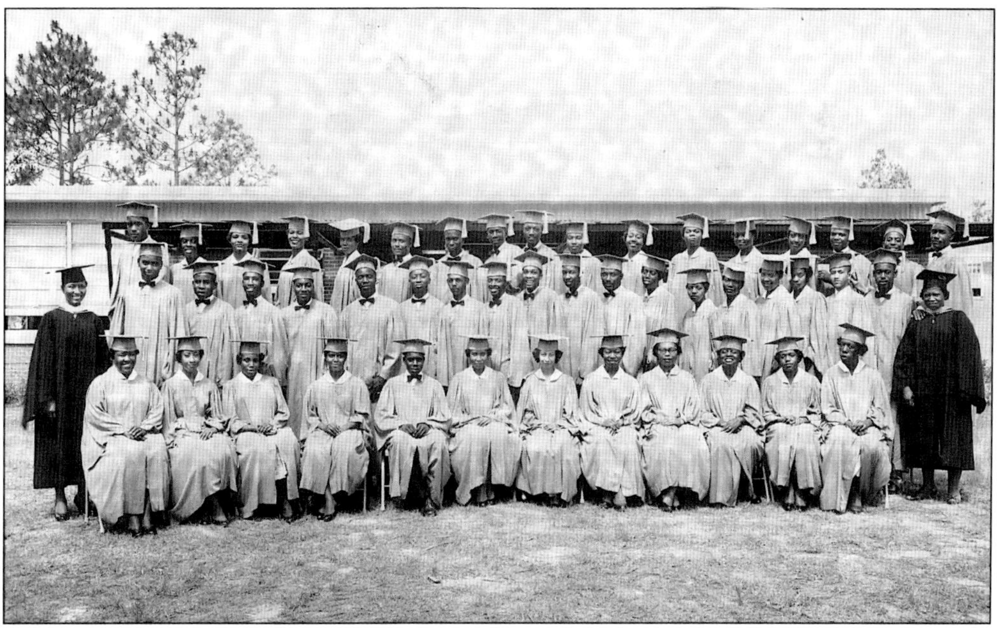

The Jackson County Training School Class of 1957 was the first class to graduate from the new high school, which opened in November 1956. The class sponsors were Lucille J. Bell, second row on the left, and Susie L. Baker, second row on the extreme right.

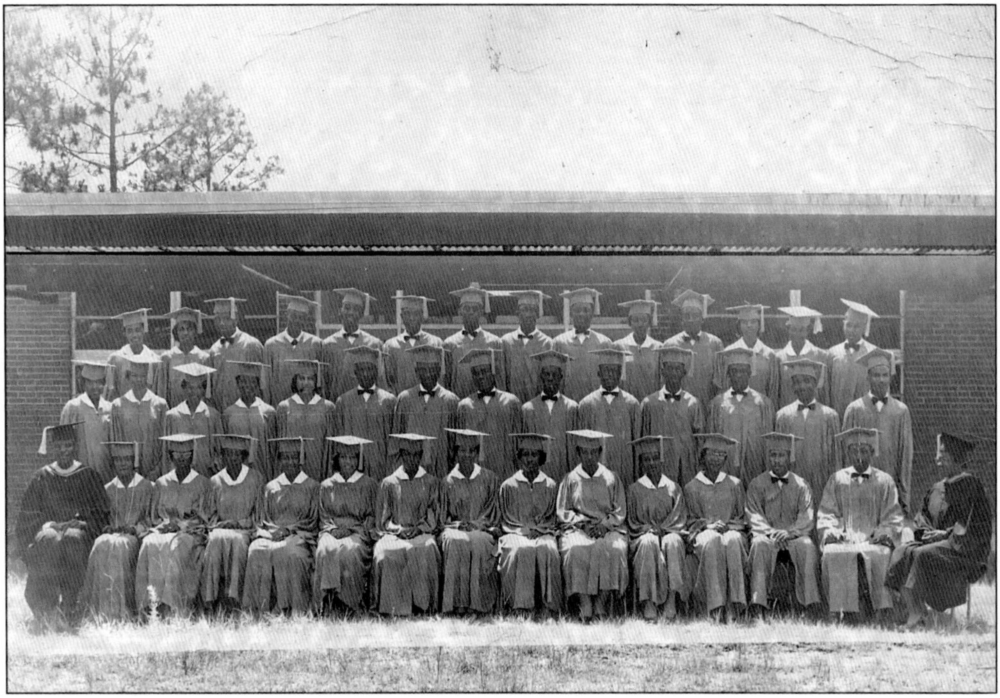

Pictured here is the Class of 1959 with sponsors King David Wilson, first row on the left, and Susie L. Baker, first row on the right.

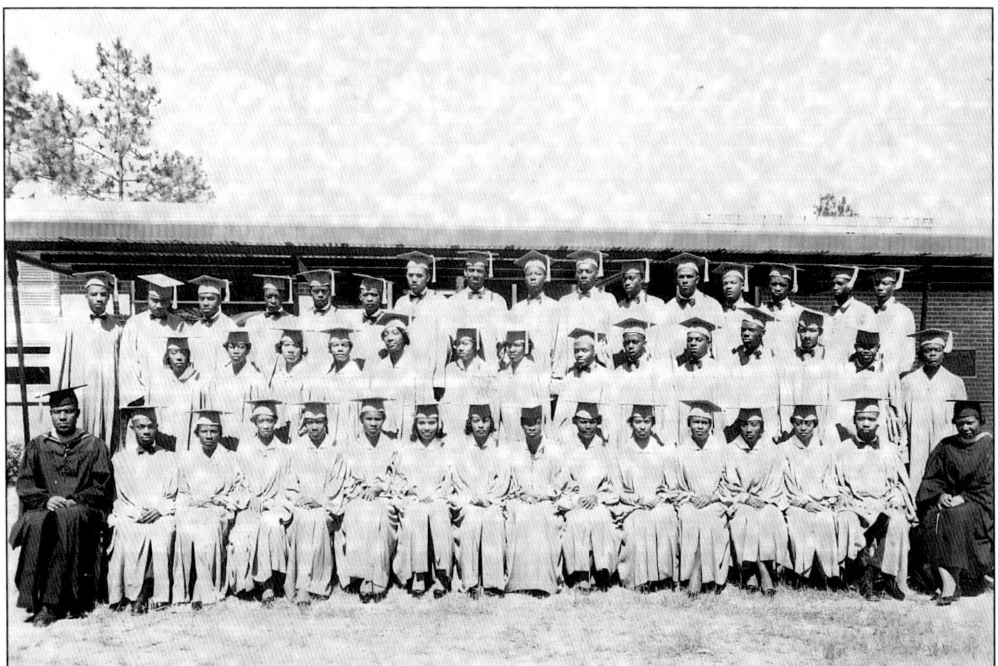

King David Wilson, first row on the left, and Susie L. Baker, first row on the right, were also the sponsors of the Class of 1960.

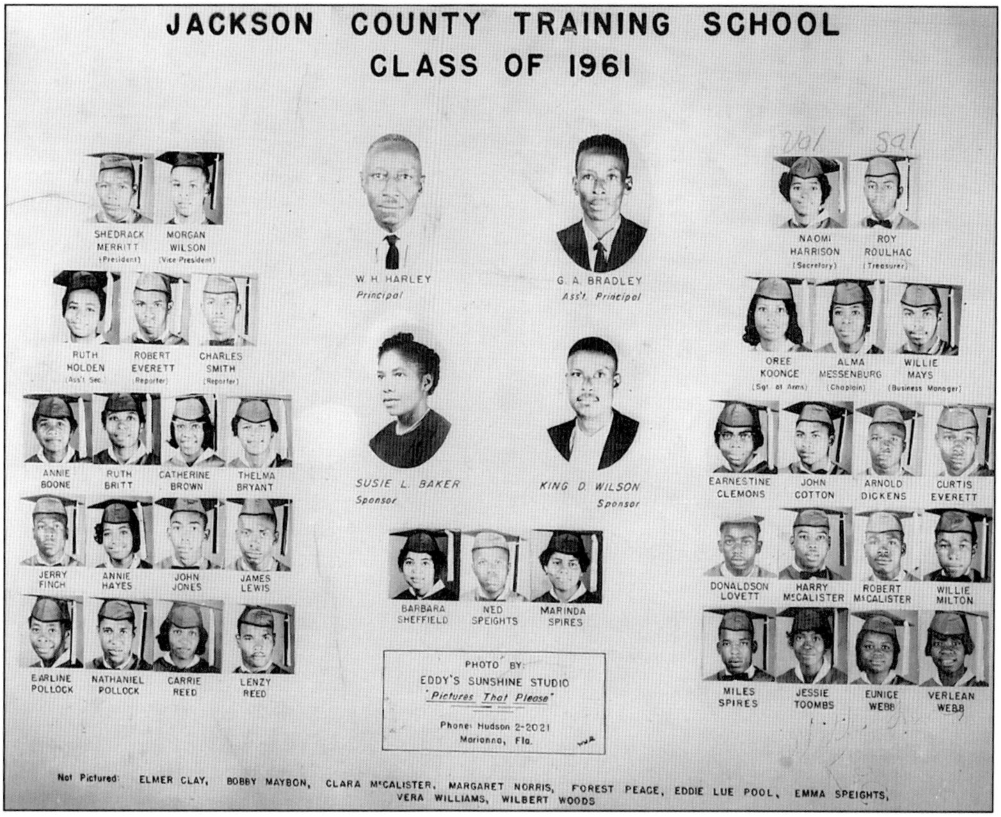

The Jackson County Training School Class of 1961 had as its sponsors King David Wilson and Susie L. Baker.

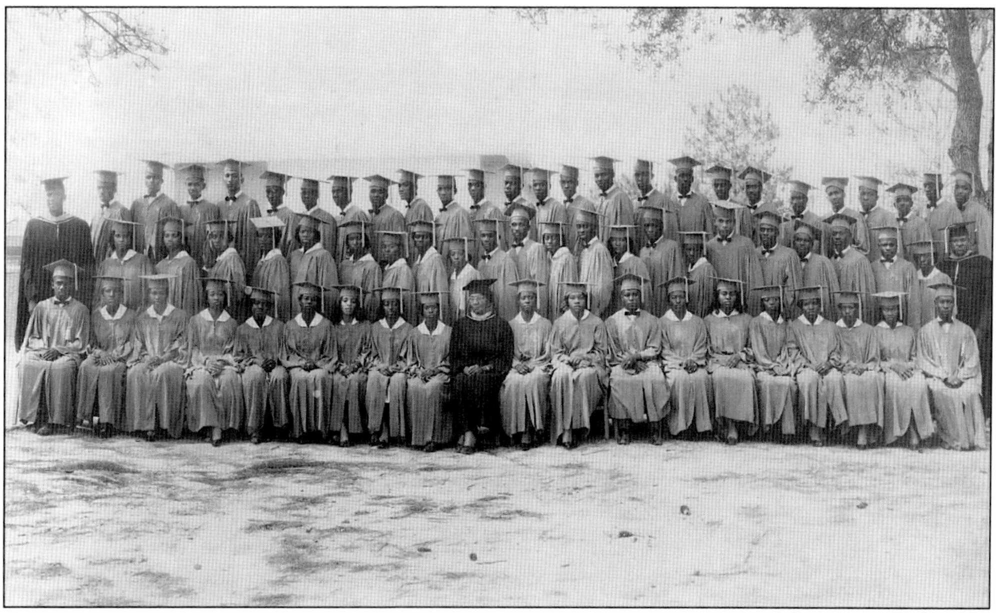

The Class of 1962 is pictured with sponsors Ms. Willie J. Hutchinson, first row in the center, King David Wilson, second row on the left, and Amos P. Brown, second row on the right.

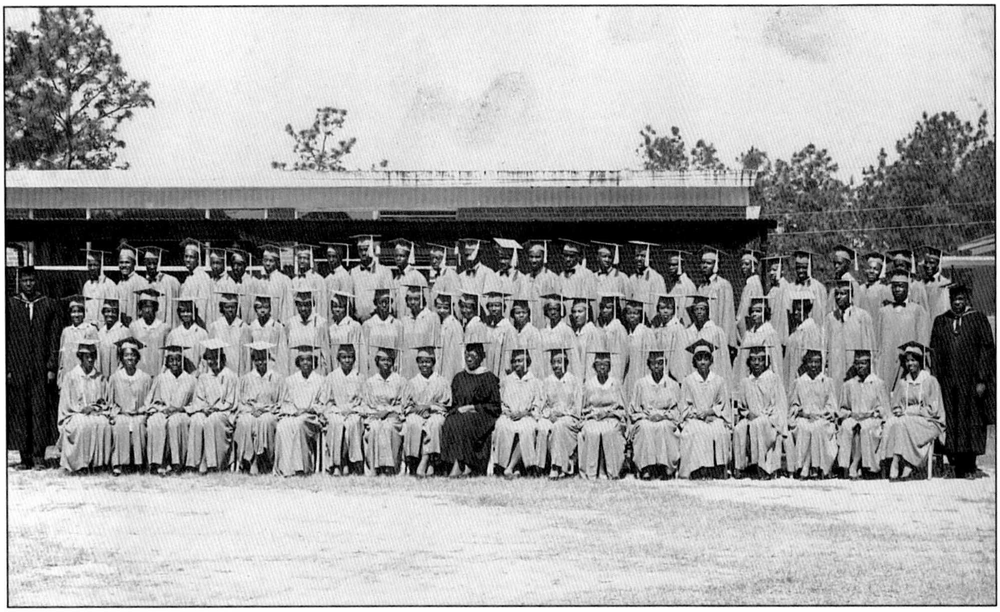

Ms. Willie J. Hutchinson, first row center; King David Wilson, second row left; and Amos P. Brown, second row right, were the sponsors for the Class of 1964.

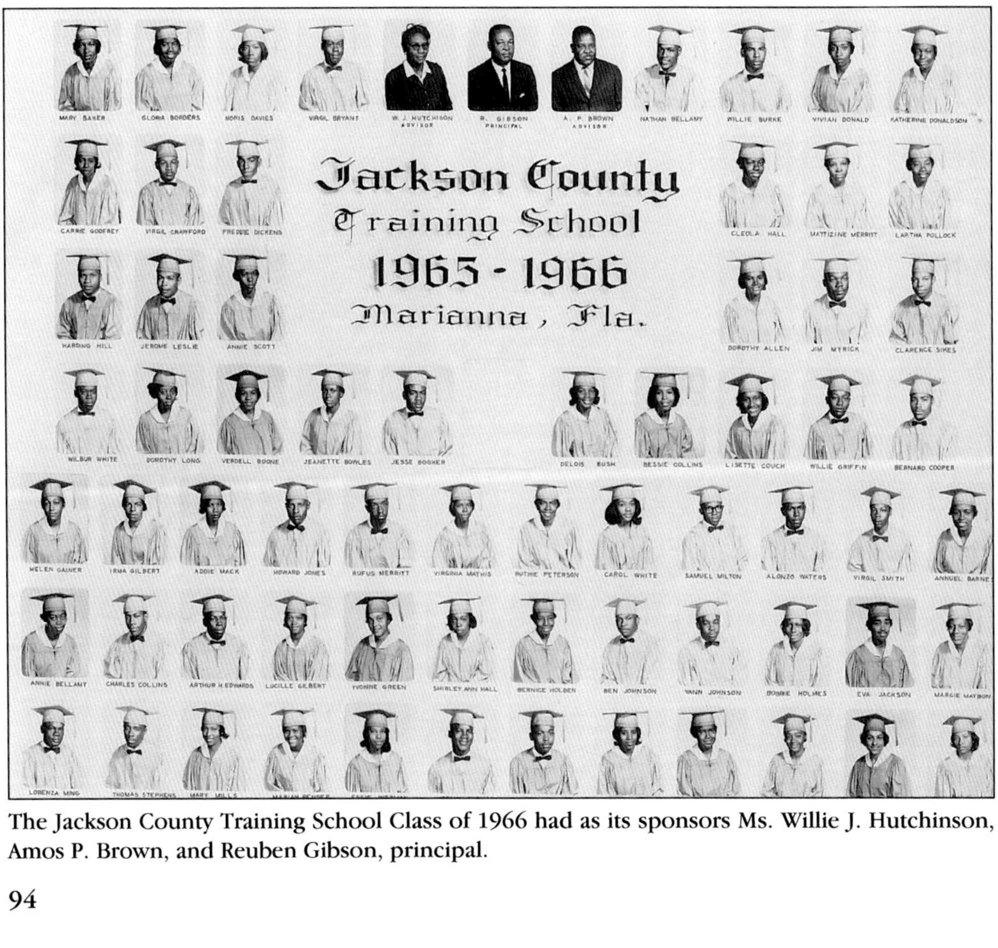

The Jackson County Training School Class of 1966 had as its sponsors Ms. Willie J. Hutchinson, Amos P. Brown, and Reuben Gibson, principal.

Lee C. Herring served as principal of Jackson County Elementary and Cottondale Elementary Schools. Later, he became Elementary Supervisor of Colored Schools.

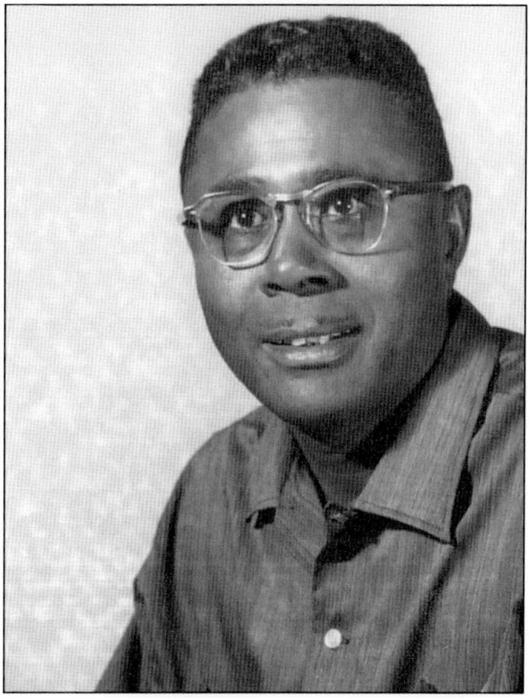

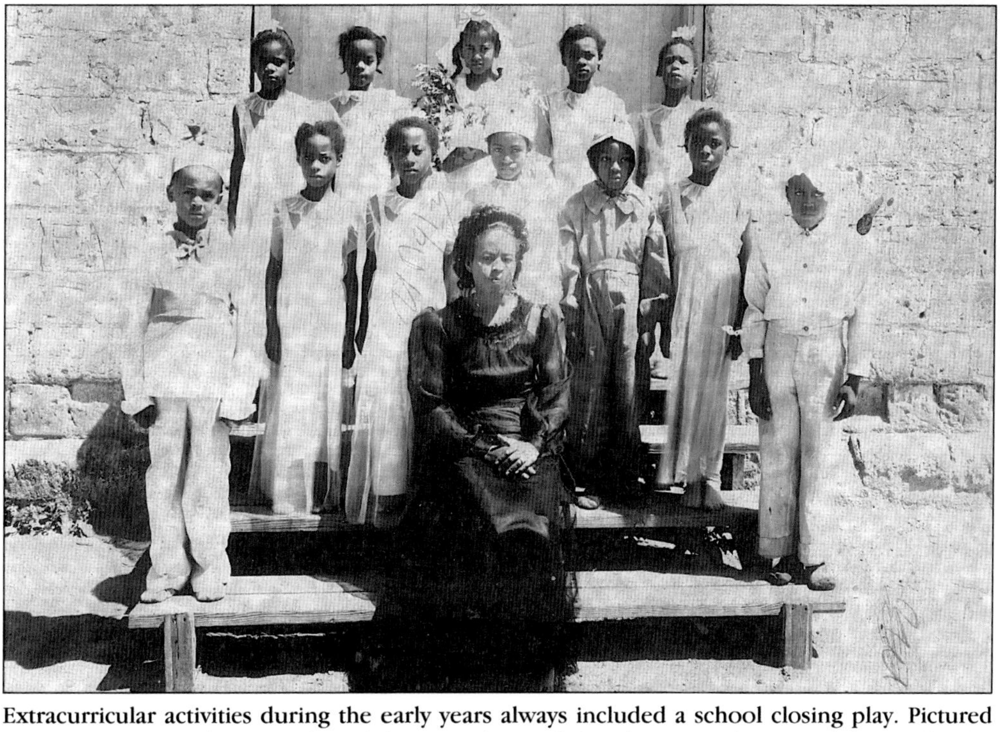

Extracurricular activities during the early years always included a school closing play. Pictured are Willie Mae Pender (seated) and the cast of one of the plays, *c.* 1940. From left to right, the players are (front row) Angus Borders, Tommie Joyce Green, Mamie Paramore, unidentified, unidentified, Effie Dickens, and unidentified; (back row) ? Paramore, Gwendolyn Pittman, ? Stephens, Helen Barnes, and Shirley Harrison.

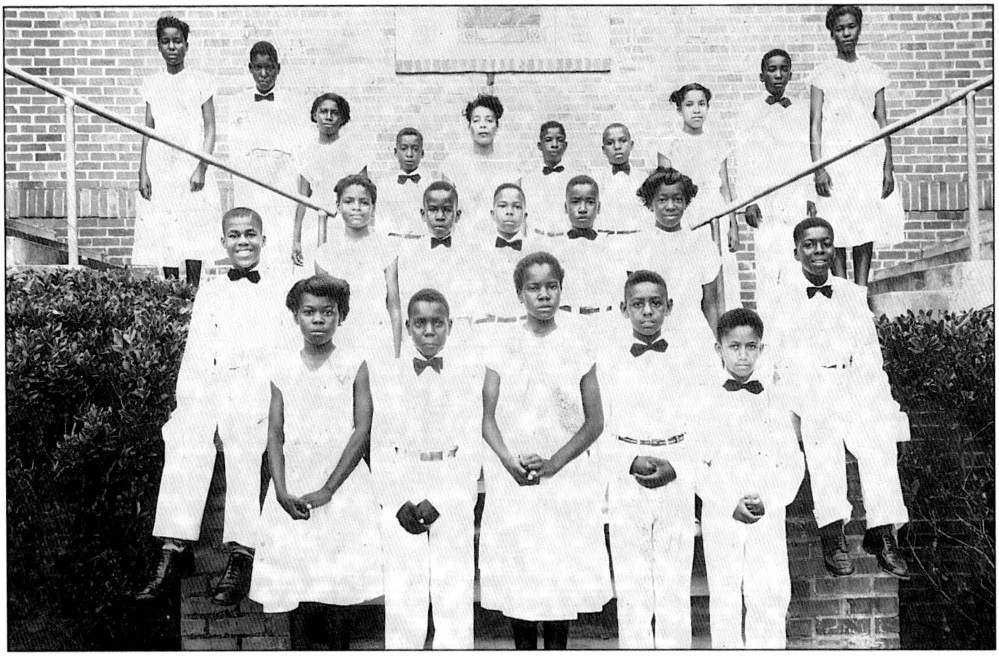

Another special event was the graduation exercise for sixth graders. Graduation took place at St. James A.M.E. Church. Pictured is the Class of 1951 of the Jackson County Training Elementary School. Elrea Daniels, top row center, was the class sponsor. The students are, from left to right, (front row) Carolyn Clay, Edmund Speights, Margaret Speights, Ronald Crawford, and Emaneul Purdee; (second row) Mathew Jack Weston (seated), Eldonia Spires, Marion Spires, Harold Wynn, Andrew Speights, Sarah Speights, and Haywood Thomas (seated); (back row) Annie J. Brown, Jack Norris, Elizabeth McNealy, Algene Gainer, Elrea Daniels, Ora Lee Dickens, Willie Smith, Betty Jean Peace, Willie Everett, and Shirley Harrison.

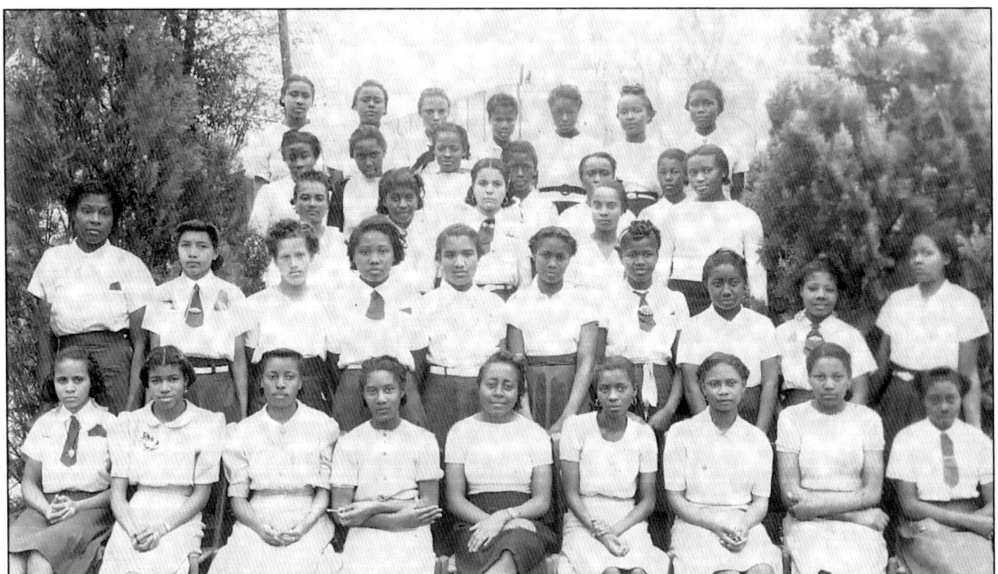

Seen here is a group of juniors and seniors of JCTS. On the front row, in the center, is Miss Thelma Lucinda Ellis, Miss JCTS 1940.

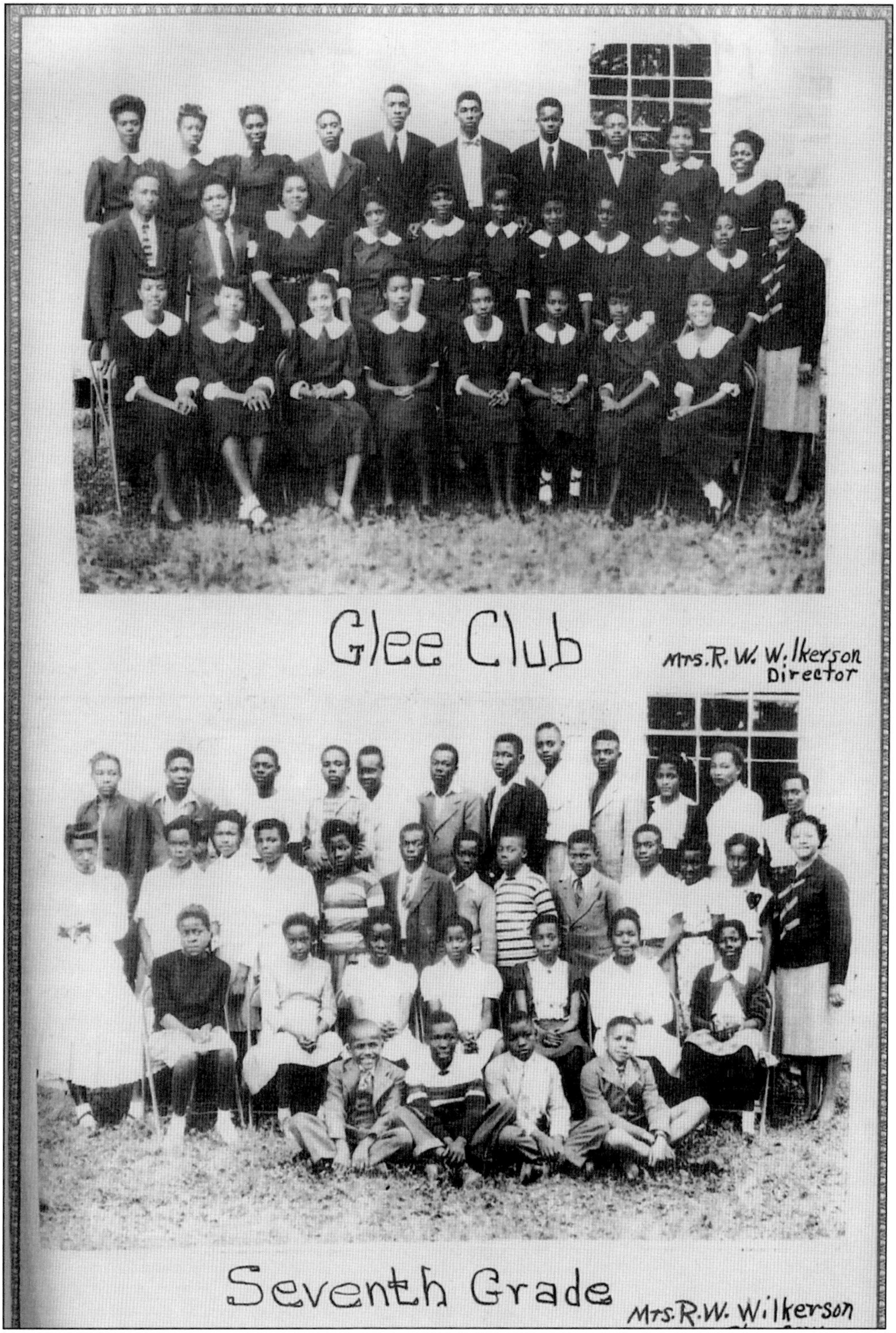

The Glee Club and seventh grade are seen in this 1949 photograph. Ruth Wilkerson Glenn was the sponsor of both.

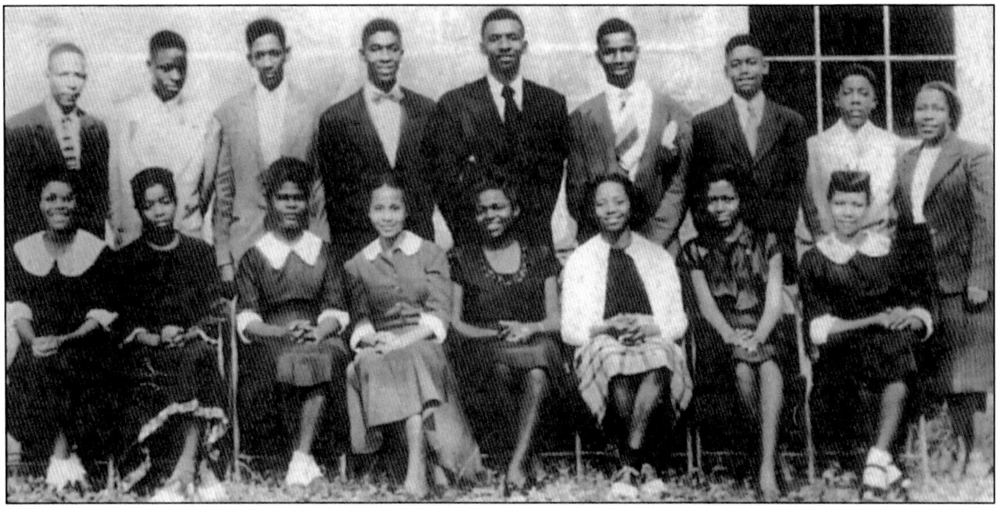

Gertrude E. Cotton (second row, right) was the sponsor of the student council at Jackson County Training School in 1949.

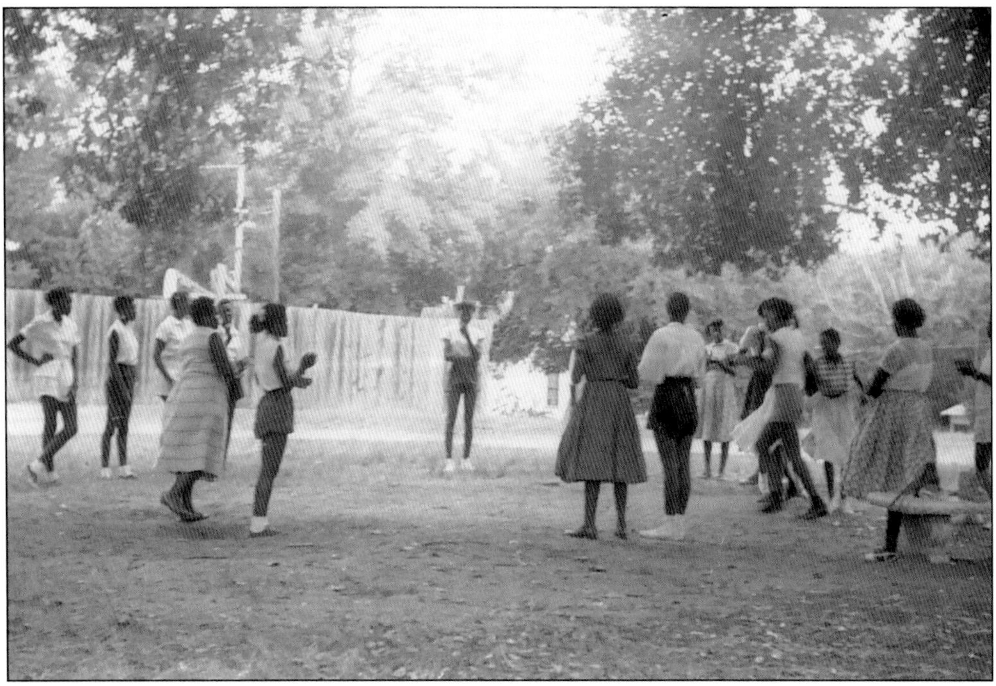

This ninth grade physical education class is pictured in 1953. Mildred McMullen was the teacher.

Roy A. Allen, right, was the fourth principal of Gilmore Academy. He served until 1950 and was preceded by the Academy's founder, Robert T. Gilmore, Emanuel King, and J.B. Williams.

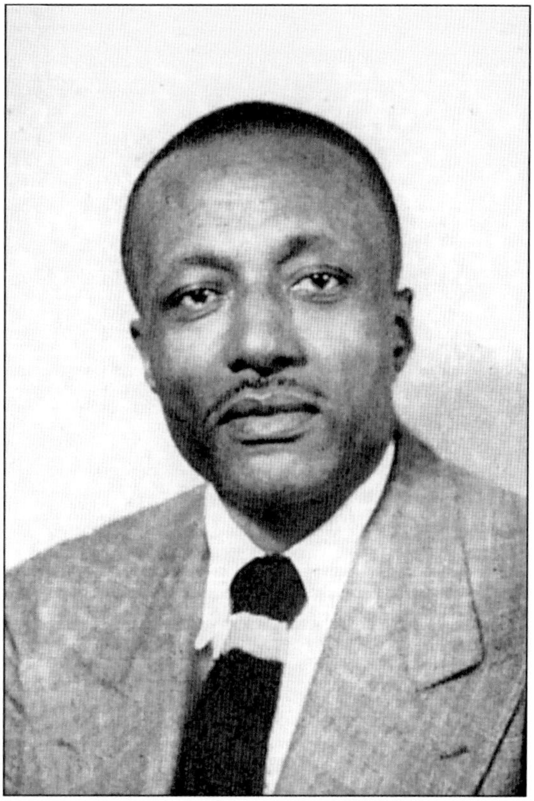

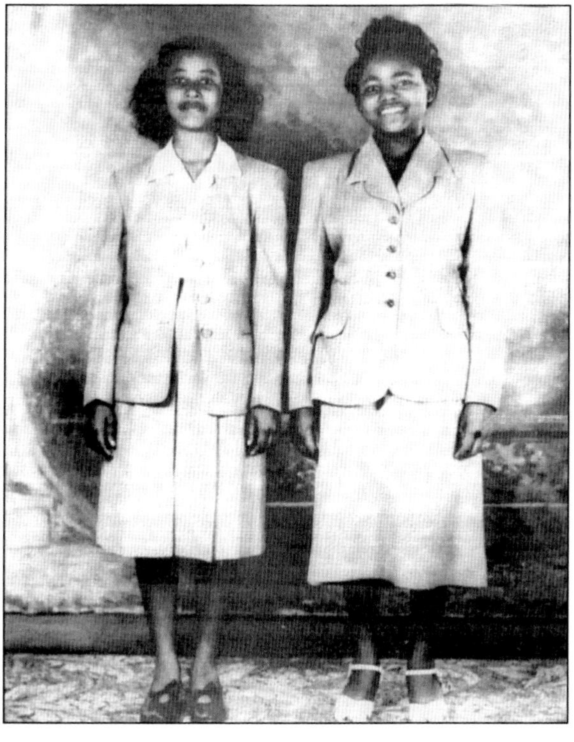

Caralee Barnes, right, was Miss Jackson High in 1949. Callie Pope, left, was her attendant. These young ladies added grace and beauty to the school and athletic events.

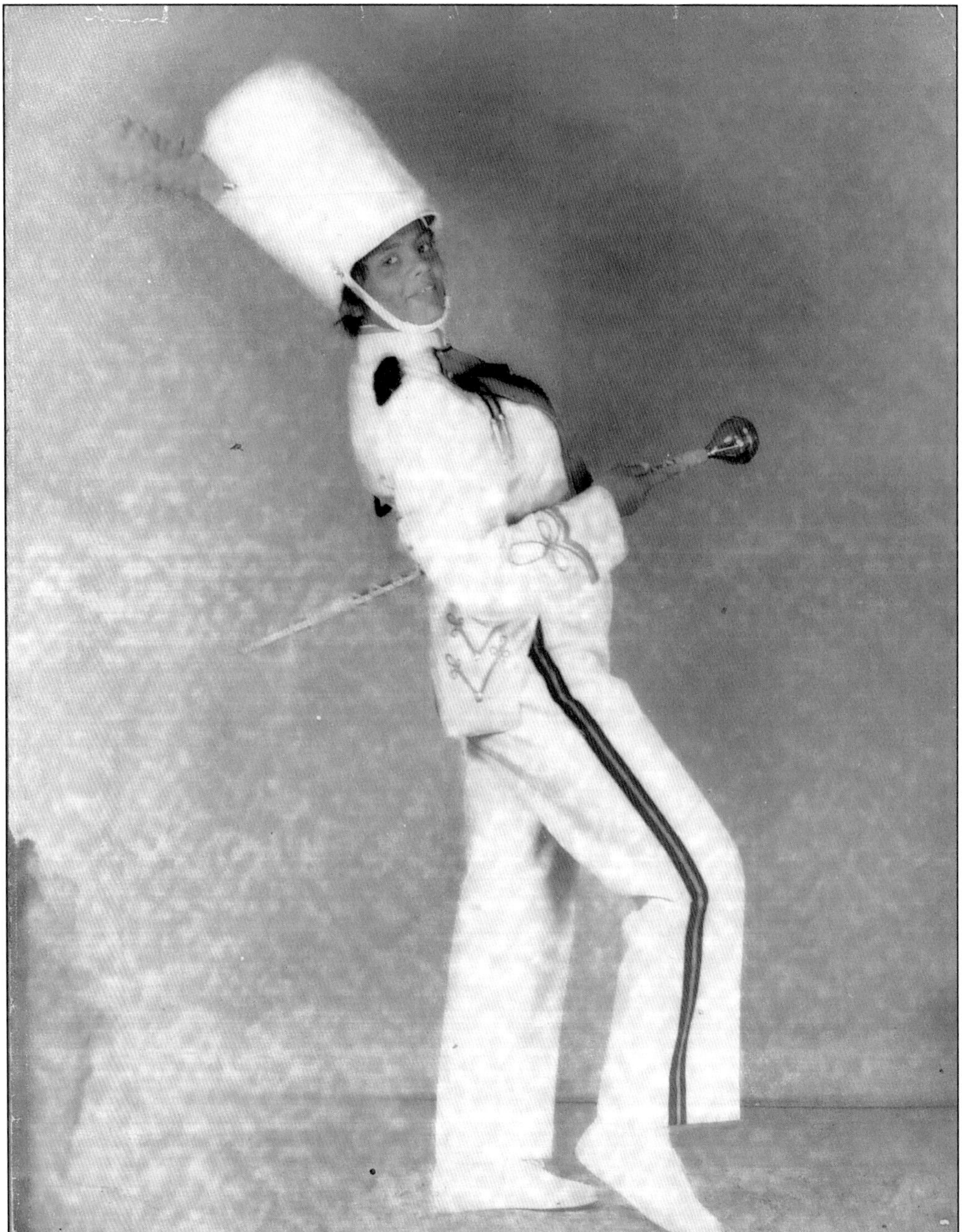

In 1960, Miranda Spires Hayes became the first drum major for the JCTS Band. She is one of the granddaughters of Armstrong Purdee, a former slave. He was the first black lawyer in Jackson County.

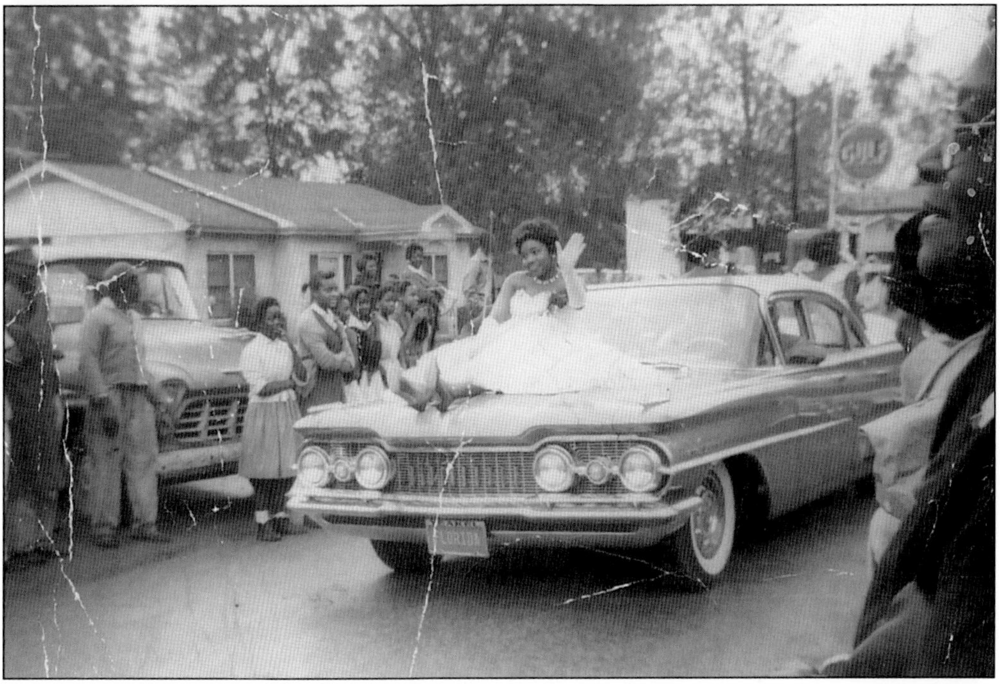

Pictured is a homecoming parade along Orange Street, *c.* 1963. During this period, JCTS, unlike the all-white Marianna High School, could not use Lafayette Street, the main street in Marianna, to hold its parades. Pictured is Marlyn Long on her class float.

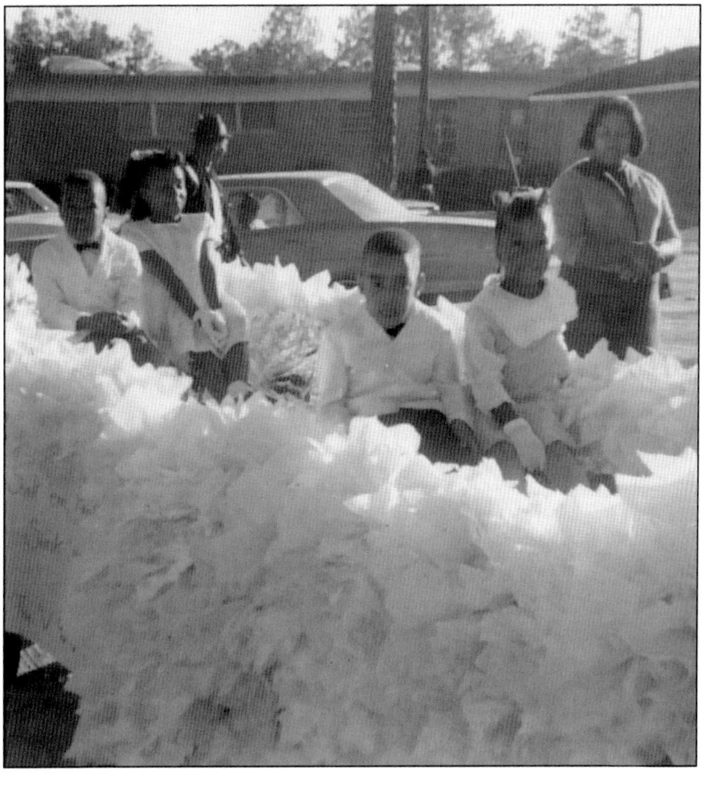

This homecoming parade float was sponsored by the Vogue and Valiant Club.

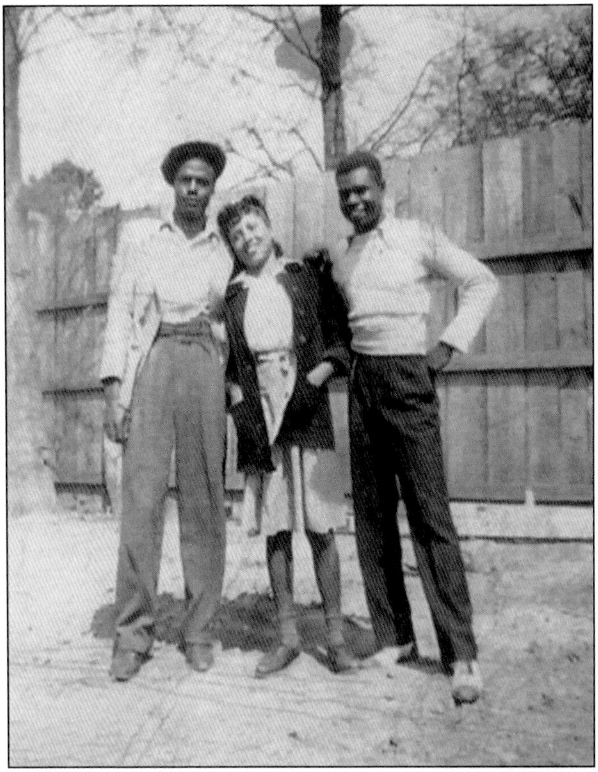

Students are pictured on the wood-fenced, clay basketball court, a favorite spot for socializing during school hours. Little did we know that this would be known today as "a privacy fence." From left to right are Abraham Wynn, Iris Dickens Gibson, and Eddie Washington.

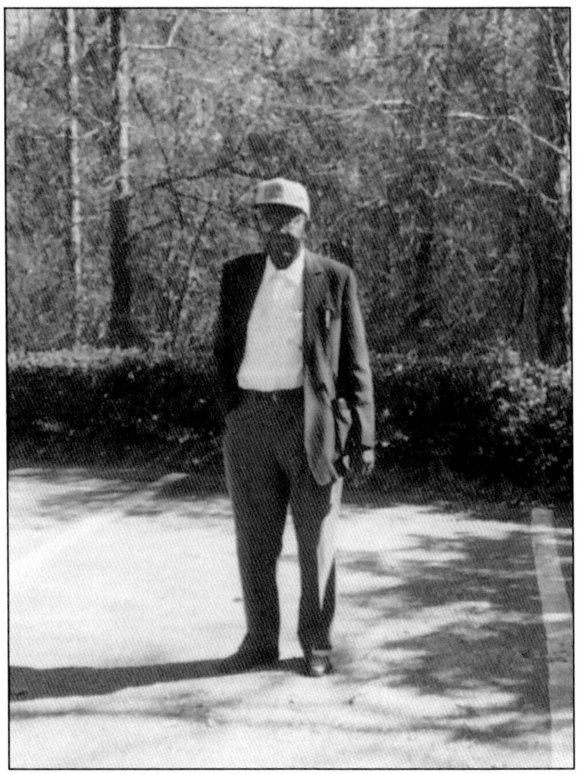

William "Stack" Jones was a member of the 1939-40 basketball team. The team was coached by Monroe Spencer and J.B. "Bull" Williams, the school principal. The team of six players was invited to participate in the Invitational Tournament at the Tuskegee Institute in Alabama. They would compete against top teams from across the United States. Only five of the six players on the team made the trip. Although two fouled out early in the game, the team managed to win with three players: Jones, Abraham Robinson, and Albert Robinson. In later years, "Stack" was a referee in African-American schools in the county.

Pictured is Carlton "Opp" Smith, physical education teacher and coach. Other JCTS coaches were Monroe Spencer, Colbert Britt, Francis Epton, Mosley Baker, Alvin Pearsall, Willie "Bubba" Cooper, Elmore Bryant, and Roger Clay. Coach Cooper led two teams to State Class B Basketball Championships. The first was in 1958 at the tournament in St. Augustine, after only two years of play in a gymnasium. The team included Arthur (Jody) Thomas, Hercules Pyles, Monroe "Bear" Barnes, Willie Thomas, Shepard Bell, and Longworth Johnson. In 1964, JCTS won again with William Harley Jr., Chambers Wilson Jr., Monzell "Breeze" Mack, Lemon Harvey, Roy Lee Caldwell, and Arthur Johnson.

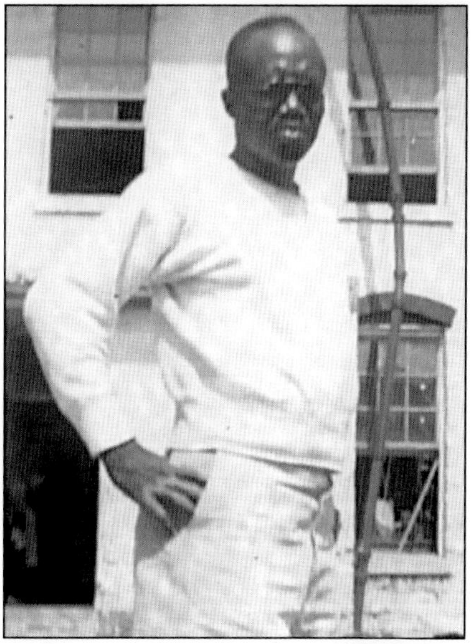

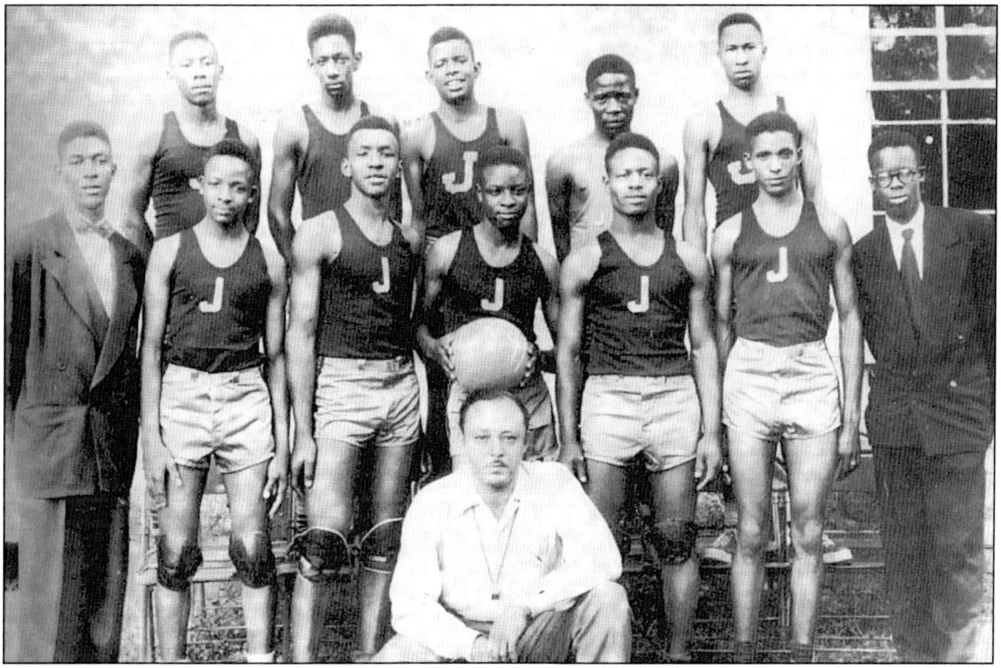

The 1948-49 JCTS basketball team was coached by Mosely Huggins Baker (front row, center). His coaching abilities were only excelled by his extraordinary expertise in teaching mathematics. In 1948, the above team was county champions in Division A. Kneepads added protection from the hazards inherent in playing on clay courts. Pictured, from left to right, are (second row) Ulysses Mack (manager), Walter Lee Robinson, Ulysses White, Roy H. Porter, Lester Cooper, Nathan Thorton, and Albert Robinson; (back row) Edward Lee Mack, Arthur Graham, Isaiah Speights, Robert Baker, and William McElroy. The last JCTS basketball team to win a state championship was coached by Robert Clay. His 1969 team included Nathan Milton, Calvin Spires, Earl Holden, Benny Heatrice, Gary Pope, Samuel Pugh, Harvey Williams, Jack Golden, Clarence Holden, and Lester Tinsley.

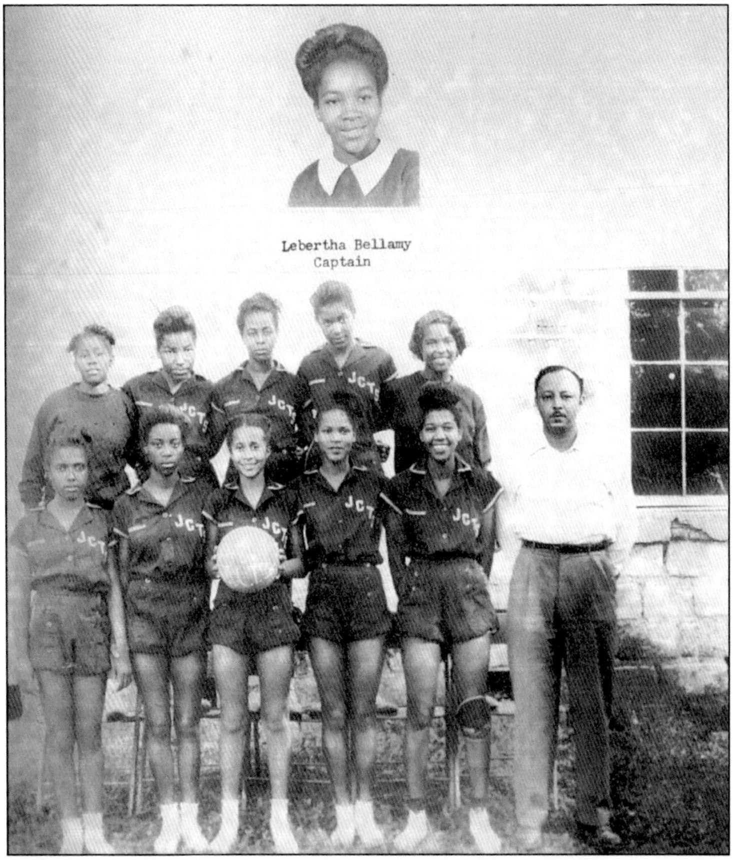

Girls basketball was a popular and spirited sport at JCTS. The rules for girls limited them to two dribbles of the ball and none of the players could go pass half court. The 1949 team is pictured here. From left to right are (front row) Eartha Bell, Lillian Barnes, Maggie Swilley, Zolena Russ, Eloise White, and coach Mosely H. Baker; (back row) Christeen Anderson, Rhoda Leonard, Naomi Barnes, Robertha Bellamy, and Henrietta Wadsworth; (top, center) team captain Lebertha Bellamy.

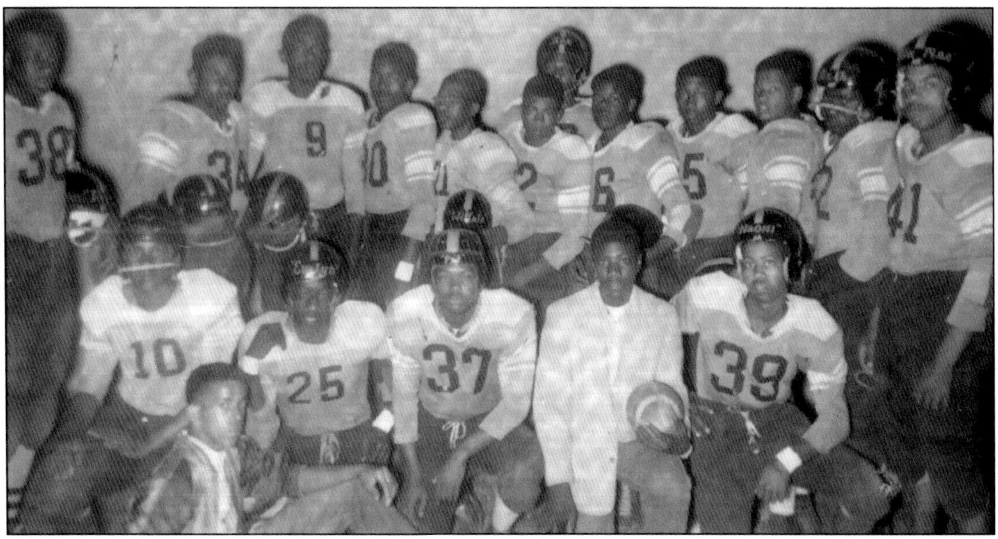

The 1959 JCTS football team, coached by Willie L. "Bubba" Cooper, is pictured above. Seated in front of the team is trainer Forrest Peace. From left to right are (front row) unidentified, unidentified, Morris White, Morris Britt, and Norman Crawford; (back row) Dan Hester, Daniel Simpson, unidentified, Waymon Speights, Eddie Roy Cooper, Gary Harrison, unidentified, unidentified, Fletcher Gibson, James Lewis, unidentified, and James Brewton.

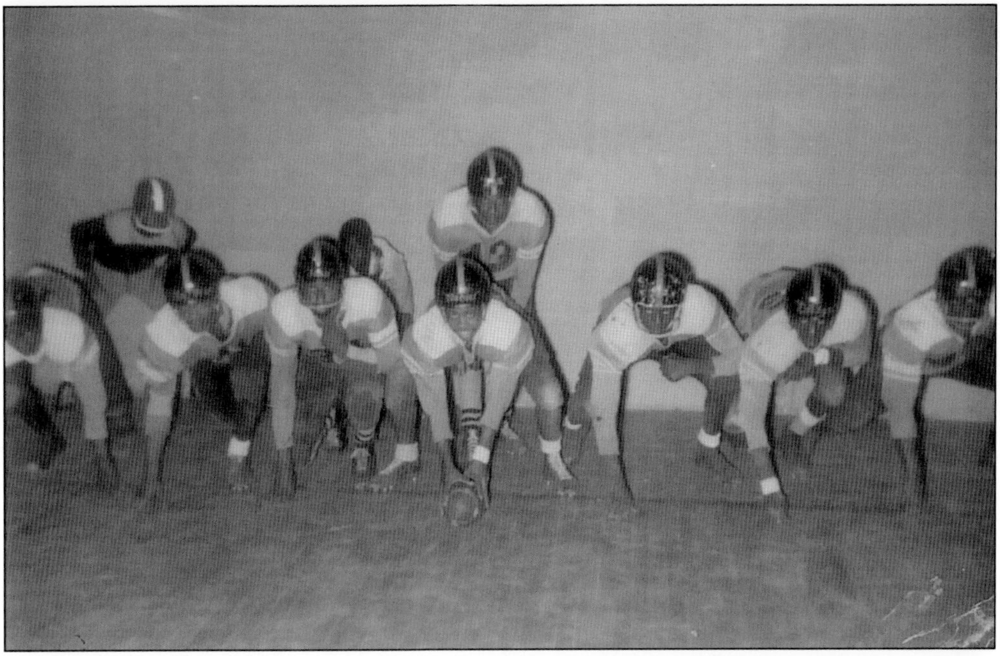

The first JCTS football team was organized in 1941. It consisted of Abraham Wynn, quarterback and kicker; William "Stack" Jones and Abraham Robinson, halfbacks; George Cook, fullback; James Roulhac, center; Joffrey Ellis, backup center and guard; Frank Moultrie and Felix Long, tackles; Carl Williams, guard; Leo Washington and Albert Robinson, ends. The team, coached by Colbert Britt, was 0-3-1. Pictured above is the 1959 football team coached by Willie L. "Bubba" Cooper.

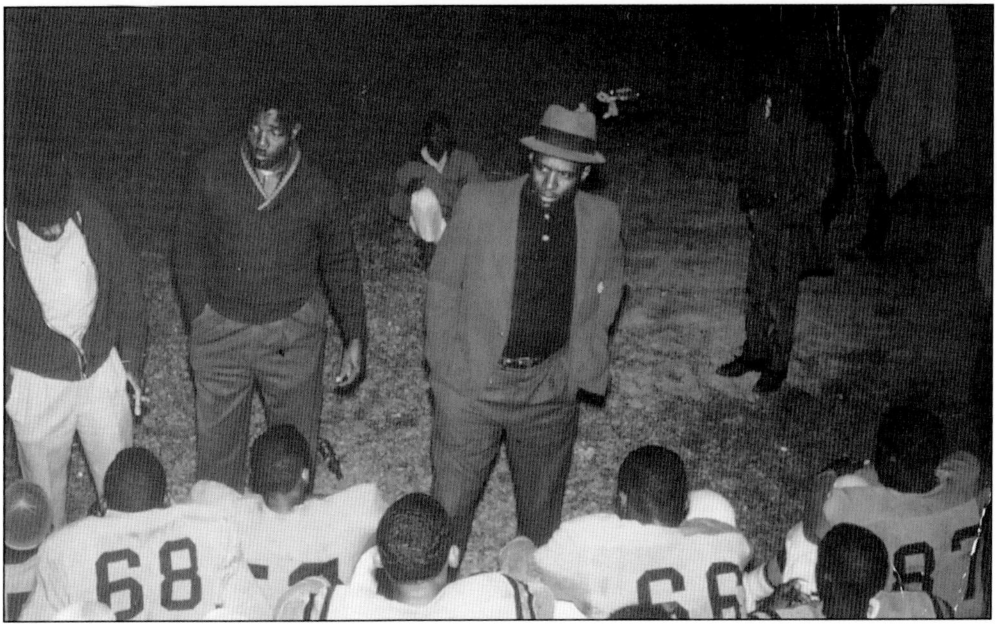

Coach Cooper, shown above center, taught physical education at JCTS and St. Paul High School for many years. He also coached junior and varsity football and basketball. Although the football team practiced at JCTS, their games were played at the Florida Industrial School for Boys because there were no lights at JCTS.

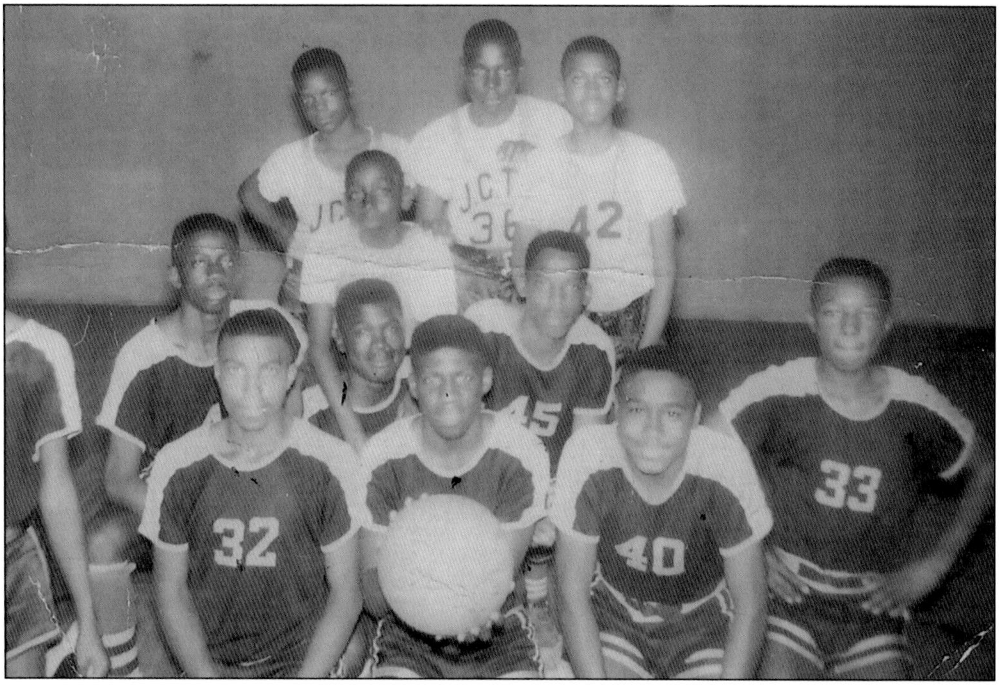

The year 1941 also marked the first year for organized basketball at JCTS. The starting players were Abraham Robinson, center; Abraham Wynn and Lawrence Swilley, forwards; Albert Robinson and "Stack" Jones, guards. Frank Moultrie, Mathis Hagler, and George Cook were substitutes. Pictured above is the 1961 basketball team coached by Willie Cooper. From left to right are (front row) Willie Mays, Stanley Wilson, Carl Williams, and Willie Milton; (second row) Roy Roulhac, Robert McClassiter, and Miles Spires; (back row) James Henry Wynn, William Harley, unidentified, and David Everett.

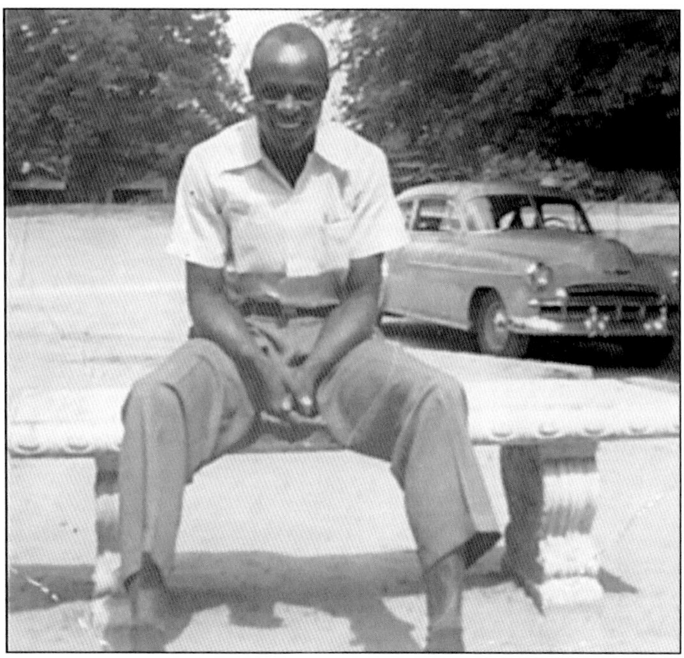

Benjamin Robinson relaxes and poses for the picture while sitting on a bench under the large oak tree in front of JCTS High School. He was a librarian there and at Union Grove High. He performed many creative dances during school assemblies.

Nine

Union Grove and County Schools

Pictured here is L.L. Hawthorne, principal of Union Grove High School from 1953 to 1970. Hawthorne, known affectionately as "Fess" by students, teachers, and patrons alike, had a long and distinguished career. Prior to his tenure at Union Grove, he was principal and/or teacher at Sneads, Buckhorn, Holy Neck, and McChapel. His success as an educator had much to do with his personal and professional philosophy: "Treat each student as you would want your own child treated." He was an advocate for students; he believed in the potential of every child and fostered that belief in the students. Perhaps this accounts for the many Union Grove graduates who entered many diverse professional careers. His advocacy extended into the larger African-American community and gained for him numerous awards, including Who's Who in American High School Principals, Outstanding Personalities of the South, and the Florida Memorial College Nathan W. Collier Meritorious Service Award. He was married to Leila B. Knight Hawthorne, who was also an educator for 53 years in Jackson County. Hawthorne also served as superintendent of the church school at St. Luke Baptist Church in Marianna. His 45-plus year career ended with his untimely death while serving as an administrator at Greenwood High School.

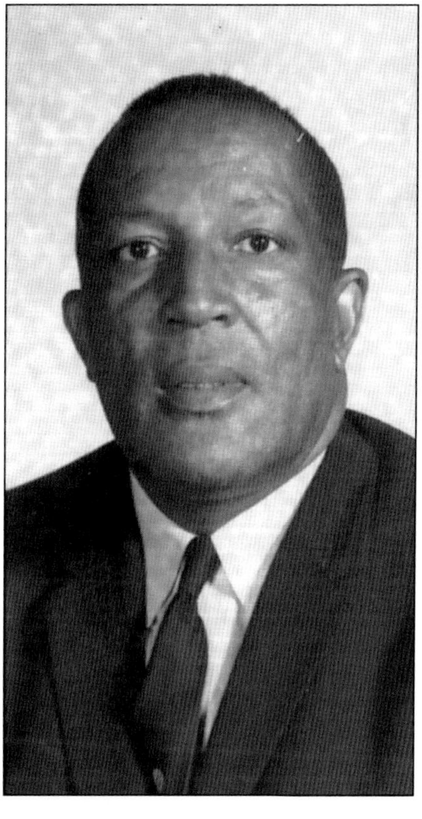

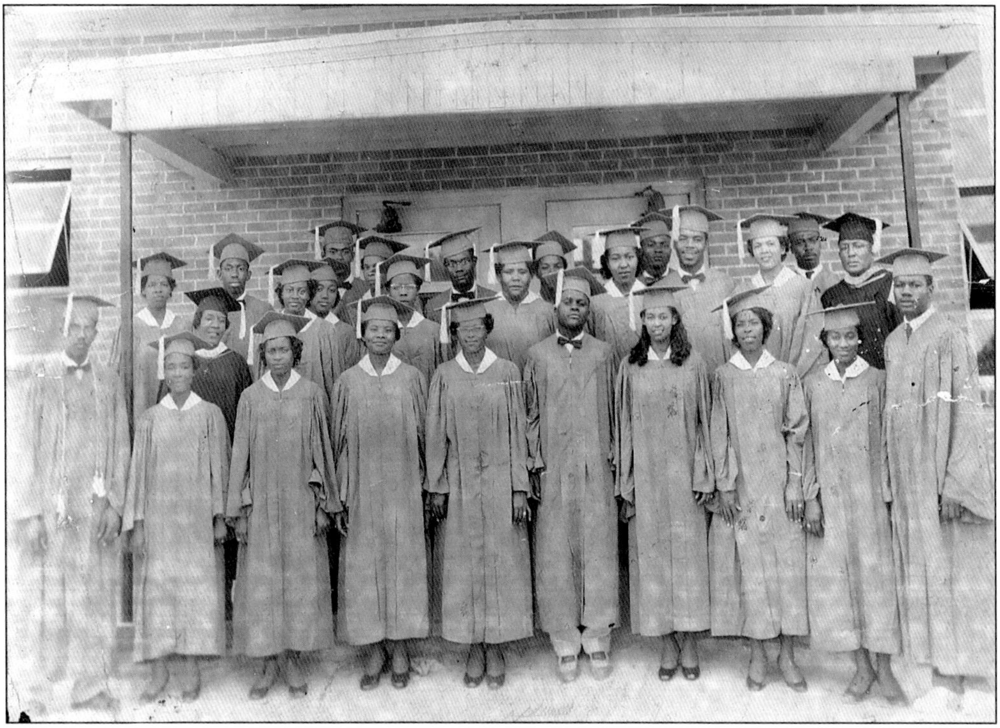

Pictured is the Union Grove High School Class of 1956. G.E. Cotton, second row on the left, was the class sponsor.

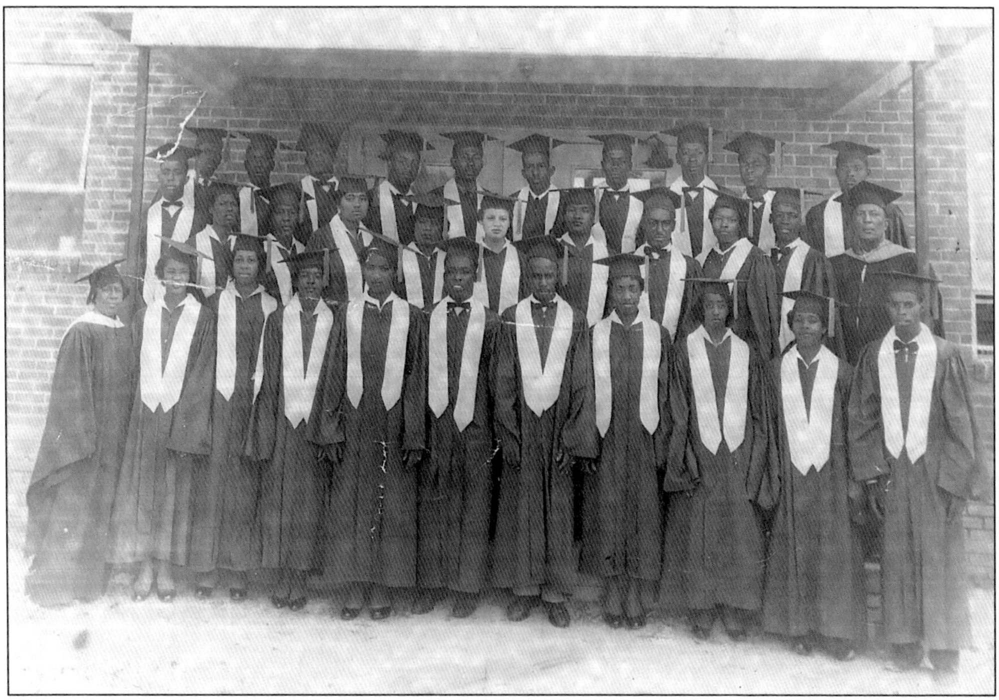

The Union Grove High School Class of 1959 is pictured with G.E. Cotton, sponsor (first row, left). L.L. Hawthorne Sr., the principal, is seen on the second row, on the extreme right.

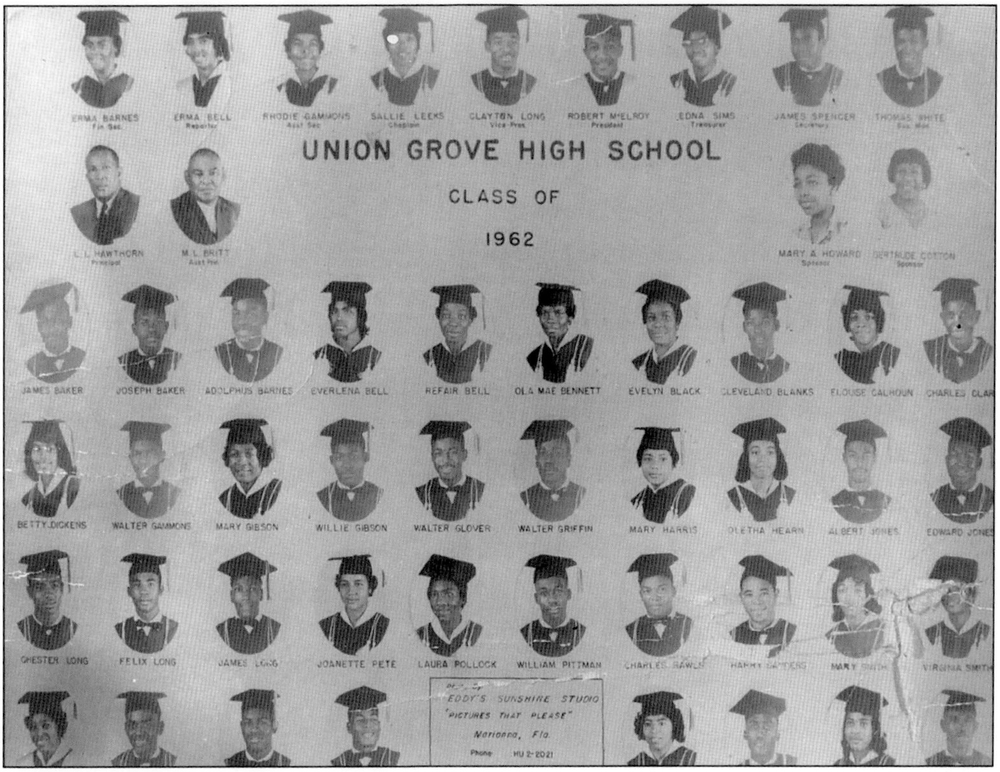

Seen in this photograph is the Union Grove High School Class of 1962. Pictured on the second row from the top, from left to right, are L.L. Hawthorne Sr., principal; M.L. Britt, assistant principal; Mary A. Howard, sponsor; and G.E. Cotton, sponsor.

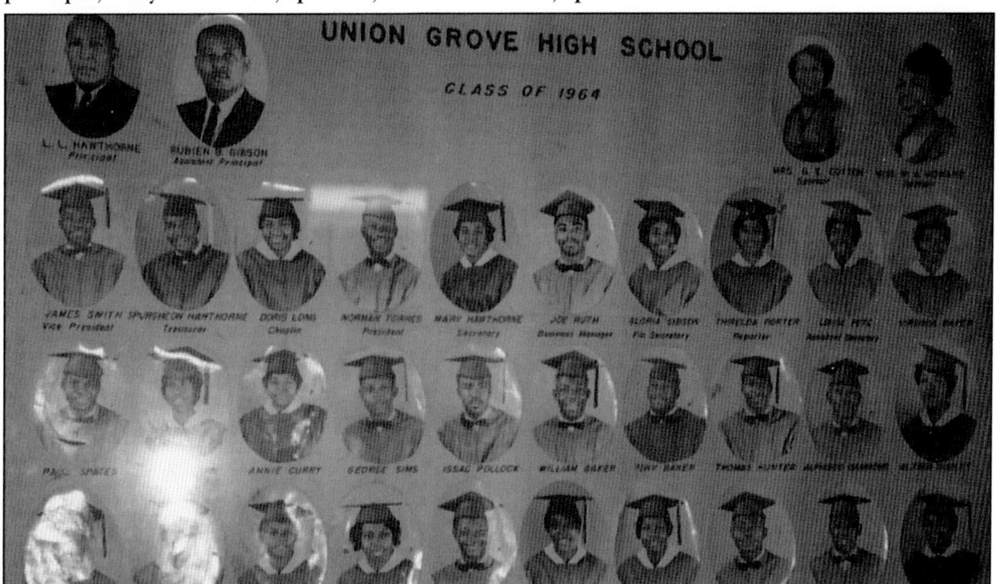

The Class of 1964 at Union Grove includes on the top row, from left to right, L.L. Hawthorne, principal; Reuben Gibson, assistant principal; G.E. Cotton, sponsor; and Mary A. Howard, sponsor.

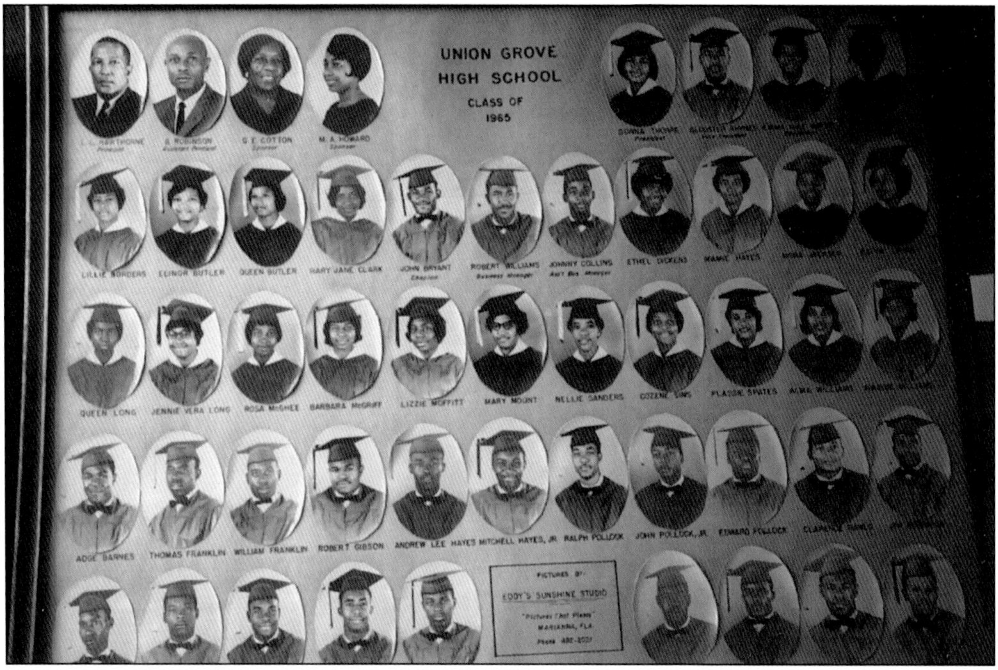

The Union Grove High School Class of 1965 includes on the top row, from left to right, L.L. Hawthorne; B. Robinson, assistant principal; Gertrude E. Cotton and M.A. Howard, sponsors.

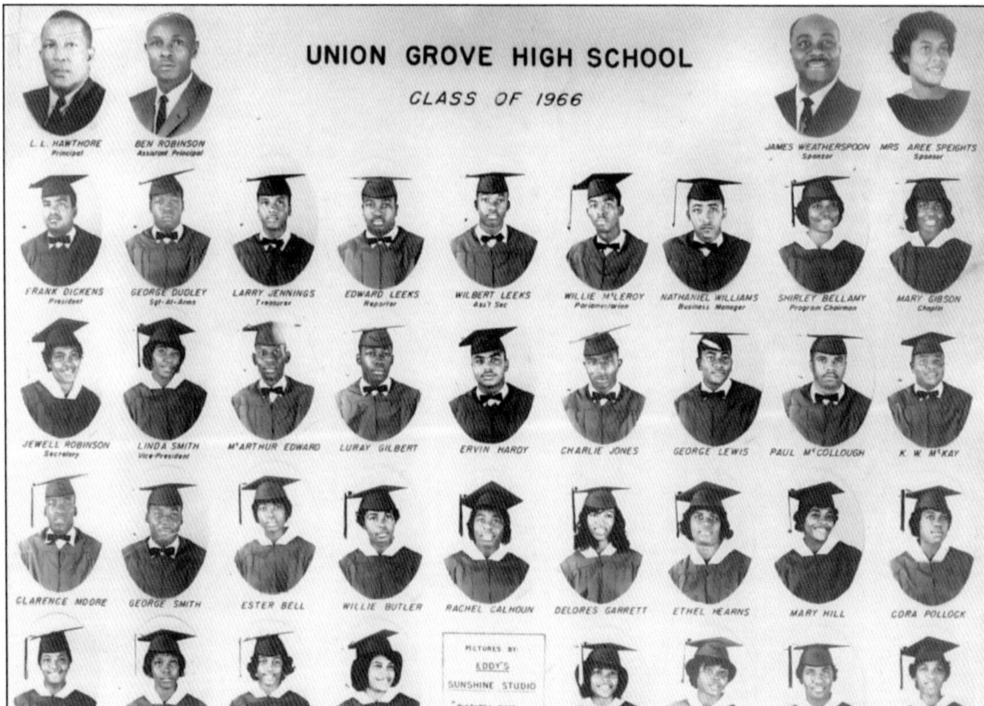

Seen here is Union Grove's Class of 1966. On the top row, from left to right, are L.L. Hawthorne, principal; Ben Robinson, assistant principal; James Weatherspoon, sponsor; and Aree Speights, sponsor.

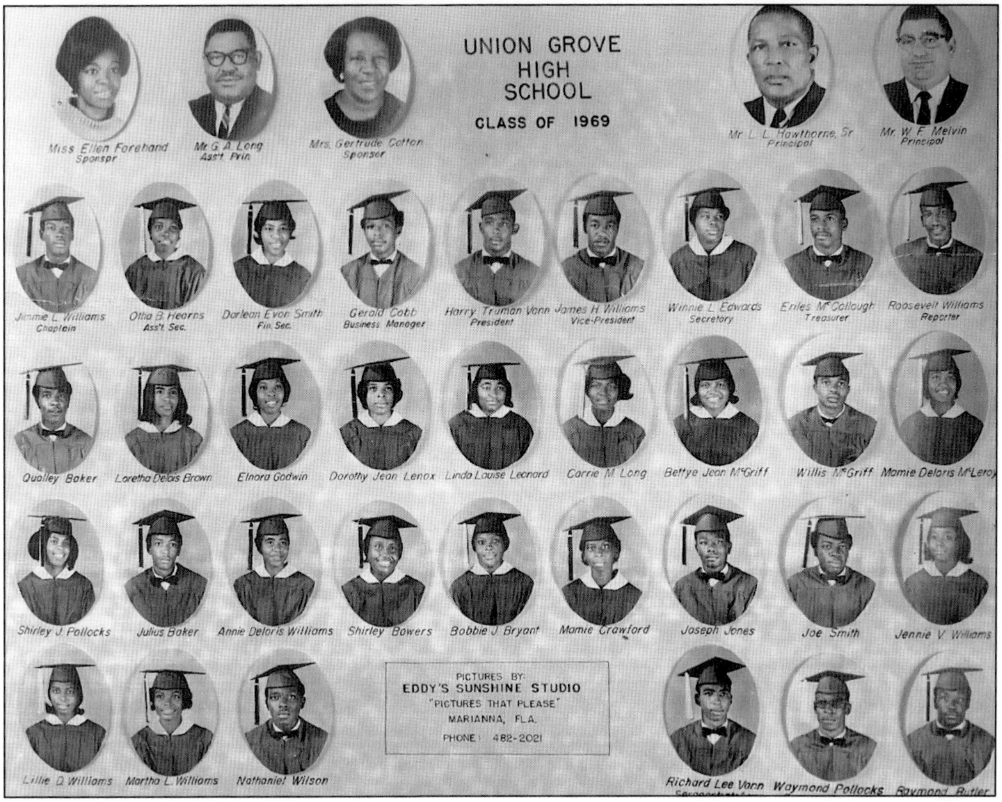

Seen in this photograph is the Union Grove Class of 1969, including, on the top row, from left to right, Ellen Forehand, sponsor; Godfrey A. Long, assistant principal; Gertrude Cotton, sponsor; L.L. Hawthorne, principal; and Willis F. Melvin, principal.

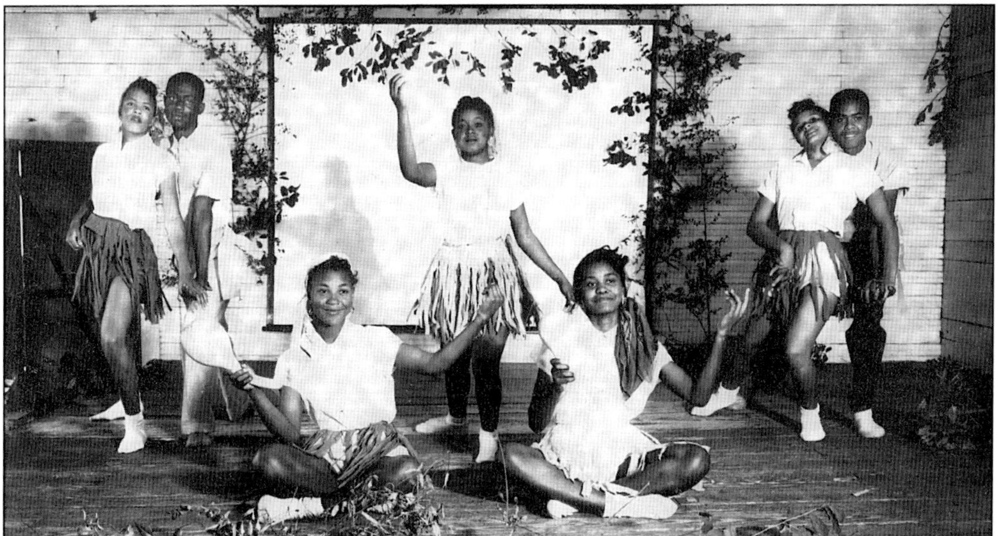

The Union Grove High School Dance Club performed gracefully during special events and assemblies. From left to right are (seated) Margaret Barnes and Jimmie Lee Long; (standing) Betty Worlds, Benny Gibson, Mattie Ethel Sims, Cleo Delores Long, and McArthur Williams.

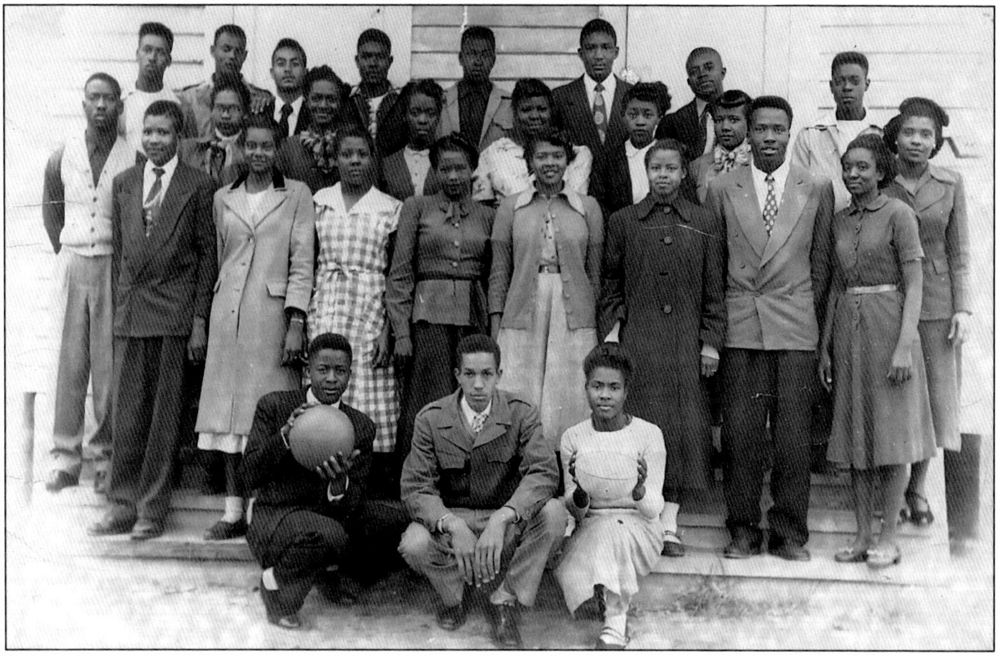

The Union Grove High School Girls and Boys Basketball Teams were coached by Howard Milton, third row on the left, and Queen B. Brown, third row on the right. They journeyed to Daytona Beach to play in the state tournament.

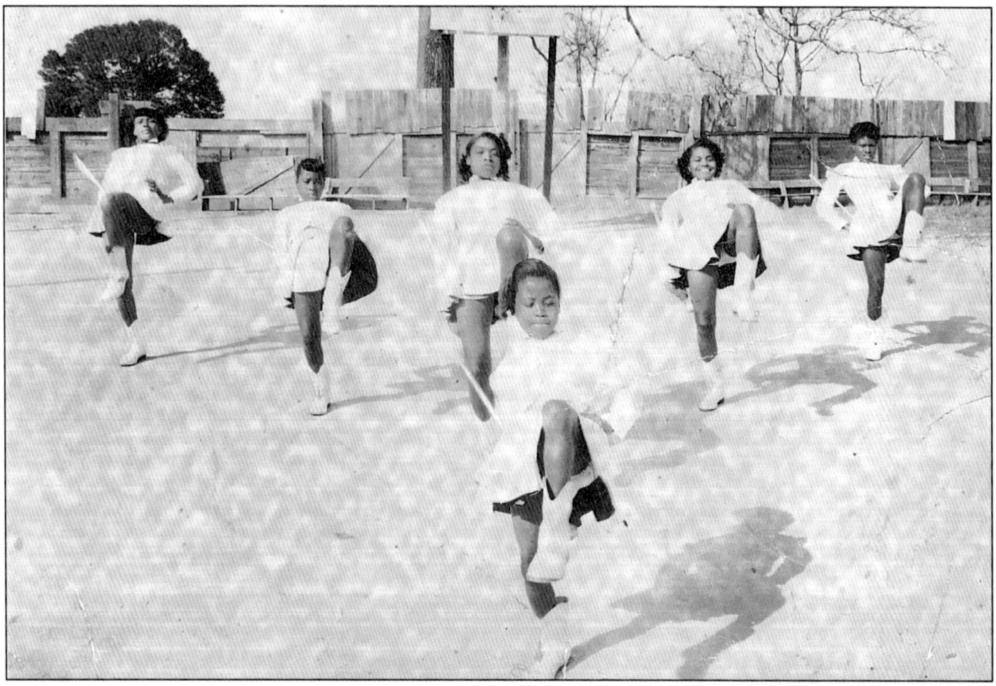

These charming young majorettes of Union Grove High School in 1954 performed during special functions and athletic events, entertaining and displaying their marching and twirling abilities. The lead majorette is Alberta Bryant and behind her are, from left to right, Margaret Newton, Leola Collins, Hattie Bellamy, Jimmie Lee Long, and Penny Godfrey.

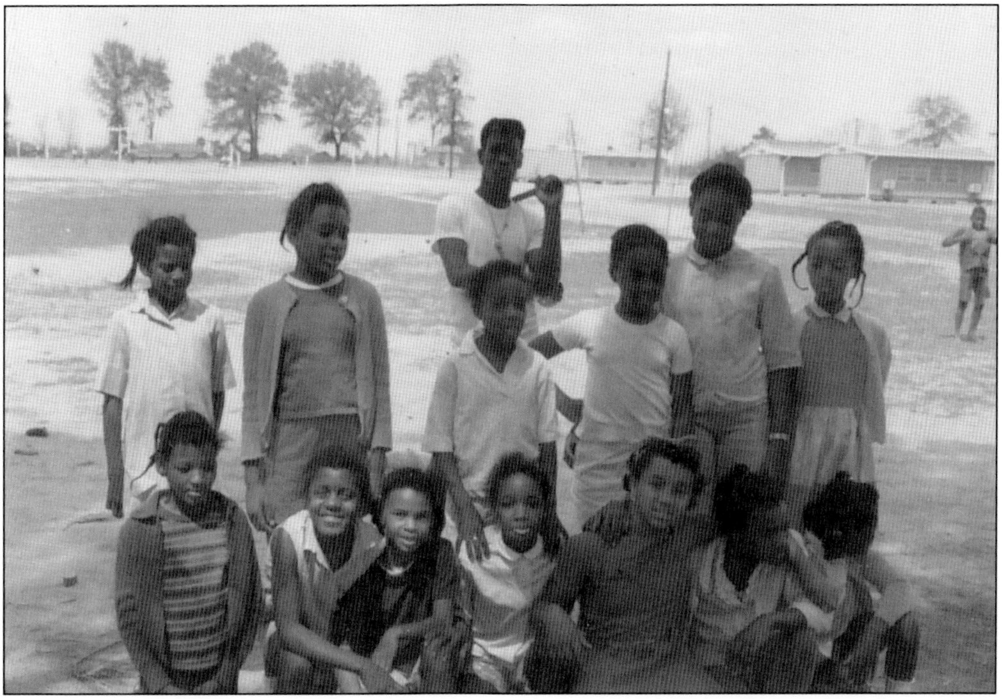

A St. Paul Elementary School physical education class is pictured in 1969. L.L. Hawthorne Jr. was the class instructor.

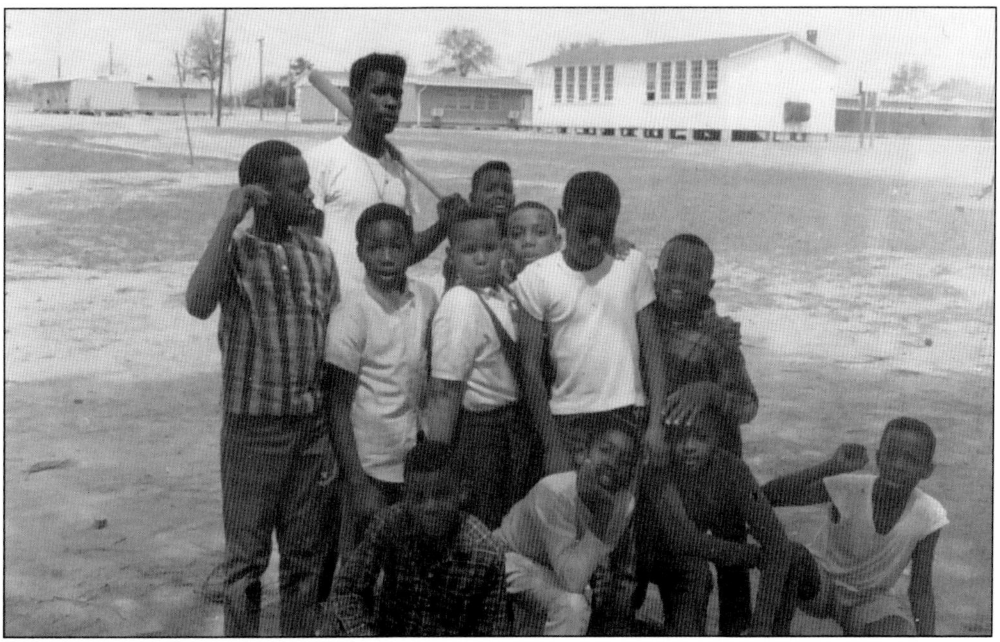

Another St. Paul Elementary School physical education class is pictured in 1969. St. Paul Elementary and High School was located in Campbellton, Florida. Built during the 1950s, the school had Herman Wilson as its principal for many years. Before this school was built, students attended mostly church-based elementary schools then transferred to JCTS, the only high school in the county for African Americans.

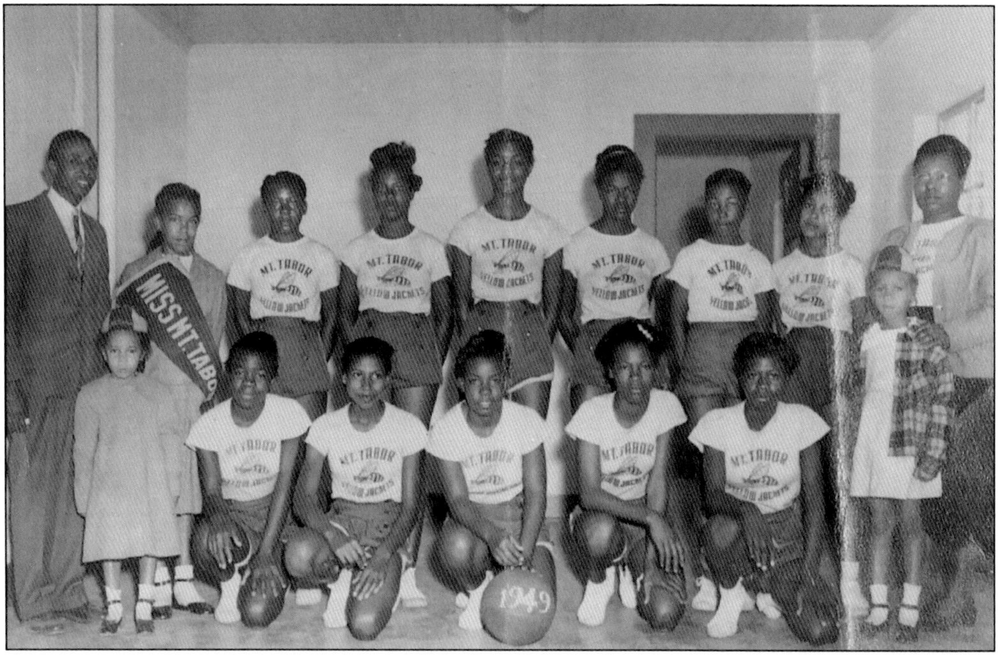

Shown above is the Mt. Tabor Elementary School girls basketball team and Miss Mt. Tabor in 1949. From left to right are (kneeling) Louise Baker; unidentified; unidentified; Careatha Bellamy; and unidentified; (standing) Principal William C. White and his daughter Emma Joyce White, Miss Mt. Tabor; Neolis Harris; unidentified; unidentified; Margaret Barnes; Ivey Gammon; Cora Bell; unidentified; Cozie Ester White, the principal's daughter; and coach Johnnie Mae Barnes.

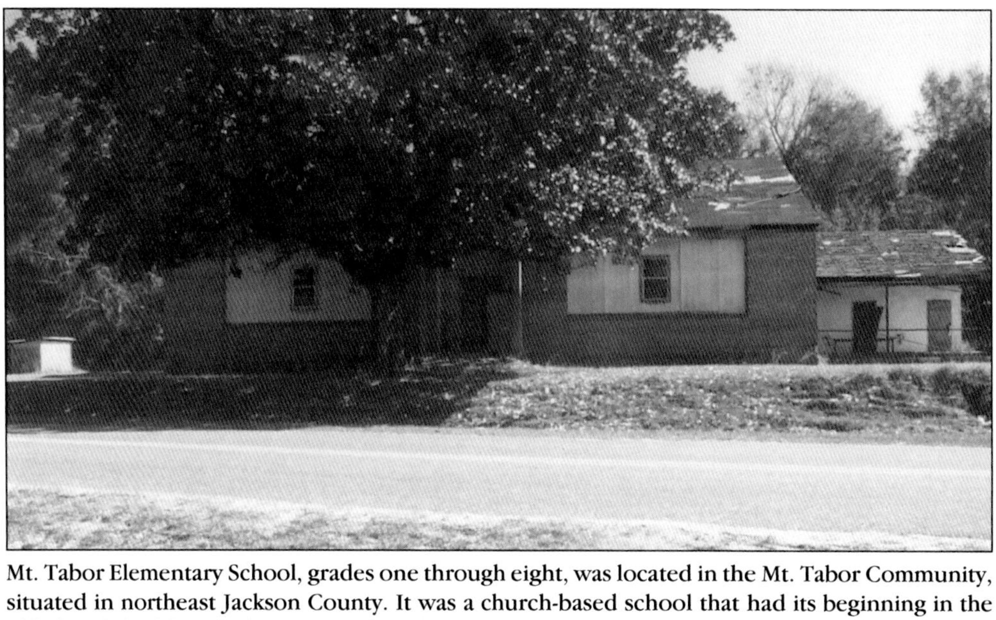

Mt. Tabor Elementary School, grades one through eight, was located in the Mt. Tabor Community, situated in northeast Jackson County. It was a church-based school that had its beginning in the old church building. In later years, the school moved to its newly-constructed building across the road from the church. Upon graduation, students attended either Union Grove or JCTS.

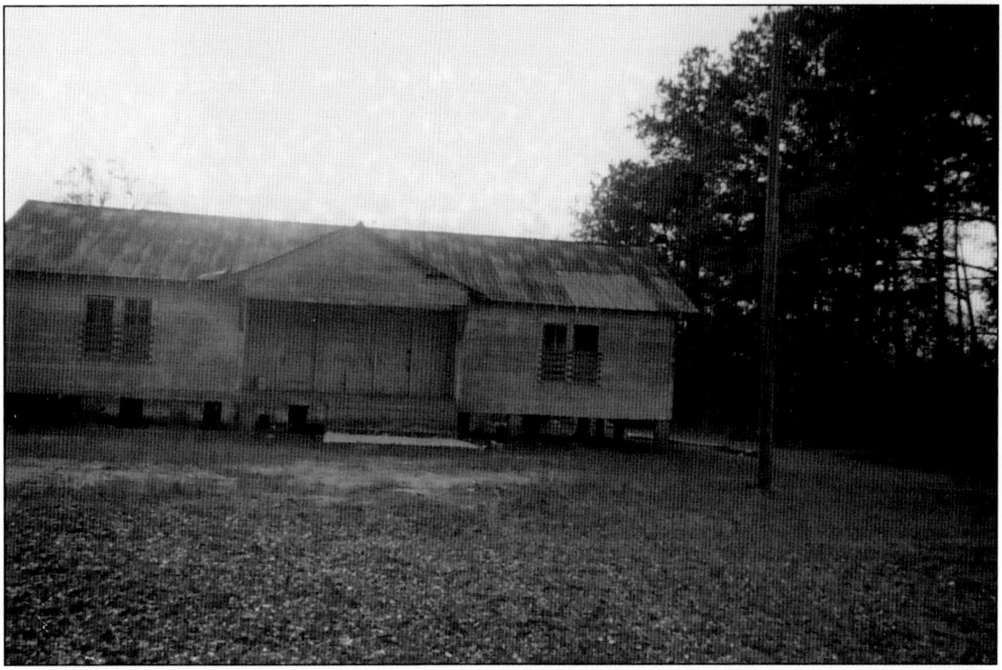

Long Branch Elementary School was a church-based school, serving grades one through eight. Long Branch was located in the Jerusalem Community at the Jerusalem A.M.E. Church site, south of Marianna. After completing the eighth grade, students transferred to JCTS.

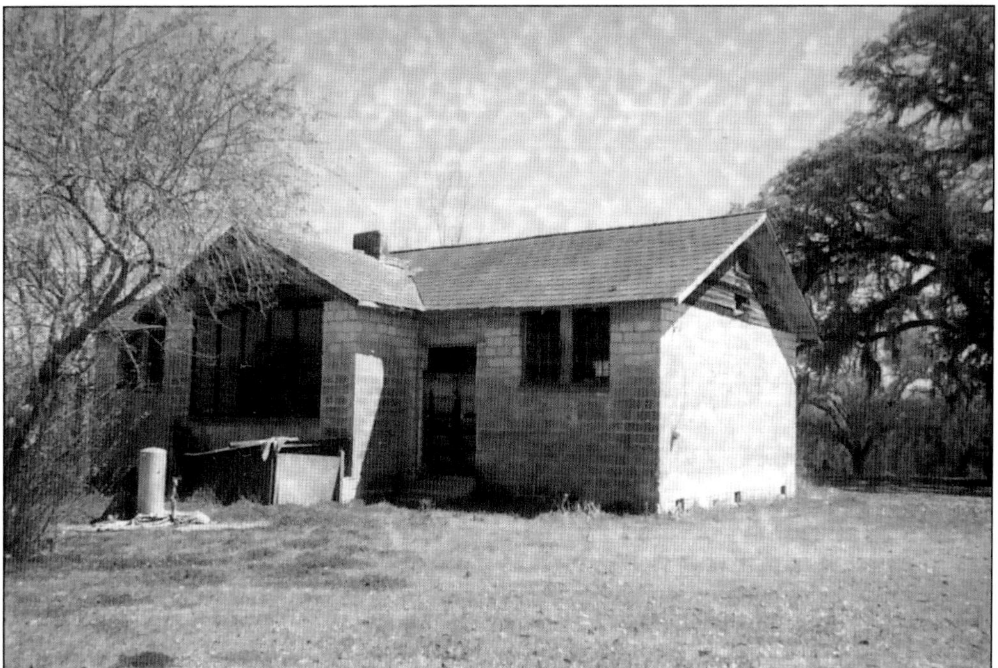

Springfield Elementary was another church-based school, serving grades one through eight. This school was located in northwest Jackson County at the Springfield A.M.E. Church site. These students also transferred to JCTS.

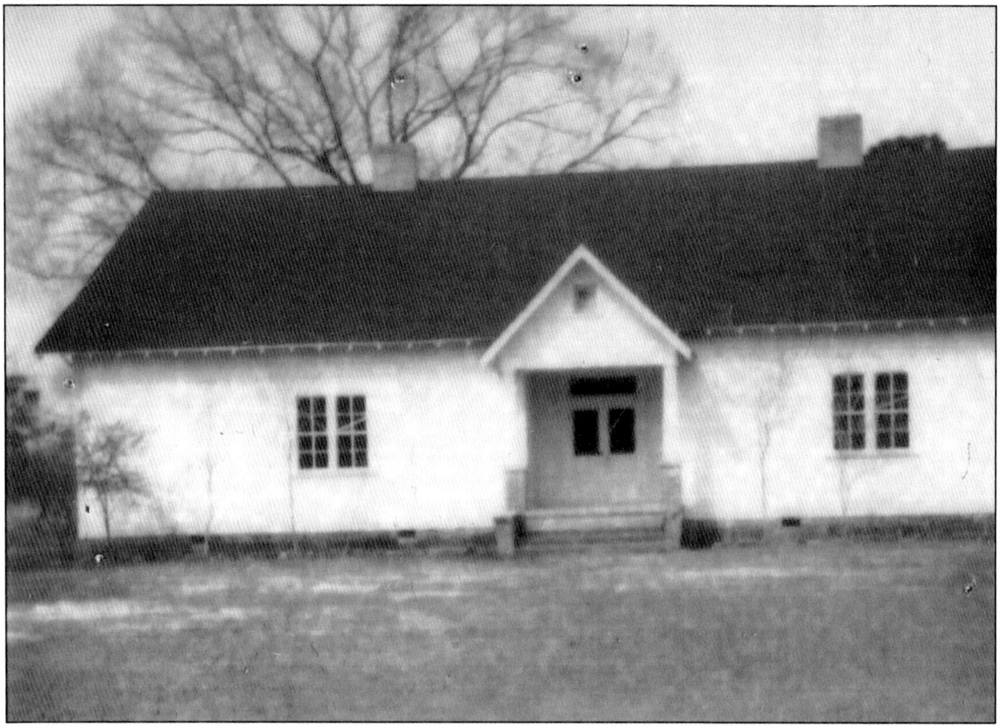

Little Zion Elementary School, a church-based school for grades one through eight, was located in the "Little Zion" community near Sneads, Florida. Most students transferred to JCTS.

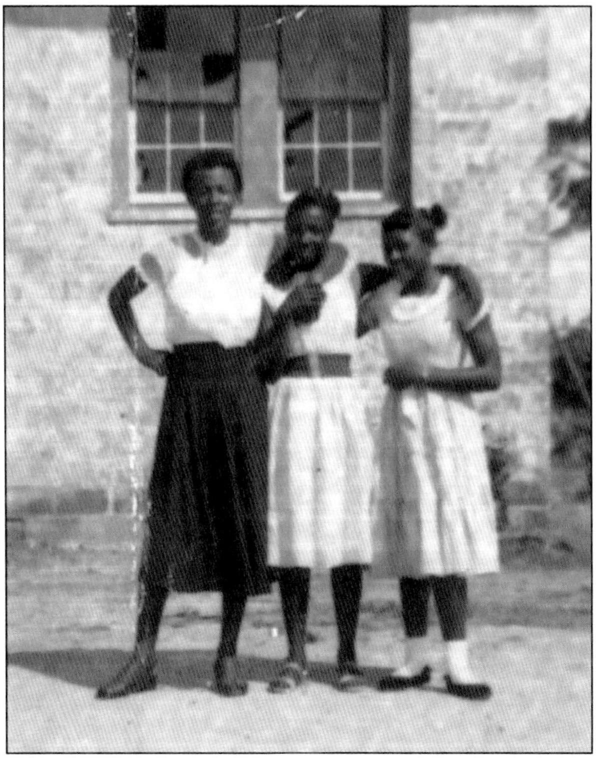

Pope Chapel Elementary School, a church-based school for grades one through eight, was located off the Blue Springs Highway at Pope Chapel A.M.E. Church. From left to right are Mildred Johnson, unidentified, and Flozell Johnson.

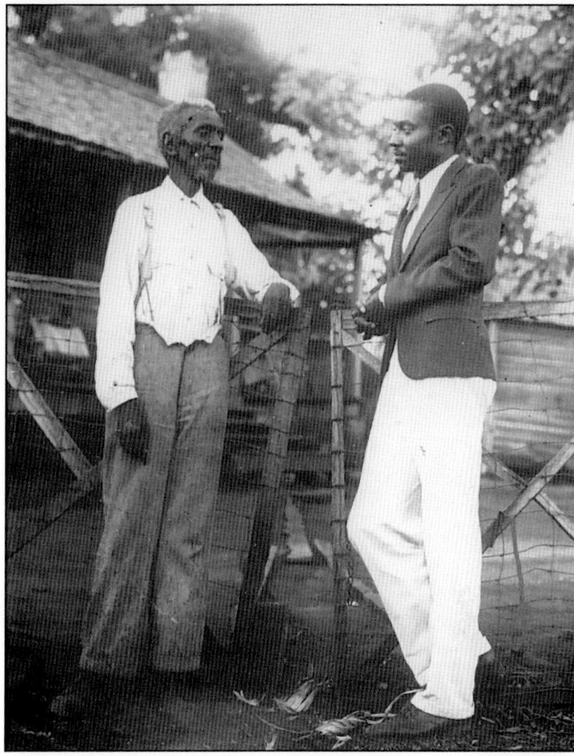

Anderson Baker, left, is shown here with his teacher LeRoy Bell. Baker, according to his granddaughter, was 99 years of age when this picture was taken on June 25, 1935. He was the oldest member of the adult education class. He died in 1940 at age 104. (Florida State Archives Photographic Collection.)

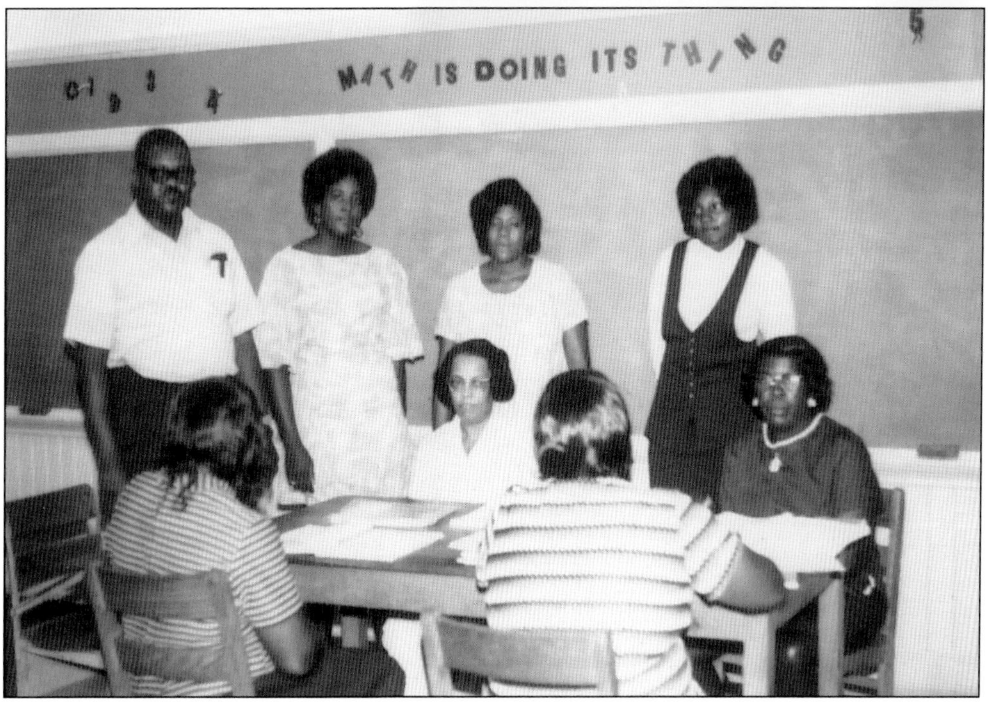

Fortunately, education was available for many adults, and it provided an opportunity for them to complete their high school education. Instructor Amos P. Brown is shown here, standing on the left.

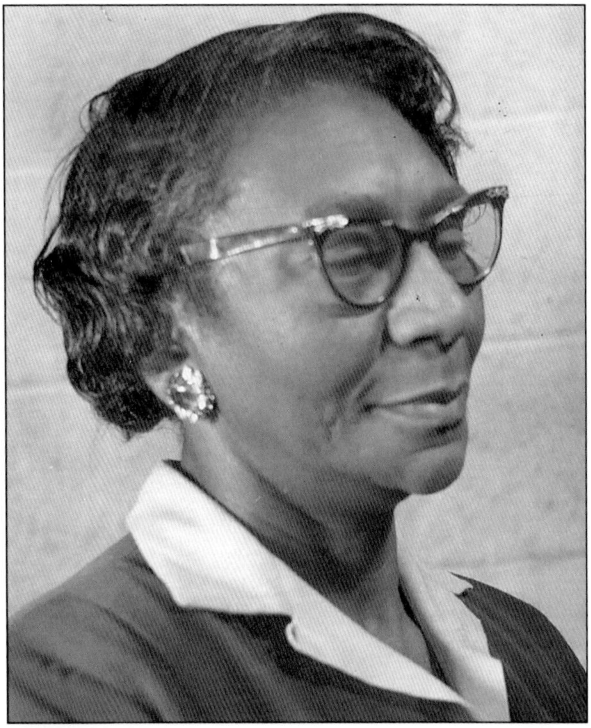

Ms. Willie J. Hutchinson was one of Jackson County's pioneers in the field of education. She was an energetic, innovative, determined, and dedicated educator who had a great concern for the welfare of people. She served as principal of Bethlehem Elementary School in Cottondale for many years. Under her leadership, a new brick school was erected. It is said that she donated the first bricks to construct the school and the land to build the A.M.E. District House in Marianna. Many children had the opportunity to receive instructions from Ms. Hutchinson in a school or church setting. She had a long career as a teacher at Jackson County Training School. She was a true humanitarian, worthy of honor.

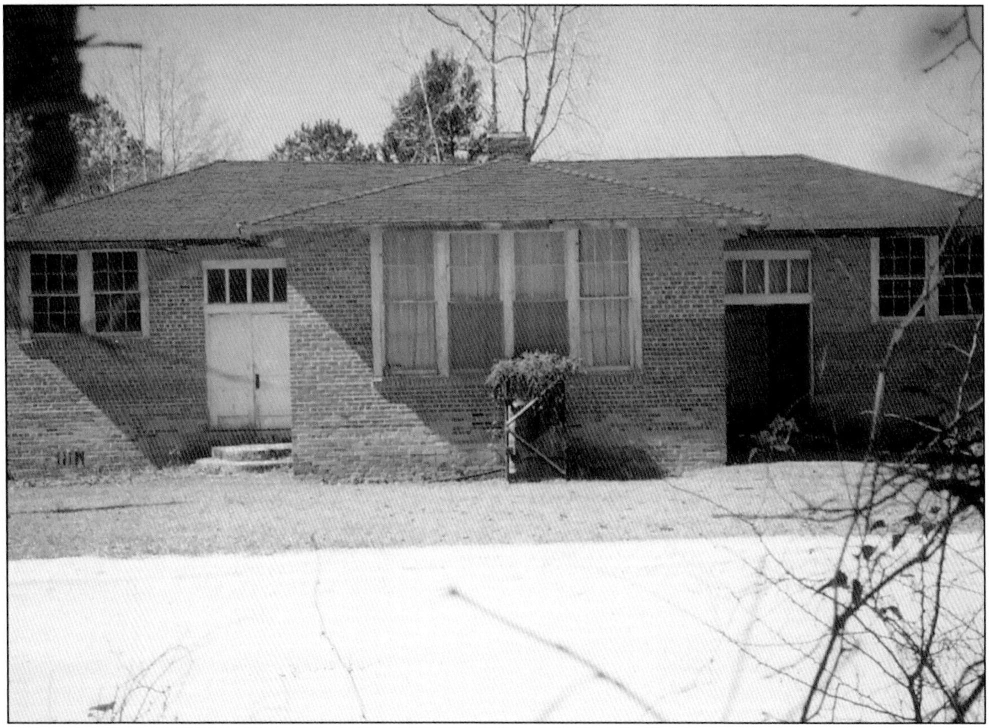

The Bethlehem Elementary School was located off the Campbellton Highway, near the historic Bethlehem A.M.E. Church—the first church of that denomination in Jackson County. This school, completed in 1946, included grades one through eight.

Ten

Clubs and Organizations

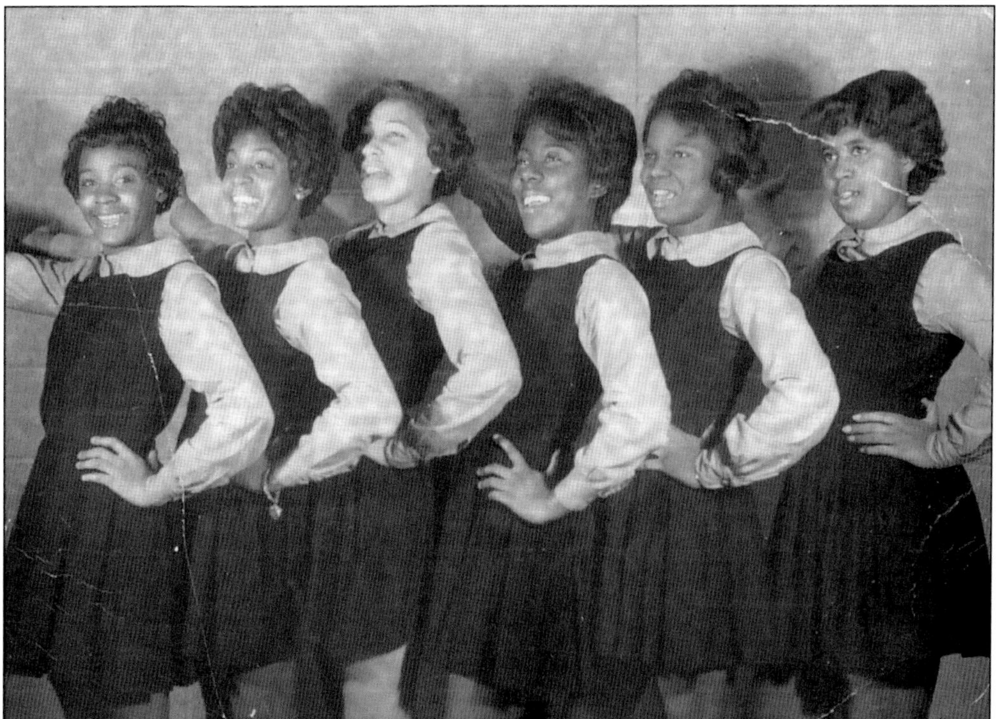

These charming JCTS cheerleaders were known to impress the audience as they performed during many exciting athletic events. These young ladies have now entered various prominent careers in their respective communities. They are, from left to right, Patricia Speights, Leatha "Sweetie" Mayes, Joan White, Carol Robinson, Linda Darby, and Dayatra Baker.

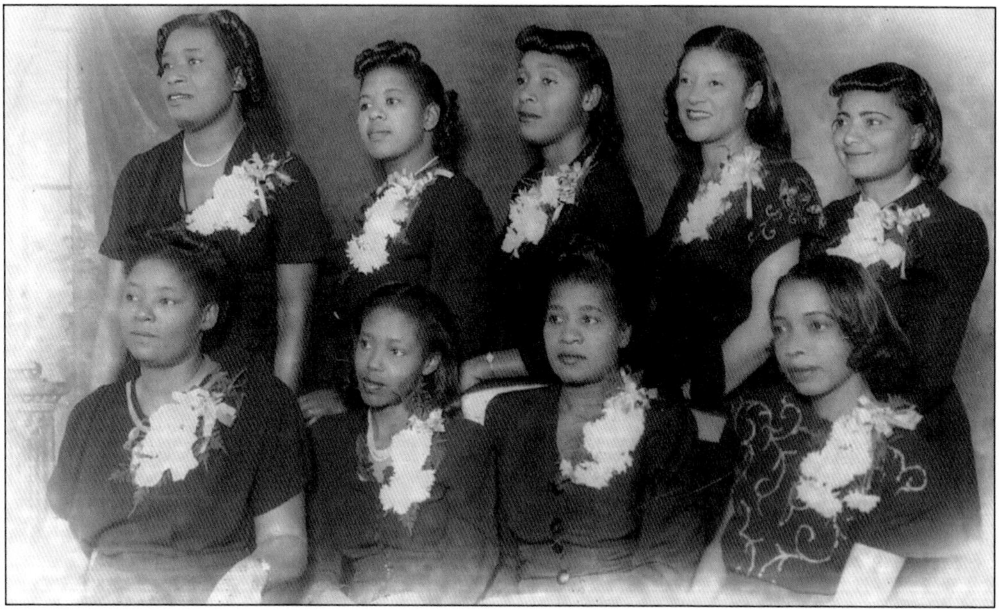

Pictured above is one of the social clubs in Marianna. It included members from various churches throughout the city. They engaged in service projects and social activities. They were called the "Just Us Club." Today, the club functions with the remaining five members. From left to right are (seated) Robert Pressley, Ollie Pender, Alice Taylor, and Myrtle Robinson; (standing) Mary Bellamy, Reola Bryan, Viola Forrest, Maggie P. Atwater, and Bessie Harris.

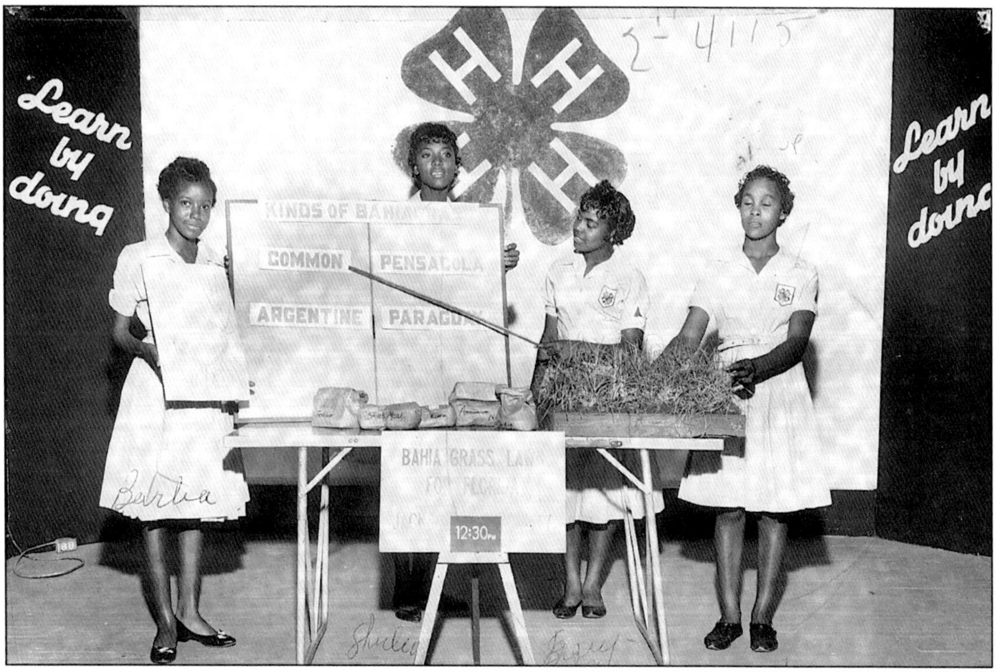

The 4-H club organization provided leadership skill for girls and boys through service projects and camping experiences. The group pictured here was active during the time Pearl G. Long was the County Home Demonstration Agent. They are, from left to right, Jeanette Bowles, Shirley Bellamy, Gloria Gibson, and Carol Marks.

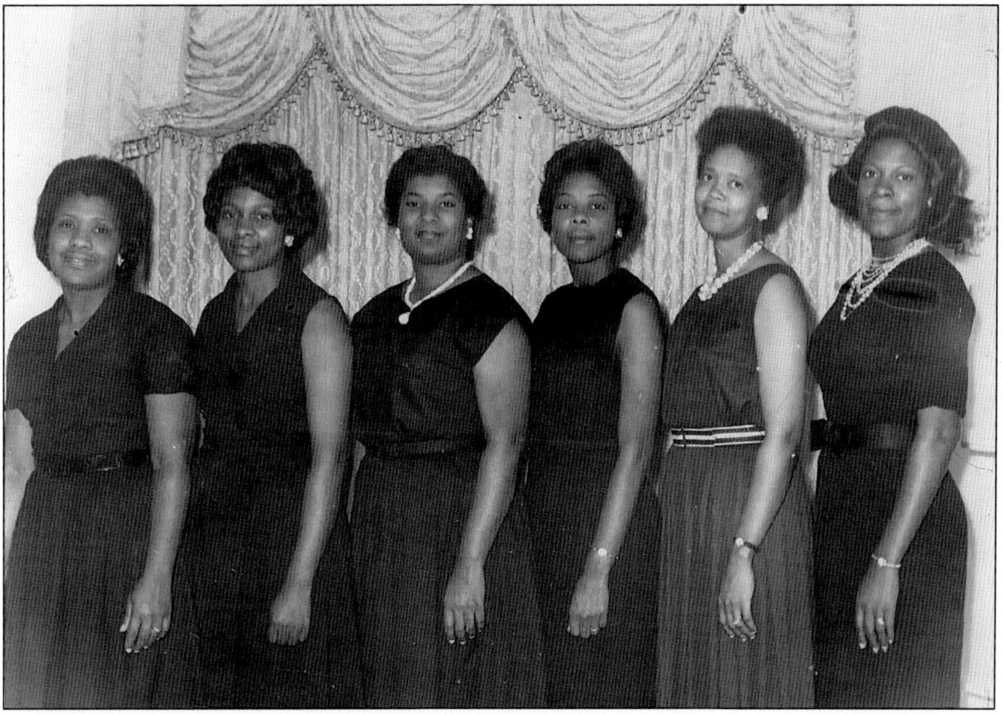

Young ladies in Marianna organized the Vogue and Valiant Club during the early 1950s. The main function of the club was to present projects that enhanced the community, especially the youthful members of the community. The club had annual social affairs. It remains an active social club with two of its original members. Pictured, from left to right, are Queen Brown, Barbara Dixon, Ella Mae Elkins Smith, Eulice Bryant, Betty Ellis, and Careatha Everett.

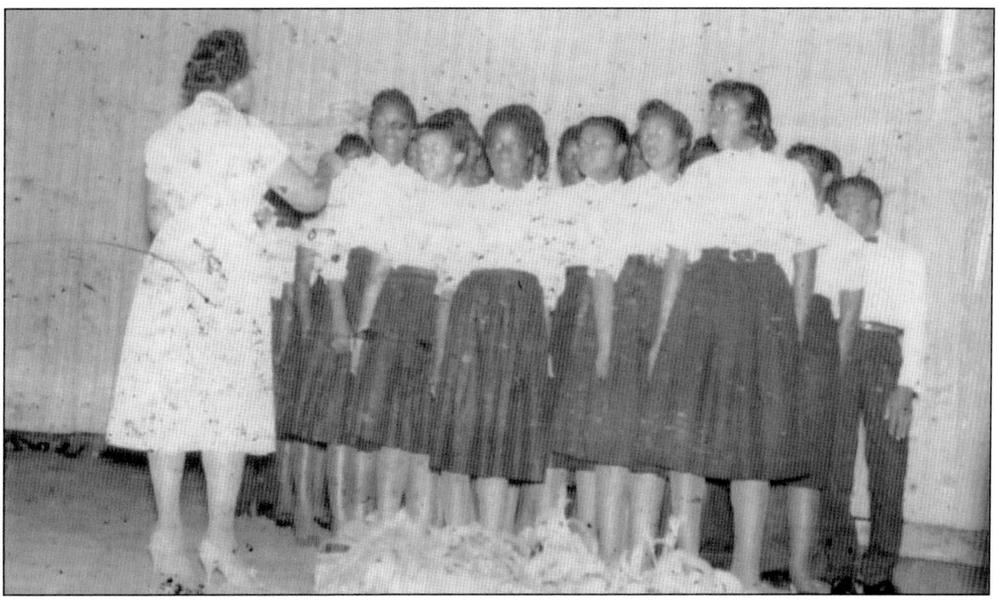

All area schools provided musical opportunities for their students—glee clubs were an important part of that experience. Pictured above is one of those clubs under the direction of Ruth Wilkerson Glenn.

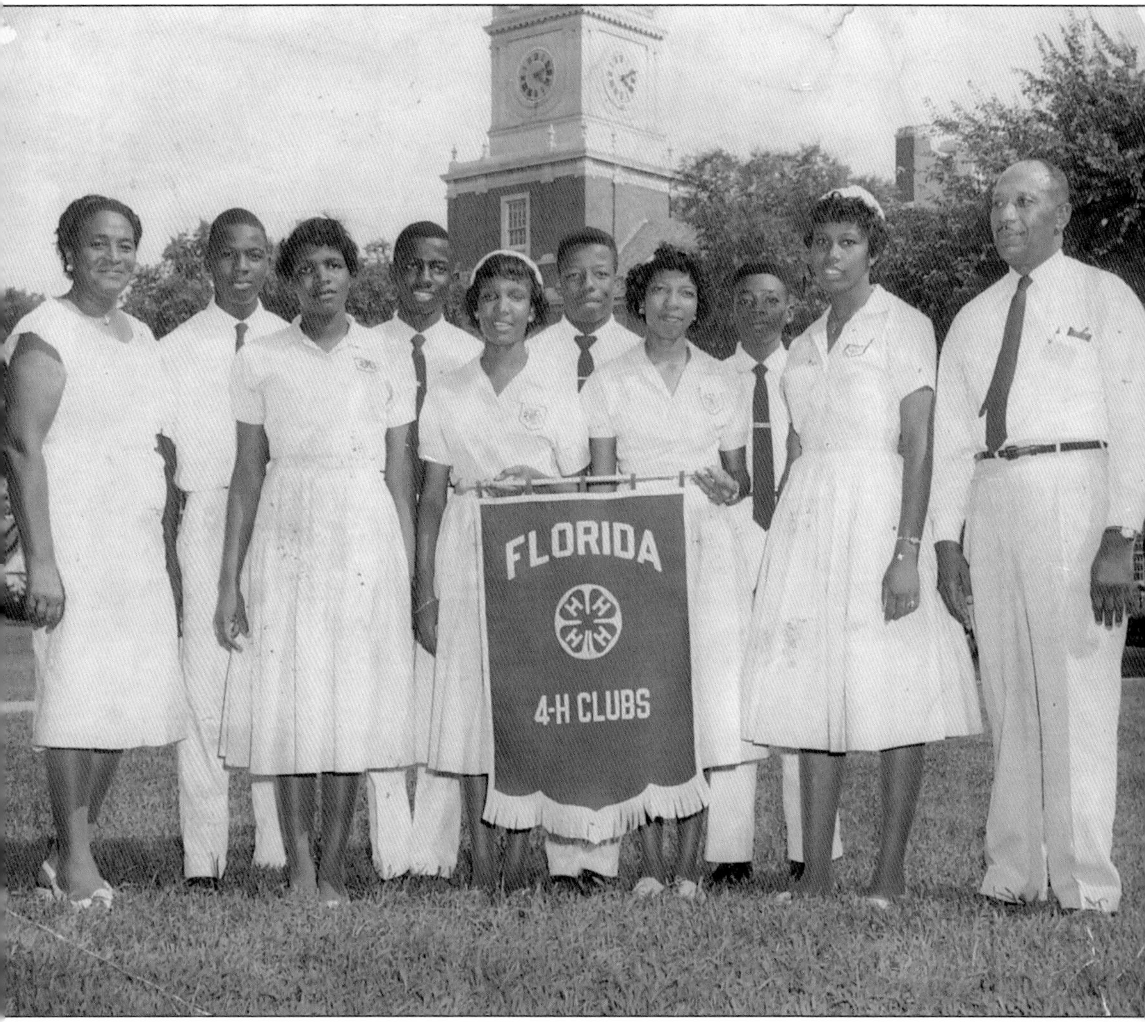

This photograph shows the Florida 4-H delegation that attended a meeting in Washington, D.C. in 1960. Fourth from the left is GA-JCTS Alumni Association president, Judge Roy L. Roulhac, representing Jackson County.

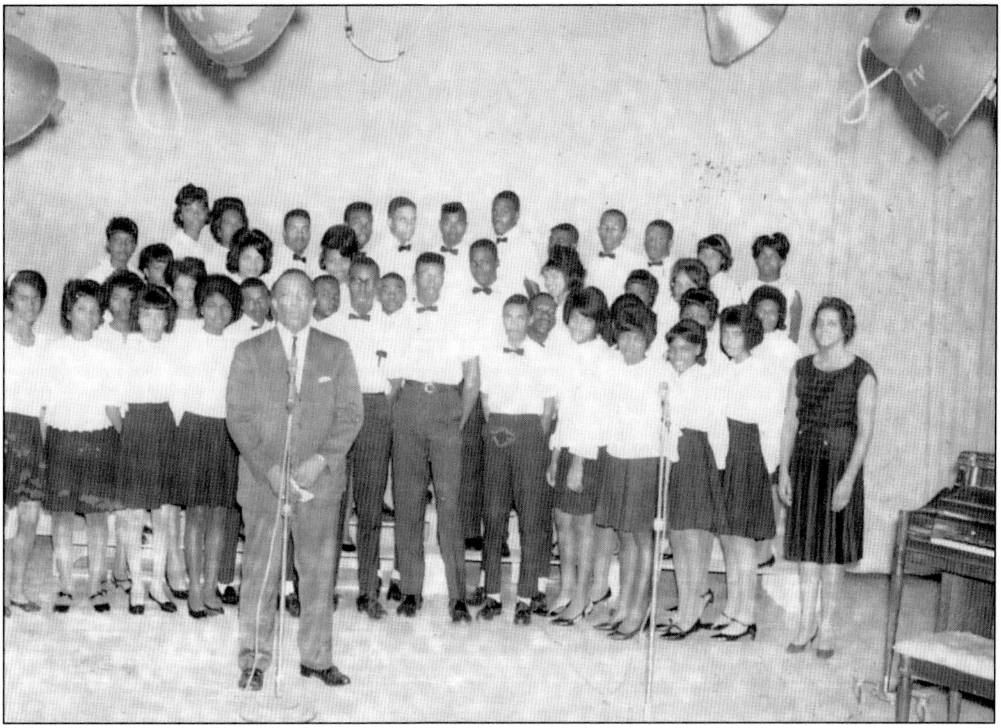

This picture shows the renowned Union Grove High School Glee Club under the direction of Rosa B. McKay. L.L. Hawthorne Sr., center, was principal of the school. The glee club made several appearances at WTVY Television station in Dothan, Alabama.

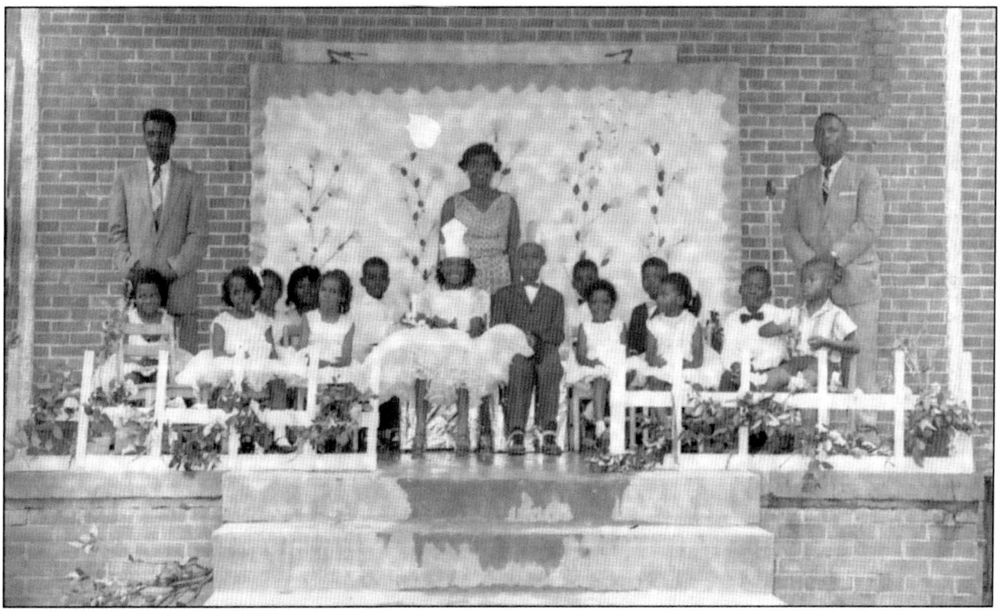

The Elementary Department at Union Grove High School sponsored a variety of activities. The picture above shows a "king and queen" coronation under the director of Leroy Crawford (standing left) and Queen B. Brown (standing center). Professor Hawthorne, the principal, is standing on the right.

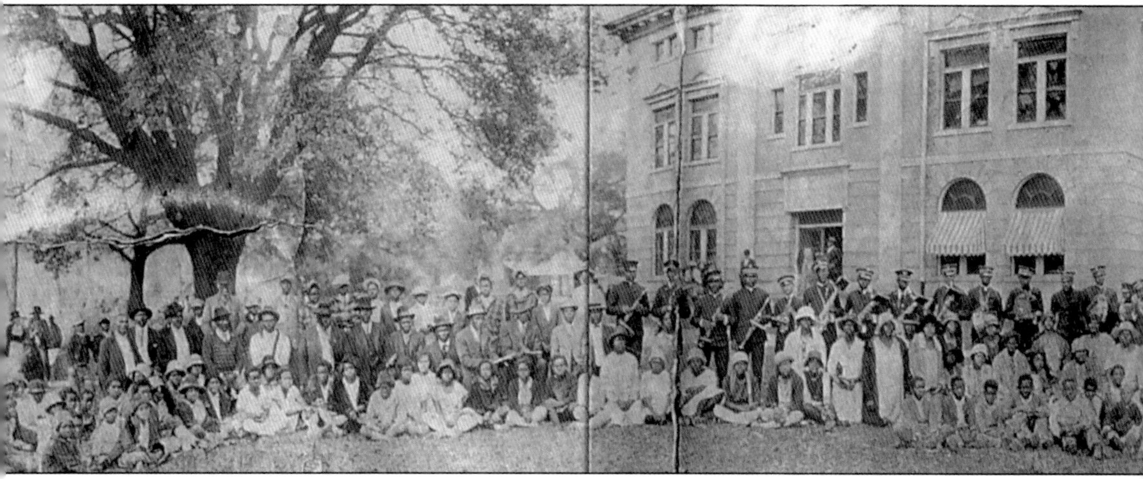

In 1924, African Americans in Jackson County held their first parent-teacher conference on the courthouse square. Gilmore Academy, established in 1922 by Professor Robert T. Gilmore, was the first school constructed that provided educational opportunities

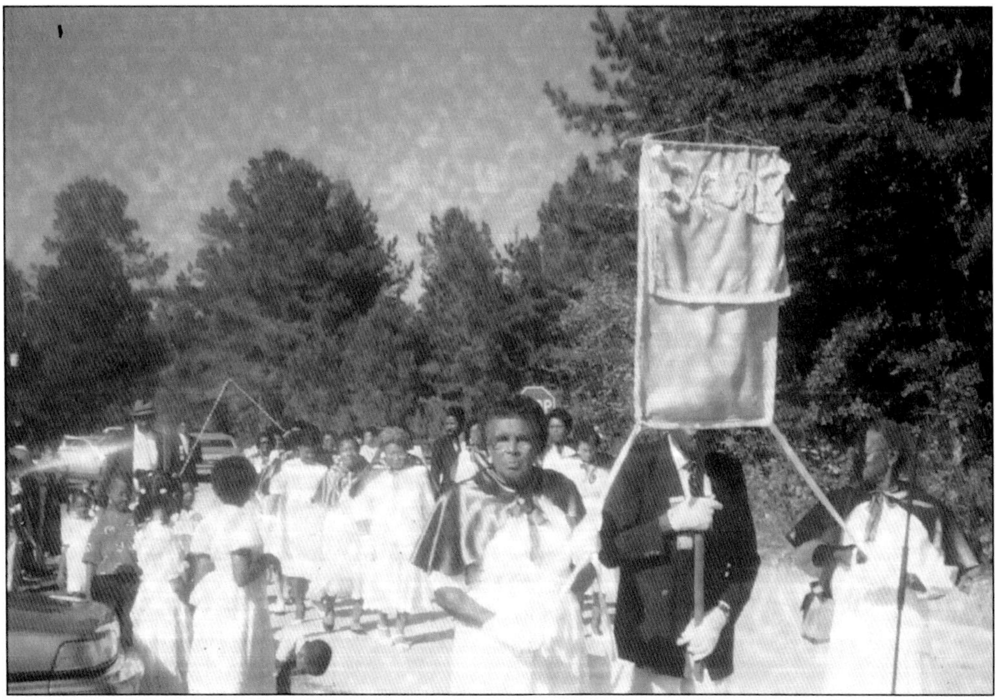

The Bethlehem Church serves as the site for the well-known Sunday Morning Band Turnout on the second Sunday in October each year. People from far and near return home to march in the parade as they chanted "What band is this? The Sunday morning band." Baskets of delicious food are shared with family and friends as they gather on the church grounds and in the old school building. Thelma Lawrence is pictured in the foreground.

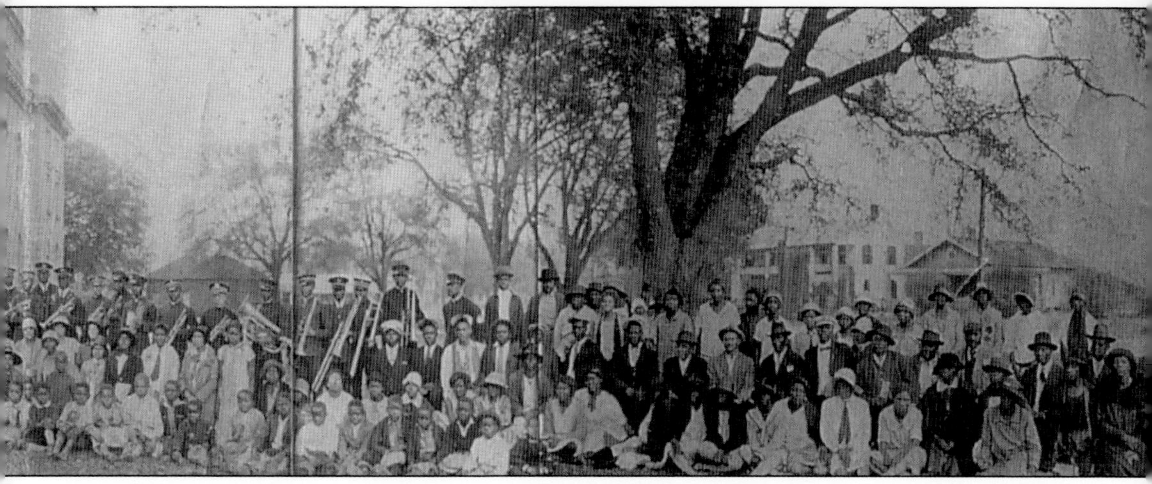

for African Americans in Jackson County beyond the eighth grade. A portion of the Florida A&M University band is in the background.

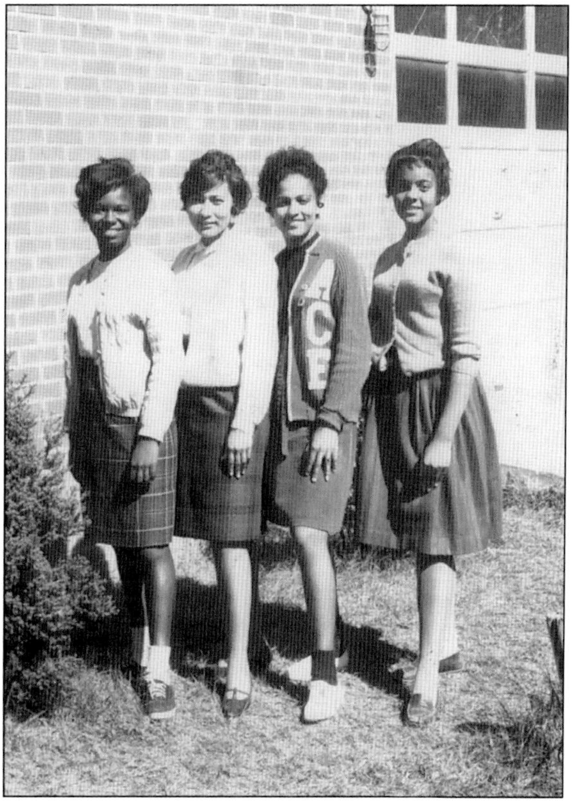

These school chums decided to take a break on campus to pose for this picture. Pictured, from left to right, are Linda Darby Jones, Joan White (deceased), Sandra Borders, and Yvonne Green. Linda and Mattie Fagan Berrien were the principal organizers of the first GA-JCTS all-school reunion, July 4-7, 1996. The homecoming, attended by over 500 former students, teachers, and faculty and their families, led to the creation of the alumni association.

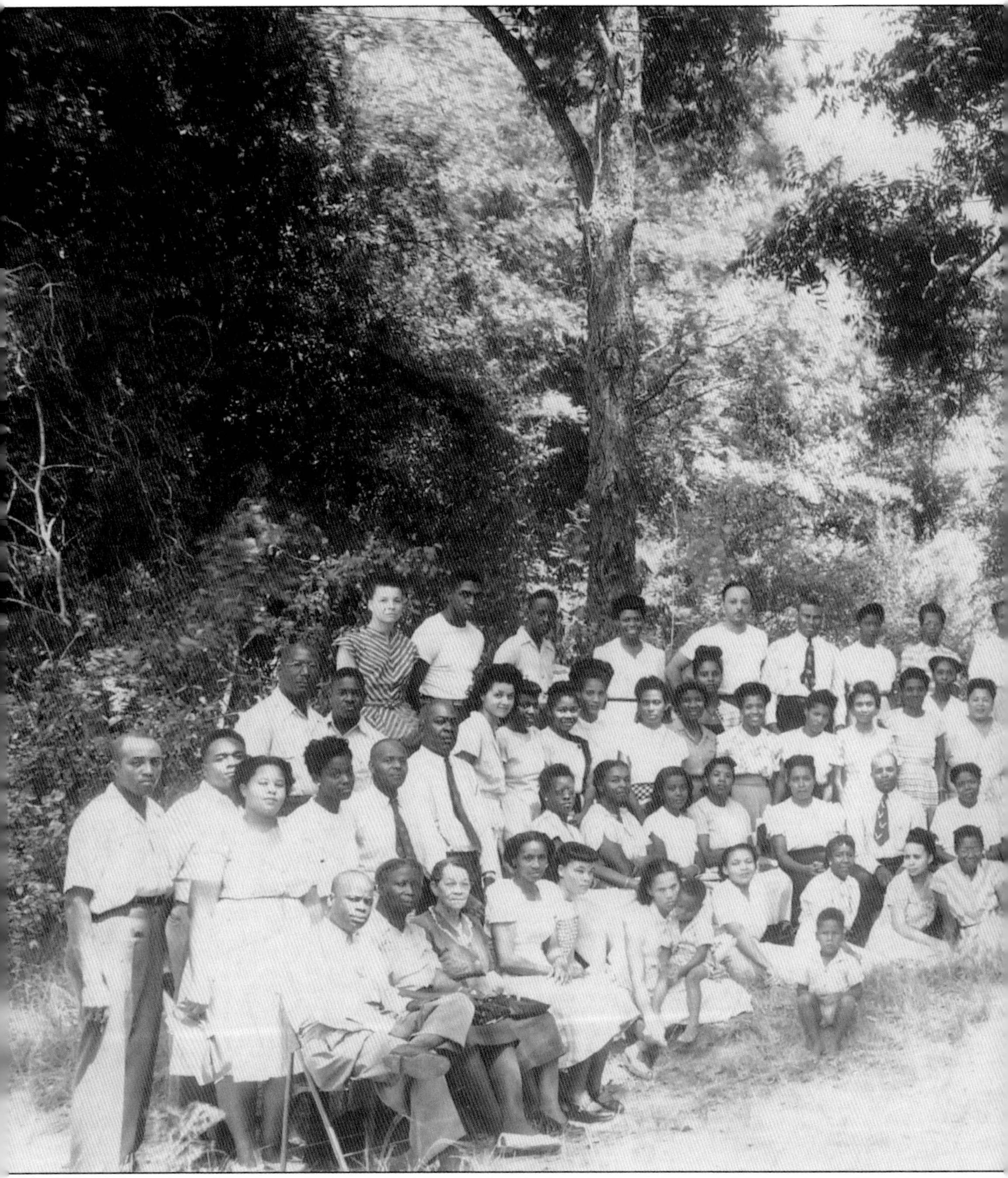

This picture includes a group of Jackson County teachers posing for a photo during a new school year's planning workshop, 1948-49. ? Rutledge, county supervisor of African-American schools, is seated on the front row, left. In 1948, the schools were segregated. However, teachers assigned to African-American schools accepted the challenge of providing a good education to children under their supervision. There was only one high school in the county for black children to attend—the Jackson County Training School. In the absence of school buses, black children used various means of transportation from towns around the county to come to JCTS

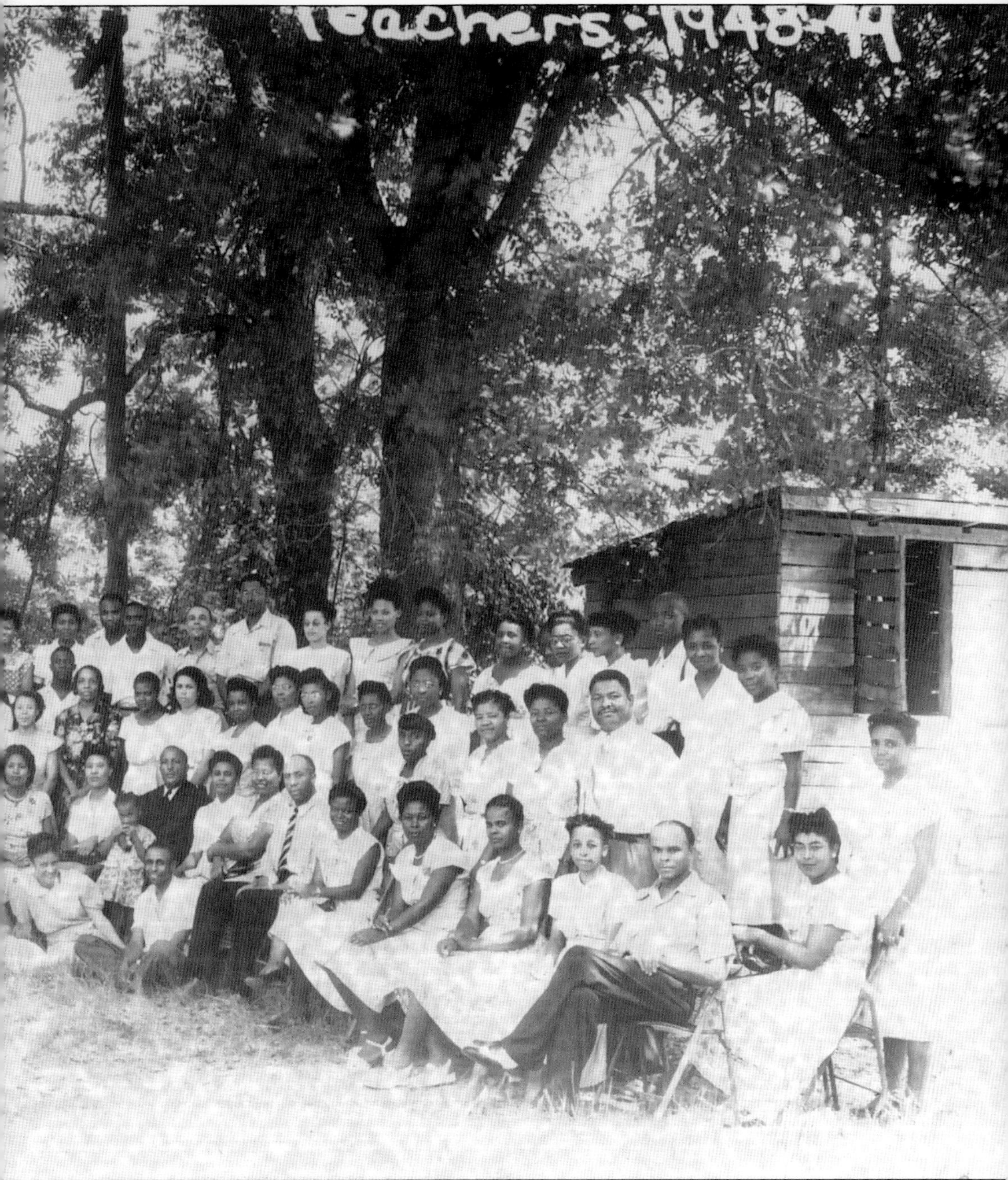

in Marianna to obtain their high school diplomas. Some children lived in private homes and walked for miles; some were brought in cars or seated on the back of trucks with covers to protect them from the cold and rain while en route to school. Regardless of the circumstances they faced, their desire to obtain an education never wavered. The dedicated teachers instilled in these children the desire to put forth their best efforts. Even though resources were limited and facilities were inadequate, many of the children have become outstanding, productive citizens.

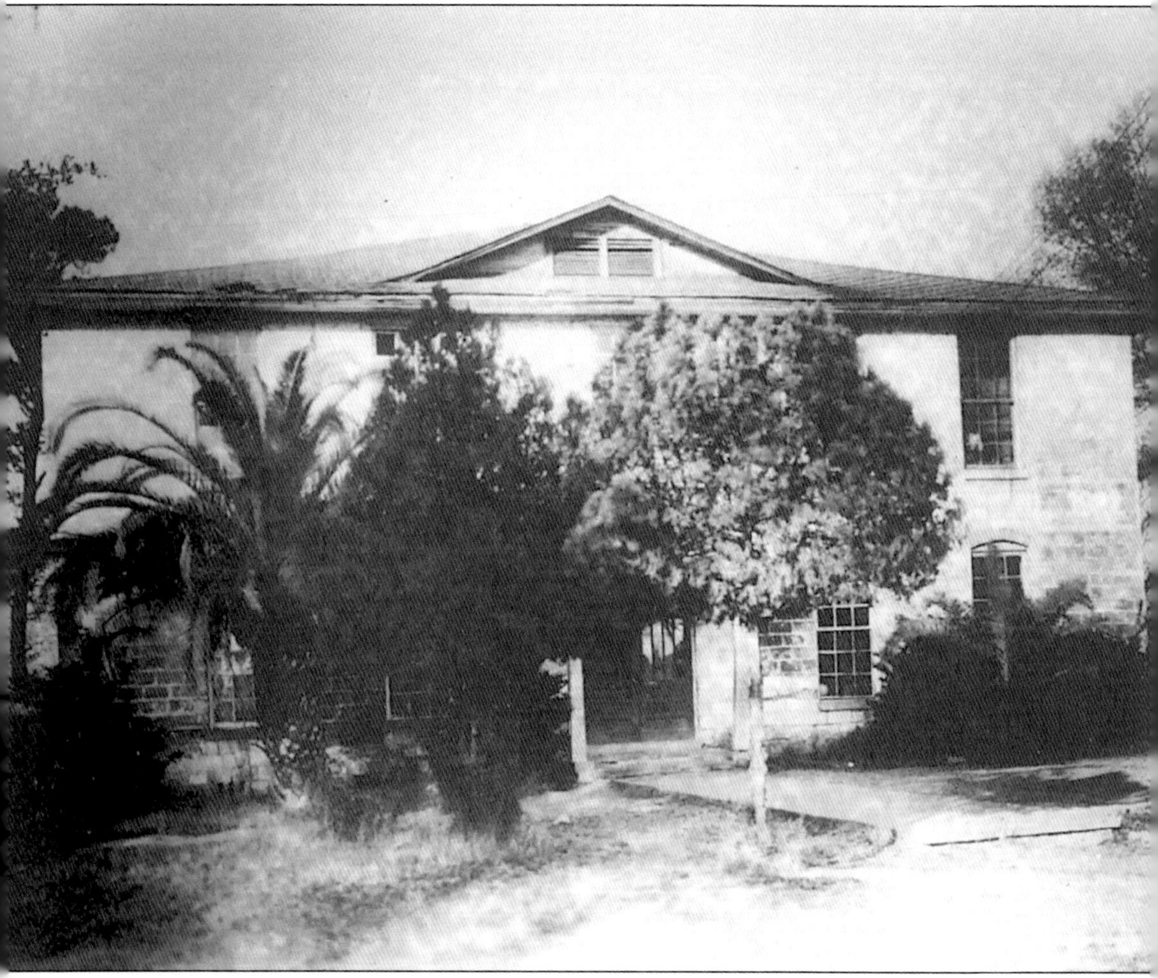

In 1922, Gilmore Academy was established in the West End section of Marianna by Robert T. Gilmore, its first principal. The two-story block structure was the first school in the county where black students could attend grades one through twelve, until many years later when Union Grove and St. Paul were established in Greenwood and Campbellton, respectively. Gilmore Academy became Jackson County Training High School in 1932. The school's mascot was the panther, and the school colors were orange and black. Many students who attended these schools are now productive citizens throughout the state and the country.

Alma Mater

Dear Jackson High,
My Jackson High
For You I'll sigh
For You I'll die.
In all my dreams,
Your fair face beams,
You are the idol of my heart,
Dear Jackson High.

Principals of the Gilmore Academy-Jackson County Training High School

Robert T. Gilmore
Emanuel King
Roy Allen
J.B. Williams
William Harley Sr.
Reuben L Gibson Jr.